INTERNSHIPS IN COMMUNICATIONS

Internships in Communications

James P. Alexander

IOWA STATE UNIVERSITY PRESS / AMES

Dr. James P. Alexander is professor of communications emeritus at California State University at Fullerton. He established the department's mandatory internship program 30 years ago when the Bachelor of Arts degree in communications was approved. Since 1980 until his recent retirement, he has directed what has become one of the largest communications internship programs in the nation, with the most students participating and the most available sites for interns. He is the author of *Programmed Journalism Writing* and *Programmed Journalism Editing*.

©1995 Iowa State University Press, Ames, Iowa 50014
All rights reserved

♾ Printed on acid-free paper in the United States of America

First edition, 1995

Library of Congress Cataloging-in-Publication Data

Alexander, James P.
    Internships in communications / James P. Alexander.–1st ed.
       p.   cm.
    Includes index.
    ISBN 0-8138-2231-9
    1. Communication–Study and teaching (Internship) I. Title.
P91.3.A44 1995
302.2′071′55–dc20   95-7273

TABLE OF CONTENTS

v

PREFACE

Most of the headlines on college career center bulletin boards these days focus on internships, which have reached into numerous career fields in the past 20 years, especially during the job-rich '80s. A national organization estimates that at least one-third of all college graduates complete an internship before graduation. Internships are still very popular in the tighter job markets of the '90s. They are an excellent way to reach major companies, to fill a gap in your résumé with professional experience and to check career options.

Interest in internships does not extend to all schools, so the purpose of this book is to help students seeking internships in communications. All chapters have helpful advice regardless of your specific career goals. If you are on your own, you can have an exciting and rewarding internship if you take the time to follow this book in its step-by-step concept.

This book grew from the author's more than 10 years of experience in coordinating a major university communications internship program at California State University, Fullerton. He worked with hundreds of students in all communications fields, visiting numerous sites each year.

If you are in a credit program and a large market, you may find that getting an internship is easy. You may accept a first offer because you are intimidated about interviewing or are pressed to find a site by a specific deadline, or for some other reason. However, former interns in professional positions report that extensive interviewing for a site pays off. You not only win an internship at an above-average company with good supervision, but you also learn skills useful in later job interviews. Thus, this important preinternship step becomes a highlight of the internship. A look at interns in communications fields other than your own can answer some of your questions. Hopefully, this book can encourage and lead you to become a stronger candidate for good internships and eliminate any fear of rejection.

The best advice is to start this process early. To search for your ideal internship, use the directories and other guides in Appendix A. You should look at all of the appendix material in the book. Although some guidelines and tips are directed to faculty and employers, you, too, as an intern can benefit by studying objectives and job descriptions and ways to make your own internship more effective.

The author believes that a key to operating an effective intern program is teamwork. For this reason, in addition to chapters and appendix sections for students, this book has important information for both faculty and employers. Appendix B includes informative material for a department chair, a faculty member just starting an intern program, and an internship coordinator with years of service. For background, faculty also should review appendix items primarily prepared for students and employers. An important member of the team is the employer or site supervisor, the one person actually working in the field with the intern. Appendix C has information to assist employers and encourage them to participate in reaching educational objectives. For both Appendixes B and C, brief introductions explain these materials.

A *Guide for Faculty Coordinators and Instructors* is available. In addition to discussing ways to establish an internship class, the *Guide* includes a section discussing the questions at the end of each chapter and material helpful for a class or seminar.

A final note. Throughout the book a few employers with advertising agencies, newspapers and stations asked that their firms not be identified. They said that at present they have limited resources for more interns and more people apply than can be accommodated.

ACKNOWLEDGMENTS

To my wife, Ilo Browns Alexander, whose encouragement and skills in writing and editing were major factors in moving this book along to publication.

I am grateful for the many interns who shared their experiences and contributed their thoughts on what makes an internship successful. Also, many faculty coordinators and administrators at schools and departments throughout the country gave their support and advice on what they recommended as basic principles for coordinating university internship programs. And to these faculty and staff members and friends, I am especially indebted: Mary Lynn Hartman, Al and Louise Hewitt, Tom and Sandy Pasqua, Ed Fink, Carolyn Johnson, Joan Joyce, George Mastroianni and James Fields.

INTERNSHIPS IN COMMUNICATIONS

The first little intern did nothing but whine.
An employer cut back and then there were nine.

The second little intern often was late.
Attendance was taken and then there were eight.

The third little intern strolled in at eleven.
Excuses were made and then there were seven.

The fourth little intern viewed employers as hicks.
He griped once too often and then there were six.

The fifth little intern acted more dead than alive.
A turn of the pay sheet and then there were five.

The sixth little intern shouted and swore.
The employer got wise and then there were four.

The seventh little intern took the job to be "free."
No work was produced and then there were three.

The eighth little intern cursed all with "who?"
Reassignments were made and then there were two.

The ninth little intern saw no work to be done.
Co-workers griped and then there was one.

The tenth little intern giggled, "Work should be fun."
No tasks were accomplished and then there were none!

Poem courtesy of the National Commission for Cooperative Education.

Cartoon by Bob Rich, courtesy of the Knoxville *News-Sentinel*.

CHAPTER 1

WHAT ARE INTERNSHIPS?

Internships: A Bridge to Careers

Internships are a vital link between college majors and courses and the professional opportunities of the work world. For many years interns have received on-the-job training in fields such as business, engineering and health sciences. In the '80s communications internships increased dramatically. Today, interns appear frequently at newspapers, advertising and public relations agencies, nonprofit organizations and radio and television stations.

What are the reasons for this popularity?

- An internship can be the first actual on-the-job application of classroom knowledge.
- You can test communication skills in a real work environment, leading to better preparation for employment after graduation.
- Part-time communications jobs and internships while attending school can give you new information on your career interests and goals.
- A summer internship before graduation can help you decide what, if any, new skills or additional courses you need. Or it can lead you to seek another career field.
- In times of recession and decreasing job opportunities, an internship may be the best and in some cases the only way to get through the door for your first communications job.

Internships Pay Off

✓ in more relevant and timely résumé additions
✓ as you learn new computer software and improve your skills
✓ in gaining knowledge of how companies and organizations function and learning the importance of teamwork
✓ in acquiring valuable work experience.

3

If you are a junior or senior close to graduation, a strong summer internship can do more than reinforce your skills. On the job, you may become aware of new opportunities. For example, if you are a reporting intern on a newspaper, you may see that adding another class or two will make you more employable for the job market later. A graphics or business writing class can prepare you for another internship.

Many interns land their first job at their internship sites. Or they may get leads and contacts through networking with their internship supervisor or other employees at the company. Some supervisors assume a mentoring role to help an intern improve his or her résumé. Writing samples and other portfolio pieces created at the internship experience increase the odds of being better prepared in competition for a job.

> *There are many different definitions for the word internship.*

Internships and part-time jobs are not necessarily synonymous. Some faculty coordinators believe that many internships should be considered part- or full-time jobs if you are receiving pay. They point out that some part-time jobs do not qualify as internships because of the job description. For example, some employers will call a clerical or receptionist position an internship, but it may be inappropriate as a learning internship.

Those involved in internship experiences define internships differently. You need to be aware of this. Also, differing views exist on the ingredients for success.

Employers' Views Vary

Frequently, companies and organizations seeking interns want to have university affiliation for credit, insurance or other reasons. Sometimes they want to know what guidelines should be followed in setting up a good program. As a prospective intern, you need to know how different employers view internships. You should be alert to potential opportunities but at the same time cautious until you get full information on all aspects of the internship. These are a few steps and concerns in dealing with employers, especially if you have little or no university assistance.

- Some employers may want to consult with faculty in establishing job descriptions and work requirements, especially when credit may be involved.
- Make sure you are aware of all of the skills required. Some employers look at interns as highly qualified graduates with a number of technical skills. The best advice is to pass on an internship that appears over your head in requirements and does not offer much training opportunity.
- On the other hand, you should reject low-level clerical or reception-type positions disguised as learning internships. Some employers do not define the skill level of an internship and are not aware that faculty coordinators reject the notion that *any* entry-level job in a company meets intern requirements.
- You may propose an internship to an employer. You need to give a detailed job description that meets your objectives for your internship experiences. You may outline a schedule of work time. Also, if you're getting credit, you need to explain requirements that your university may establish.

Supervisors and Interns

Supervisors are the people who work directly with interns at the site. They may have various job titles and range from an entry-level person who might have been an intern just last year to an experienced employee with several years with the company. You may meet a site supervisor at your initial interview for an internship, or one may be assigned after you start your internship. Site supervisors are generally dedicated to the idea that the internship should be meaningful and consider the educational goals of the intern. Many recall their own intern supervisors and strive to be effective mentors.

Supervisors with public relations and advertising agencies say that interns bring to the work world new ideas and fresh insights from recent classroom experiences. Many enjoy seeing their interns grow in responsibility and attitude, enhancing their likelihood of future employment in the field. Many site supervisors stay in contact with their former interns for years.

In many situations the site supervisor representing the company or organization will conduct the initial interview. It's up to you as the intern to question and seek out information about the internship—especially with these major considerations:

- If you accept an internship offer, you should have the skills required and be able to manage the tasks.
- Be sure you can work the required days and hours. Check at once for any holidays, interruptions in schedule, school conflicts, etc., before starting your internship.
- A critical ingredient for internship success is a good rapport with your supervisor. This may be difficult to assess initially. If the supervisor is going on a long vacation and refers you to several other supervisors for assignments, it may be better to look for another site.
- Although some routine tasks must be assigned and completed, be sure to tell your supervisor your internship objectives and ask if time will be available for you to pursue them.

Faculty Coordinators and Advisers

The faculty coordinator is the person appointed to administer the internship program. In some schools without any intern program, a faculty adviser may answer questions. Some schools discourage internships because they don't want to provide credits or be responsible for supervising interns. (For more information on how college programs operate, see Appendix B.)

Universities that do encourage internships vary so much in operations that no "correct" method exists. Some interns receive credit and pay. Some schools deny credit if pay is involved. A few schools require internships for graduation. More schools give elective credit, some toward the major and some for non-major credit hours.

When credits are available, they may range from 3 to 15. Presumably, students attending communications programs where credit is freely awarded will finish several internships before graduation. It's important to see how much faculty assistance you will have in finding an internship site.

Let's look at university programs from the perspective of faculty involvement. Credit programs are generally run by one or more faculty coordinators. Their overall load may be reduced to permit time for them to orient interns to prospective sites, to meet with site supervisors and to establish requirements so that student interns can earn their credits.

Depending on the number of majors and students served in a credit internship situation, there may be some or all of these characteristics: a faculty coordinator will maintain a directory or listing of good intern sites so that you will be able to make a selection; an orientation meeting may be held to inform you of procedures in getting an internship and explaining requirements for credit; there may be an office where faculty list part-time jobs that give experience but may not qualify for internship credit; and final reports of interns who have completed their work may be available for review to help you compare and judge potential sites.

Some of the communications and journalism departments and schools that provide time for a faculty member or members to coordinate activities of student interns report very positive results. Alumni surveys list internship classes or seminars as among the most popular college courses. Coordinators also report that when job placement and internship activities are handled in the same office, site supervisors and employers assist significantly by calling in job openings on a regular basis.

R Assistance Varies

Requirements regarding internships and credits vary even in the same school. At an accredited university program in Ohio, advertising students must locate their own internships. This is an optional requirement for advertising majors who can get elective credit. But at the same school, public relations majors have a mandatory internship program that includes a formal class. Faculty members teaching the class assign students to internship sites. One reason for this may be that in a smaller or medium-sized market internships in public relations are more readily available than in advertising.

A faculty coordinator may teach a formal class or seminar about internships. In this situation credits may be required for the major or count as elective units. Such a class may be scheduled before or during the students' internships. One objective of these classes is to explain to you how internships operate. Site supervisors, employers and former interns may be invited to speak to the class.

Faculty advisers may encourage you to arrange your own internship, especially in the situation in which no credit is available. You can ask advisers questions about application procedures at different sites, deadlines for applications to be mailed, what clippings or work samples are necessary, etc.

A faculty adviser may maintain a notebook showing some of the major national internships and their deadlines and requirements. You may then need to apply yourself, using care to do the following:

- Complete all parts of the application and attach any materials requested.
- Watch for items that need immediate attention so as not to delay your application. Potential employers may request transcripts, which can take weeks to obtain; clippings or work samples that also may take time to assemble; and letters of reference, which should be requested well in advance of your mailing deadline.
- Update your résumé if necessary.

H ow to Prepare for an Internship Independently

Another situation in which no credit is given arises when no faculty or staff member is available for help. In other words, you are on your own.

The chairperson of the department or dean of the school may be a source of help. Or perhaps the career development center or job placement office on campus maintains lists of internships that can lead you to some contacts. This book may also be helpful to you as you develop your own strategies to search out an internship.

If your college is accredited by the Association for Education in Journalism and Mass Communications (AEJMC), you will probably be limited to three semester units or equivalent credit for any internship you take. Probably, you will be able to do other internships if you wish, but on a no-credit basis. Departments or schools not accredited by AEJMC sometimes award credit for several internships or may grant credit for staying at the same site for longer than a semester or year. Some AEJMC-accredited universities do not grant internship credit or have an organized internship program.

> *As internship opportunities in communications increase, many students must seek out their own site and make their own arrangements.*

If you are in a situation in which you don't have faculty help in finding an internship site, you need to use other university services as much as possible. The process of finding an opportunity on your own can be complicated and time consuming. As you look through the chapters in this book, you will observe some of the pitfalls to avoid and see some of the techniques other interns have used to make their jobs and working conditions improve.

If you locate a site where credit is required and none is available for internships in your department, check elsewhere on campus. Internships have different titles, such as practicums in work experience, experiential education or independent study. They come under various course headings, such as cooperative education or fieldwork or as a special class scheduled through the career development center. If credit or registration is required to win an internship, you may have to register at another school or community college. Thus, the credit units may give the green light to authorize your internship, but they might not be transferable to your own university.

As internship opportunities in the communications field increase, many students must seek out their own potential sites and

make their own arrangements for applying and interviewing. It isn't unusual for a student to travel many miles from home to get this professional experience, frequently at his or her own expense with no prospect for a salary. Nonetheless, some students are eager enough for an internship to travel to Europe and other international destinations.

You need to size up the internship site market early in your college career. If there is no credit or faculty help in locating a site, you need to take responsibility and start the process early. You may wish to take one or two summer vacation periods for an internship or two. A list of some communications organizations helping interns appears in Appendix A.

Communications Defined

Within the context of internships and careers in this book, communications is broadly defined, and all communications jobs are included.

Journalism

Journalism is part of this exploration. In the past some have narrowly defined journalism as being the route to only a newspaper career. However, internships exist at newspapers, magazines and many other publications. Today, many journalism and communications graduates are moving into a more general genre of publications work but one that still demands writing and editing skills. For instance, you may have specialized interests or expertise

- in working with computers
- in writing and editing technical publications and magazines
- in producing photos and writing accompanying articles
- in producing and writing radio and television programming.

Advertising

Advertising is a big part of the internship picture, with interns working in all areas of advertising agencies, from creative to media to traffic. Advertising interns reach into promotional departments of companies and organizations. Do you have good oral communications skills? Some work experience and an interest in business? You can qualify to serve as an intern in marketing or in sales departments.

Decisions . . . decisions. Keep an open mind about a specific work goal within communications. Your internship may help you adjust your goal.

Advertising internships also are available with in-house ad departments of large companies. Interns with strong art and writing skills are especially sought. Advertising draws many majors, not only in business and marketing but also from graduates in liberal arts and social sciences.

Public Relations

Public relations is another major area of communications with a number of growing career paths. Internships are found in all areas of the PR business, from those that assist communications directors in many non-profit organizations to those at the highest level of corporate communications.

Public relations is closely related to journalism in the internship arena as many PR interns work on publications, newsletters, reports and other tasks involving a great deal of writing, editing and polishing. Although PR agencies often come to mind first, opportunities are available at a host of other PR sites. Interns contract for assignments in hospitals, governmental agencies, all kinds of companies and even police departments. All of these PR internships have some media relations tasks at the core of their activities.

Electronic Media

The electronic media are a popular part of the communications world, with a wide variety of internship opportunities. Radio, television, film and photography sites attract students and graduates interested in technical and creative work.

The news media look for people seeking broadcast journalism careers. A starting point for this might be your own backyard if there is a cable television station. You can join the interns there and move from various jobs as you learn the business. Interns ultimately can produce and direct shows, be the on-the-air "talent" for a local newscast and operate cameras and other production equipment.

Attitude and work habits rank high when employers screen internship applicants.

It's common to find that communications, journalism or broadcasting graduates have gained experience in different areas of the communications field. As the chapters ahead will show, the more experience you have in the different areas of the communications field, the more flexibility you will have if you want to change jobs. You may reach your ultimate goal by adjustments to your study program. A second major or minor in a related field can be a decided asset. Also, special skills through courses or workshops may give you an edge in future job hunting.

According to many communications employers, there is a need for quality applicants. Hard-working, dependable people with enthusiasm and energy to give to a job are in demand. Good work traits can shine in an internship and lead you closer to a much-desired job.

Employers and Personnel Directors

Employers and personnel directors respect good college preparation by their applicants. But this may not be enough. The added advantage of knowing that their entry-level people have proved themselves on the job can make a difference. And this is one reason internships can be part of that difference.

Tom Gorman was a talented student who followed a prudent course of varied internships and part-time employment to pave his way to success as a reporter. Gorman, a *Los Angeles Times* reporter for 15 years, is now assigned to the newspaper's San Diego bureau. He describes his journalism training beginning at age 15:

I wrote a letter to the editor on some incident in the news when I was a high school sophomore. He liked my letter, put it on the Teen Page and gave me a job on this weekly for a year. Most of my pay was gas money and freebies of one kind or another.

At age 16 I moved to a daily newspaper—the *Daily Pilot*—in a nearby community and covered night meetings, writing news, features and sports, with much of my instruction coming from very helpful editors. My work continued into college.

My previous experience qualified me as a freshman for a news bureau job with the student body organization. It was a $150-a-month grant, and I kept the job all four of my years in college. In those days it helped meet college expenses.

In the summer following my freshman year and after I had completed the basic news writing and reporting classes, I did an informal internship with a county public information office, writing features and doing PR work. Through a contact with my teacher, a *Los Angeles Times* editor and part-time university copyediting instructor, I was able to get a summer internship in a zone section of the *Times*. This served as my required credit internship at the university. It might also be described as a vacation relief assignment, handling news and features.

Following graduation I had to work at both a daily newspaper part-time and at a PR agency where my writing skills could be used. The *Times* offered me a full-time general reporting job in two years, chiefly because of my previous internship there.

There is absolutely nothing to compare with internships! It's not only the improvement of your writing and learning the skills of reporting but also the excellent interaction with caring editors.

Every university has its "stars": students who, through work experiences or internships, or both, can move directly from college into higher levels and very well paid communications positions. But these are the exceptions, and competition today in all areas of the communications field has increased the number of intermediate steps you need to take in your career.

> *Consider how those who work with interns as supervisors view the process: what do they expect from an intern? What are their needs?*

Winning a reporting position on a large metropolitan newspaper within two years of graduation, as the Gorman example shows, happens only with a sharpening of skills and work habits through a variety of interrelated jobs—all in the field of communications. The combination of jobs and internships can lead to a successful career.

The following examples are not necessarily typical of how all employers view interns. But they do provide some insights into what can be expected by communications employers working with interns.

Jim Scott is a partner at a successful advertising agency owned by three professional colleagues. He comments:

We take interns from a couple of colleges but not on a regular basis. However, there may be two or three interns here in a given semester. The media director seems to have the most need, but interns are also used in account services and traffic. Occasionally, we will have an intern in creative, working either with me or with one of the other creative people.

Our philosophy is simple. We work closely with the college in evaluating the interns and assuring each intern of significant work experience—no phone answering or clerical work. The intern's supervisor meets with faculty who visit to evaluate progress. The intern gets college credit for their hours. We start paying them when the credit hours are finished.

For example, one of our creative people worked with an intern last semester to complete his 170-hour college requirement. After that we hired him on an hourly basis. He still works with us this semester part time helping with some print and radio copy.

We greatly prefer advertising majors who are dedicated to going into the business. Last summer we had an excellent intern who was a young woman from the University of Oregon.

Jay Goldberg, who owns his own high-tech public relations agency, has had interns from two colleges for the past eight years. He often speaks to PR students at a nearby university. He comments on pay and what he looks for in selecting an intern:

I believe that each intern should be paid regardless of whether or not the school is awarding credit. I pay each intern $5 an hour for two or three days work a week. Usually, there is only one intern aboard at a time.

I must have good writing skills. Sometimes I give a small writing test to check grammar, spelling, etc. I don't think that I should have to teach that. While we have technical companies as clients, I can teach the interns the technical side as long as they have good writing and organizational skills.

I prefer to pay because in truth the intern is doing all the work that an entry-level PR person will do. This includes some phone and mailing work.

Most of the intern's work is in handling PR releases, media contact work, special event pro-motions and related tasks. Probably about one of three interns is hired by us on a part-time basis the semester following their internship period. Most are good. Some have become full-time employees here but leave after a year or two. I can't compete with larger PR firms on salaries.

I enjoy working with interns a lot. What do I look for in an intern? Good writing samples and other evidence of related skills such as graphics or photo skills. An interest in public relations business certainly helps. Most important, I want an intern not afraid of work, one who has a good attitude and will be here on time tomorrow. That's not asking a lot.

An analysis of these examples should be helpful to you if you are trying to decide between advertising or public relations. Some agencies will accept communications or any related undergraduate major as long as the intern is seriously interested in advertising or public relations.

As the advertising agency owner implied, media internships are often more readily available than those in account services, traffic or creative. Many agencies with large media-intensive accounts may assign interns to media planning or media buying. (See Chapter 6 for more explanation of the work assigned to media interns.)

You may have noted that the intern was getting some credit and that a faculty coordinator would visit the site. This may account for the remark that no phone or clerical work was assigned. Even though clerical tasks are often part of entry-level job descriptions, conscientious supervisors will want you to avoid this work and concentrate on all that you can learn about the advertising business. Secretaries and receptionists, they say, are available to answer phones and handle routine tasks.

Pay Is a Complex Issue

Pay is often available to journalism, photography and public relations interns, but it generally is not offered for advertising, radio, television or film interns. However, you shouldn't conclude that it will be impossible to get a paying internship in advertising. Pay is possible if you have strong art and/or graphics skills or you are particularly talented in writing. Some internships in advertising sales and marketing departments are paid, but most of these paid positions are in urban areas with larger ad agencies or in-house advertising departments of large companies.

> *Pay depends chiefly on the area of communications.*

A study of several western colleges with internship programs in 1989 showed that about 80 percent of the PR interns were paid an average of $6.75 an hour. The other 20 percent included interns with non-profit organizations and some who accepted unpaid internships. Those working in the non-profit sector were awarded stipends or scholarships, the costs of which were not figured in this study.

The issue of pay is controversial, even among college and university advisers. And, of course, the possibility of pay by a company or organization reflects the economic climate. Some recession-hit companies eliminated pay for interns as one of their first budget cuts. Later chapters discuss pay more. For now, here's a summary of some of the practices relative to pay:

- Some companies insist on paying interns as a general policy. Credit may or may not be awarded, depending on the participating school.
- Some colleges have their own rules about pay and credit. For example, interns who are getting paid cannot receive credit. You need to check the policy at your school.
- A paid part-time job in communications may interest you and greatly benefit

your résumé building. You may gain valuable work experience and learn a lot about the company or organization where you are working. But, if this is a receptionist position or a job with largely clerical duties, it may not be appropriate for an internship. Faculty coordinators say that these communications jobs should be posted on job placement boards, not on internship lists.

- The question of pay is closely tied to another issue of great concern to employers—the writing skills of college graduates. Many internship site supervisors, recalling their own good education in writing and editing classes, are unhappy with the ability of today's graduates. They complain frequently about encountering students who can't spell and who know little about grammar and word usage. Some have developed their own writing tests that they give to entry-level applicants and internship candidates.
- Some public relations internship sites have increased their hourly wage to attract interns with superior writing and editing skills. The rule at many corporate and PR agency sites is not only to require substantial writing samples when you apply for an internship but also to ask you to pass a writing test before any interviews.

> *Interns with computer skills can often teach something to their supervisors.*

Computer skills are a different matter. Most interns arrive with only basic skills, but they can be trained quickly. Some sites send interns to workshops or classes, often paying any tuition or costs for the instruction. Then interns can master programs they will be using while working at their internships.

A smaller number of interns can increase their pay by bringing to the site higher-level computer skills. In fact, interns trained in state-of-the-art computer labs at universities may bring some unique skills to their sites. Some have helped train their supervisors in desktop publishing and introduced new software packages.

Regardless of pay or other issues, when you embark on an internship, always keep asking yourself: How do I ensure a quality experience for myself? How do I avoid problems? The following chapters of this book will help you answer these two important questions.

Probably your own campus newspaper has run stories or columns on the negative aspects of internships. Such off-the-top-of-my-head articles appear occasionally, even at colleges where the internship program grants credit. Such an article may describe the endless trips an intern "go-fer" had to run or the experiences of conquering old copy machines or responding to the unreasonable requests of employees of the firm. Often, the writer is soured on all internships based on one unhappy experience, so the articles never tell you that good internships exist and how to get them. The bad news drives out the good news.

It's true that a percentage of students in all internship programs have some negative experiences that don't fully test or expand their skills. But such unhappy situations can be avoided. Just remember to be careful in considering internship openings. The next chapter will help you avoid the pitfalls and learn the preparatory steps to guide you through a good internship. The more you know about what to expect, the better your chances for success.

Before moving on to Chapter 2, let's look at some questions posed by students who were prospective interns seeking information. Answers are supplied by experienced faculty coordinators and employers, including one who has supervised many interns at a large communications company.

Questions and Answers

Q. I understand that one needs a high GPA for most major advertising agencies. I hope that I can be considered with an overall GPA of about 2.75. I have some experience at a small ad agency, and I really want to enter the field. I would like to get a creative internship at a big agency. What are my chances?

A. In the first place, what is your GPA in your major? If your major is marketing or advertising and your major GPA is better than your overall GPA, you should have no problem. Emphasize on your résumé your experience at the small agency. You may need a letter of recommendation from the owner or manager stating what advertising work or projects you completed.

Getting a "creative" internship at a big agency is another matter. This can be a big problem because few large ad agencies offer creative internships compared with the number available in media or account management. You need to lower your expectations a bit to get your foot in the door. You may be able to get an account management internship or one in media planning or media buying. Then you'll have a chance to meet and impress people with your good work habits. If you're a good intern, you may get a job in media or traffic and later on move into the creative area.

Grades are still important in screening applicants for ad agencies.

The competition for large agency internships can be tough, and you may have to move to a major media market. Those who employ interns say they want only the brightest and best. If you were working in an agency and had a chance to get an intern, you also would want to select the very best. One frequently used gauge, unfortunately for some, is grades, especially in classes that teach specialized skills.

Q. Some employers seem to think that any job with their company should be eligible for internship credit. But at our school some jobs do not qualify for internship credit. What is the policy at most colleges?

A. There is no one strict policy, which will vary by school. Some colleges try to monitor their internship programs carefully to make certain that interns are actually producing for the newspapers, magazines and various companies where they're working. At our credit program, we want to see that interns are collecting writing and other samples from their internship work. We also encourage sites to pay interns.

To separate approved internship sites from employers seeking interns for mostly clerical work, we maintain a job notebook. A PR agency may call wanting to fill a receptionist position and says that the person can work into an account executive position in six months. The pay is entry level, and we would list it in the notebook and post it as a job. But this job doesn't meet the requirements for internship credit because the worker is doing mostly clerical work.

Q. What about phoning prospective internship sites?

A. Some university internship programs deal with the same sites each semester or each year and may have a listing of these regular sites. In this case, it may be best to simply call the contact person at the internship. Some request that interns do this so that a brief interview on the phone can disclose whether the intern is either not qualified for or not interested in what this particular site has to offer.

However, when you're getting your own internship, it's best to send a résumé and cover letter outlining your skills as a first step. If you get no response (be sure your

phone number or a message number is on your résumé), phone after a week or two to see if your résumé has been received and if you can set up an interview.

Phoning can be a problem. The right person to reach (potentially your site supervisor) may be very busy and not easily contacted. Explain on voice mail, if available, who you are and that you need an appointment and then leave both day and evening phone numbers.

Experience Is Rated as Top Hiring Factor

A survey of San Francisco State University (SFSU) students who graduated in May 1993 and are now employed shows that *work-related experience, including internships,* was the single most important factor in their getting hired. According to Don Casella, director of SFSU's Career Center, who conducted the survey, employers value work-related experience much more than academic major, GPA, job contacts or the personality of the job seeker.

Comparing the current survey of SFSU grads with similar studies conducted by the center since 1980 shows a clear trend, Casella said. Although the importance of work experience has been increasing consistently over time as a factor in respondents' getting jobs (from 35 to 56 percent), the degree to which the academic major plays a role has been declining (from 30 to 13 percent). Other factors respondents rate higher today include the role of personality (from 10 to 30 percent) and knowing someone who has the power to hire (from 7 to 15 percent).

Q. I have good skills and a high GPA. Our college doesn't offer credit for internships. Why should I try for an internship that may involve my giving up a good part-time job? Since I have work experience, is it that important?

A. Obviously, not all graduates need internships. Some can't complete internships for a variety of reasons. The question about how helpful such training will be depends on the type of job you have. Is it related to your career plans? Are you able to apply some of the communications skills from your courses? Today, most graduates have been employed in several part-time jobs before they finish college. Experience in the workplace is important, but much depends on what kind of experience you're getting.

As an intern, you get "special" treatment. You may advance on your internship into assignments and job tasks close to those given entry-level workers. But you aren't under the pressure to perform as a real employee. Hopefully, the internship is designed to give you necessary training to test your skills.

The results of a good internship experience produce much more than simply the training you have received. A letter of recommendation—a valued addition to your résumé—samples of work assigned, networking with employees, experience in dealing with a supervisor, etc., are among many possible outcomes.

Q. I'm a journalism major seeking a summer internship. I mailed cover letters, résumés and writing samples to more than 15 daily newspapers with few or no results. They were directed to the managing editor at each paper. I have a 3.2 GPA and am currently managing editor of my campus daily. Also, I work part time in sports for a nearby daily, so most of my clips are sports news and features. Why didn't I get a better response to my queries?

A. One possibility is that you weren't including the right kind of clips. If you are applying to a daily for a general reporting or non-sports assignment, you will need to include a wide range of clips, including hard news and features. Samples from both your job and campus paper would be needed. If

you were applying for sports, varied sports clips including sports features would be required.

You also might not be checking with personnel people at the paper to find out whether there is a contact person who handles initial internship applications. Completing and filing an application by the deadline each year may be a requirement. Paid internships on medium and large newspapers are very competitive, and most have early deadlines. One editor said he selected his summer interns by January 1 to get the best candidates.

Check directories and watch for announcements at your school from newspapers of interest to you. Frequently, you need to get the specific name of the person handling internships. Résumés are easily lost if they aren't sent to the right person. A daily is a busy place.

Q. I'm an advertising major but I don't want to go to an advertising agency for an internship. I have good writing skills and am interested in PR or marketing sites. I have a marketing minor. I am willing to go anywhere. What should I do to improve my chances?

A. You need to start early. If you live in a rural area, you may have to look to larger cities and markets. Check directories of PR agencies and large companies with publications, communications and/or marketing departments. One key is to make the company understand that you have no problem in working and finding housing in a distant city. A college near the city may offer inexpensive dorm housing, especially in the summer. State in your cover letter how you can handle room and board and whether you have a car, which may be necessary in some situations.

A call to a company may get you the name of the marketing manager so that your cover letter and résumé will be directed to a specific person. Learn as much as possible about the company so that in your cover letter you will be able to discuss the company's clients or products. If you have business experience with similar clients or products, note that as well. You may need to be available for an in-person interview.

Q. You hear a lot about networking, but what can you do if you have no work experience and don't know any people working in the communications field?

A. There are at least two good sources for you: alumni and professors at your college. Send a résumé and letter to several alumni who are working in the field of communications that you prefer. Ask for an appointment for career advisement, telling them that you are graduating from the same college they attended. The odds are good that you'll get an appointment for an interview.

After you ask for career advice and tips on getting a job or internship, you can start networking. If they like you and are interested in helping, you may get an introduction to the personnel director or someone who has an opening. Often, it's best to avoid personnel or human resource departments. Try to go directly to the person in the department with the job.

Search for alumni who are active in your alumni association because they care about the school and the students. The alums who are officers or are on planning committees may appear to be busy, but many will make time to talk to an interested student.

Professors can also be a good networking source. They may have worked in the field and may know of agencies or companies that take interns in the summer. Or they may have contacts in a city where you would consider an internship. Some belong to organizations such as Women in Communications, Inc., (WICI) that have established programs to help interns seeking sites.

Q. I'm a PR major looking for a non-profit agency or organization for an internship. Where do I look?

A. In addition to directories of internship sites, there are many listings of non-profit organizations in almost all cities. Some-

times networking can help. Checking with the PR directors of non-profit agencies in your own area can lead to contacts in other cities. For example, the American Heart Association, the American Lung Association and the American Cancer Society and other organizations may know who the PR people are in their organizations in other communities.

Don't overlook small non-profit groups. Organizations such as Prevent Blindness, Mothers Against Drunk Driving and Easter Seals may need an intern. Fund-raisers, promotional projects and public relations activities exist in all groups. Hands-on experience is very possible for an intern, especially if you can show that you have skills in areas such as writing, graphics and newsletter production.

Often, these organizations don't pay interns, but some may have enough budget to offer a stipend or scholarship. Some will pay mileage, tuition and other expenses. Getting some kind of credit from your college can go a long way toward alleviating problems of insurance or requirements for university affiliation.

If you're a professional or student member of an organization, you can write to the organization's national headquarters to request help in locating in another market. Or check with members of your local chapter for help. WICI, the Society of Professional Journalists (SPJ) and the International Association of Business Communicators (IABC) assist graduates with both internship and job leads. However, SPJ would assist on news site requests, not PR non-profits. In writing your query, stress two points: (1) explain why you want to work in a non-profit public relations area, and (2) indicate a specific city or region for the site. For the latter you would need some compelling reasons, such as you want to move to this city or you have personal or family reasons.

Q. Does it matter when during my college program I do an internship?

A. This question has two different

responses; first, from a faculty coordinator. Of course, much depends on the skills of an intern—what courses are completed and previous internships or related work experience. Some internships are earmarked for freshmen or sophomores. Some magazines and newspapers reject seniors or graduate students. They want only juniors who are returning to school. This is probably because they don't want a senior to be disappointed if he or she doesn't get a job after the internship. Some newspapers don't hire entry-level people.

If you are well prepared and have good writing and computer skills, go ahead and do an internship when you're a junior. Many students do several internships, and some don't get credit for any of them.

A site supervisor answers this way: I find that the best interns are those with the maximum skills. For a communications major, probably the senior year will allow the addition of a business course or two. Or maybe the completion of a skills course as a senior will make the internship applicant much better prepared to handle the assignments I have.

I prefer a senior just getting ready for graduation and willing to do an internship with us before hitting the job market. I see no problem with the "no job" situation. We are honest with interns and tell them that it's unlikely that a job will develop during the time they are here with their internships. If they want more of a guarantee of a job, they should go elsewhere. If a position should suddenly open and the intern is qualified and has been doing excellent work, then he or she can certainly apply and probably will be one of the top candidates.

Q. As a broadcast journalist, I want to get as much hands-on experience as possible. Some internships at our school are limited to production assistant work. At times, these don't test the skills I have developed in broadcasting. What should I do?

A. As you probably already know, you're in a very competitive field. You

should start with a non-credit internship that may include some production assistant work to get some experience on your résumé. Maybe a local cable television or small radio station can help. You will then have an advantage over others in seeking a better site for a second internship.

> *Television interns start at the bottom of the ladder because the field is competitive.*

Directories of radio and television stations may supply some leads. Try to look in places where potential jobs show up such as ads in *Broadcasting & Cable* magazine and at listings from radio and TV placement services. Some of these stations may be looking for a good intern willing to work hard. Maybe a job is possible there. Of course, your chances may be better in a smaller market where there is less competition.

In addition to a good résumé and cover letter, a performance tape from your school showing you covering an event or story definitely can help in introducing your skills.

Q. What if the internship is boring or isn't providing any real experience? Can one just quit?

A. Quitting may reflect unfavorably on you and your school. It may be best to stick it out, but the decision depends on several factors. Is the initial job description being followed? Can you discuss the problems with your supervisor or perhaps the person who hired you for the internship? Ask yourself "What would make this a better internship?"

It's possible that the supervisor is too busy to see what you are or aren't doing. It's possible that you aren't getting the assignments that you were promised. It also could be the case that you haven't completed one assignment to their satisfaction and they are afraid to give you more of this type of work.

If you're on your own with no university support, you'll need to remind the site supervisor that the tasks in the job description are not being assigned to you. If the work assigned is what you and the site people agreed to initially, you may just have to finish the internship. The good news in this is that you've learned that you don't want to work in that particular job. Many interns test their career interests this way.

If you simply can't get along with your supervisor, you may have to take steps to terminate the internship. Check with your university faculty adviser if you're getting credit. If not, give sufficient notice before leaving.

Q. What effects do business recessions have on internships?

A. Obviously, many paid internships are put on hold or dropped permanently during times of economic recession. For example, in the early 1990s many newspapers had to cancel internships because of budget cutbacks. While one directory author said that 90 percent of newspaper internships are still paid, he added that there are far fewer of them than five years ago.

In the areas of broadcasting and advertising where there are fewer paid internships to begin with, internship opportunities may increase as business conditions improve. Many companies and agencies want unpaid interns. They help to fill positions of entry-level workers who were victims of layoffs.

For Thought and Discussion

1. Some employers want interns to do minor clerical or routine secretarial tasks. Most faculty advisers try to keep such jobs off of their internship lists. Discuss three other problems that communications interns may face when employers and site supervisors write job descriptions that do not give the intern a sufficient learning experience.

2. Explain how an internship could derail a career-bound student and lead him or her into an entirely different area. Discuss both positive and negative outcomes for the intern.

3. Discuss some steps that can be taken by each person involved—intern, site supervisor and faculty adviser—to arrange what might be described as an ideal internship.

4. Assume that you are the PR person for your college. The news director of a local radio station has asked you to prepare a radio program on your college's internship program for airing soon. Prepare an outline showing all information and sources that will present a positive approach, especially seeking to encourage local businesses to participate.

5. Compose a sample letter for critique by your instructor or classmates as a model for the student seeking an internship with a non-profit organization. Give reasons why you want to work with a specific non-profit group. Also, sell the idea of doing the internship in a specific city, giving reasons for your choice.

6. Some faculty members and employers debate on whether a student should receive academic credit, pay or both. Divide into small groups and spend 15 minutes discussing the subject. Have a spokesperson from each group present to the class their views and position on the subject.

CHAPTER 2

PLAN AHEAD: PREPARATIONS FOR INTERNSHIPS

PREPARATIONS FOR AN INTERNSHIP can take a substantial amount of time. As you go through the steps necessary to search for that ideal internship, consider how Susan Hamerski applied initiative and hard work to find herself a public relations internship. Across the country, more and more students are following her example. Frequently, it takes a big effort on your part, especially if you have little or no help. A senior PR major at Winona State University in Minnesota, Hamerski decided that she wanted to find an internship in a major city. She compiled a large list of potential internship sites.

Targeting chiefly corporate communications, hotels and hospitals, Hamerski mailed out 150 letters of inquiry along with her résumé. She received about 80 responses, many reporting that no intern program was offered by the company or organization. But she got some positive responses too and narrowed her list to five sites that she seriously considered. Only one, at an insurance company, promised a salary. This was attractive, but it was a new program and Hamerski

would have been the first intern there.

So she chose a hotel site in a major market far from home. It was an unpaid internship. The chief reason for her selection was that the hotel's PR coordinator had supervised several interns from a nearby university over several years. Hamerski believed that working with a supervisor who had previous experience with interns more likely would produce meaningful assignments for her. She explains:

This internship from late March to May gave me five quarter units of credit and allowed me to return to Minnesota for graduation in May. I had a faculty supervisor at my college should any questions or problems arise. I maintained a log of my activities, showing what I did and what hours I worked in the hotel's public relations and marketing department.

Working from 20 to 30 hours per week, I completed a major project in addition to a number of writing assignments. The project was a questionnaire I developed for use by the hotel to query customers on services, etc. in the hotel's several restaurants. I did a lot of writing so that samples were available to show my faculty adviser as well as any future employer.

> *"I did a lot of writing so that samples were available to show my faculty adviser as well as any future employer."*

The story continues with comments by Janine Fiddelke, Hamerski's on-site supervisor and a public relations coordinator for the hotel:

Susan was a good intern, one of the best that we have had recently. A good writer, she was able to handle a number of writing assignments. I prefer journalism interns as they generally have better writing skills than those with PR majors, but Susan performed well.

Tasks in our department assigned to interns include work on a newsletter that spotlights entertainment acts in our restaurants and lounges, in-house communications such as guest directories, tent cards for booths in the restaurants, letters and memos, and participation in seminars and programs for travel and restaurant writers. There is some contact work in the city convention bureau as well as media relations work.

We ask the interns to compile a reader while here. A reader is simply a file, much like a portfolio, showing copied samples of all work including business letters, press releases and memos to me and my assistant on projects started or completed. The reader reflects, in effect, what the intern did and shows us the variety of tasks that we expect all interns to do. We closely supervise the work of all interns.

This example has a happy ending. After her graduation, Hamerski returned to the area where the hotel is located and soon got a job as a PR writer with an agency specializing in financial public relations. She said that the reader—the showcase of her internship—was a big factor in being hired.

It will be helpful to analyze this example more fully. Some aspects may be helpful to you as you seek your own internship.

- First, note that as a senior Hamerski was able to get academic credit for her internship. She mentioned this fact in her inquiry letters. Since the hotel had been dealing with a university giving credit for internships, this information was considered important by her prospective supervisor.
- Second, note that Hamerski started the search for the internship early the previous year. Remember that Hamerski had to mail out more than 100 cover letters and résumés. She had to accept a good deal of rejection because most of her respondents were not interested.
- Third, a major hotel in a large market proved a good choice. After Hamerski's graduation, PR employment opportunities were available if she decided to stay in the area.
- Finally, note that Hamerski's only "pay" from the hotel was two complete meals given free to each intern each day worked. Travel and housing expenses may have made this internship too much of a financial burden for some. It would help many people to have friends or relatives living in the area and willing to help you out with inexpensive housing.

Remember Hamerski's comment that the hotel's several years of experience with interns helped her in getting significant work assignments. Also, the site supervisor had an assistant, making it easier to get help if needed.

Checking Your Skills

A big step in the preparation process for an internship is to have the confidence that you have the necessary communications skills. Knowing the basics is very important. Your competition is well prepared.

In addition to having basic computer skills, you need a thorough knowledge of the organizational methods for communications writing. A news story or PR release may be required. This background may come from a high school journalism class, basic college courses and/or a previous part- or full-time job in the field.

> *Earlier work experience can be an advantage in developing skills and understanding the demands of the workplace.*

Earlier work experience, related or unrelated to what you may be assigned to do at your internship, is an advantage. You may have important skills in working with colleagues and clients from your previous job. An understanding of the demands of the workplace can help you in adjusting to assignments.

Some Ways College Interns Started

Seniors who were candidates for internships noted these previous experiences on their résumés:

✓ Sports or feature writer for a local weekly newspaper.
✓ Assistant to a hospital's community relations director.
✓ Production assistant for a local cable station.
✓ Photographer for a local magazine.
✓ Newsletter editor for a local church publication.
✓ Assistant to a high school teacher assigned to produce football programs and sports publicity.
✓ Volunteer for a non-profit organization.

Some students with communications interests start working in the field early. It's common to hear professionals in journalism and public relations describe their first experiences as reporters on their high school newspapers. Also, some have community organizational work as volunteer high school interns. If you have this experience, you learn the importance of team work and the values of contact with the public and community leaders.

Sharon Finsterbush, PR director of a chapter of the American Lung Association, maintains a regular year-round program involving high school students interested in communications.

We work with the top academic/athlete students from several high schools. They are selected for their leadership skills. This successful program draws students in several times a semester for publicity, special events and public relations tasks involving a variety of community activities.

High school students are capable and willing to work. While there are always tasks involving filing, mailing and clerical chores that entry-level public relations people also have to do, these students become very involved in special events, too. Those with photography skills have worked out well. Now with desktop publishing, students with basic computer skills and interests in design and production can produce newsletters.

Regardless of how or when you develop necessary skills, you must be sure that you meet the requirements of a specific internship. Job descriptions may lack sufficient detail to show what skills you will need. Explore this very carefully in any initial interview or letter.

There is no model internship program to follow. If you're getting credit (usually elective, rarely required), you may meet a faculty coordinator for directions. You may even be assigned an internship location or given leads to check. Or you may be on your own. Some schools allow credit, but you must discover your own place to work. The preparatory steps take much longer without a faculty coordinator to help guide you.

Let's look at two faculty coordinators to see what they do to help interns. Polly Flug, internship coordinator at Drake University, says that internships there may be on a credit or no-credit basis, depending on arrangements with the student's adviser. She adds:

We encourage students to do two or three internships, if possible, as today's job market requires it. They need strong writing samples and portfolio items to compete.

My principal job is to locate sites. A number of Des Moines ad agencies and public relations organizations participate in our program. But some students, chiefly in advertising, often intern in the summer and live at home. Many sites are out of this area.

Students keep a diary of their activities at an internship and file a final report at the end of the internship.

Leonard Hooper coordinates an advertising internship program at the University of Florida. Students work both full- and part-time internships in his program. He comments:

We award from one to three units (the latter if a full-time 40-hour-per-week summer internship) of elective credit. About two-thirds of the advertising majors complete internships during the summer, fall or spring semesters.

Some go home for internships. One of my tasks is to maintain a book of available local sites. In advertising there are retail and department stores as well as restaurant chains with in-house ads to do. Some interns produce radio-TV commercials and brochures while others are involved in direct marketing firms and sales sites. Some go to ad agencies.

We ask that supervisors assign significant work to evaluate each intern. This is the way to learn the business. *Regardless of where they intern, our students get exposed to background which may be applicable to many parts of the advertising business.*

Timing: A Critical Consideration

As one of your early preparatory steps, you need to decide on just when you will do your internship, although depending on your site, the actual decision may be out of your hands. Many public relations and advertising firms refuse interns during the summer when business slows down and there isn't much challenging work for interns. Managers of some companies ask for interns to start in late summer or early fall. Other companies or organizations with special needs search for summer interns, sometimes to fill in for vacationing employees.

> *Coordinate your schedule with the needs of the company.*

One of the major reasons for a negative report on a site is that the intern says there was insufficient skilled work to do. Timing can be a critical factor in the success or failure of your internship experience. An agency may lose a client or two and experience a sudden drop in work. It's appropriate for you as a prospective intern to ask a supervisor if there will be projects and assignments for a meaningful work experience at the time you want to intern. If the answer is "no" or even a tentative "perhaps," you need to look elsewhere.

You may need to discuss with your supervisor the best time for you to work. Evenings and weekends are preferred by some broadcast journalist interns because fewer regular reporters are on duty those hours. If your college classes allow, you may wish to work several days in a row to increase the chances of completing assigned projects quickly.

MFigure Your Time

Many television stations in major markets have a number of internships for production assistants. Some have specific hourly requirements that may exceed those needed for credit at a university. They may list more hours than you as an intern can devote in a given semester or quarter. It's up to you as the prospective intern to ask for a definite agreement at the initial interview regarding the schedule of hours, days and weeks.

One intern left an internship at a TV station when the completed hours met those required for university course credit. The station's intern coordinator refused to sign off, stating that the station's internship guidelines called for an additional 50 hours beyond university requirements even though it was an unpaid internship. *Clarify your hours before you start.*

Obstacles to Meet and Beat

As you look for an internship, consider questions that will help smooth your career path. Be positive that your selection is on target toward your goals. Collecting internships merely to add to your résumé is not an answer.

▪ **What are your professional goals?** Make a list of companies or organizations that will help you move toward your goals. Don't include attractive organizations that may appear to be fun or entertaining but have little to do with plans for your career.

Since applying for an internship approximates what you will do in looking for your first job, focus sharply on prospective sites that seek your interests and skill level. Your list needs to include a number of possibilities because some sites will be deleted as the process progresses.

▪ **When are you available to do an internship?** Some sites want juniors or only seniors. Prerequisites frequently are an obstacle to overcome. Also, some sites may wish advanced computer skills, so you will need time to attend a special workshop or take an additional unexpected class. *This is why you need to consider internship planning at least a year ahead of when you will actually intern.*

Some sites may have a particular semester or quarter in mind for bringing in an intern. If you aren't available in the fall when an intern is requested by a site, you may have to strike that site from your list.

At many universities internships are offered through cooperative education offices. These are usually organized on an alternative semester plan; you will work one semester full time and then return to school full time the next semester. Or there may be variations. Such internships all require long-range planning, especially for financial and academic scheduling considerations.

▪ **Are you overqualified?** You'll discover that a few locations require minimal skills and the tasks are limited and routine. You should pass on these, as well as on anywhere the workload duplicates your previous work experiences.

You may not want this particular internship, but you are attracted to the company. It may meet some of your career objectives. Ask for help. A personnel manager or interviewer may steer you to other internship opportunities within the company that will meet your long-range planning objectives and for which you are better qualified.

▪ **Are you underqualified?** The higher pay and working conditions at some of the more prestigious internships are certainly attractive. But if you lack the right skill level, you may have to leave them off your list. This is especially true if you don't have solid writing skills.

Al Hewitt, a former Scripps-Howard editor who as a faculty internship coordinator has placed hundreds of interns, says the high level of grammar, spelling and punctuation skills required may prove a handicap for some students. Supervisors complain that they can't be guaranteed that an intern's writing will be up to requirements, so they schedule skills testing after receiving résumés (see Appendix A for sample tests).

Hewitt recommends that students get more experience on smaller newspapers and at public relations sites where writing is not the chief assignment. Then he suggests applying at a large newspaper or major PR firm after all writing courses are completed and basic skills mastered. He points out that many internship applicants at major newspapers have several internships under their belts before applying at a well-paid, competitive site.

As some of the examples in the chapters ahead show, you don't want to repeat job descriptions merely to have another company on your résumé. A second or third internship should move you significantly up the experience ladder. You can learn more as well as perfect new skills. A second internship should represent a new challenge for you.

> Although many companies list a preference of major for their interns, many internships are open to any college major who has good skills.

Before looking at the information on specific job descriptions, glance at this list from the site directory of a university department. These examples give you a brief look at what can be available for juniors and seniors.

Journalism

Brentwood Daily Star. Internships available in news or feature writing or both. News includes coverage of evening city council and school board meetings. Photo skills helpful but not required. No pay but part-time work available after internship for qualified people.

County Daily Progress. Internships available each semester in newspaper's special community editions published twice a week. Both news and features. Sometimes business news internship open. Flexible hours. Pay is $5 an hour for 240 hours per semester. Plus mileage. A writing test is part of application procedure.

State Magazine. Internships primarily in research and fact checking. Opportunity to observe all phases of magazine production work. $200 month stipend for 12 to 15 hours (flexible) per week for semester. Send along writing samples with an application letter.

Public Relations

Multiple Sclerosis Society. Wide variety of hands-on experience including writing news releases, chapter newsletters, fundraising events and other PR-oriented activities. Working with public relations coordinator. Opportunity for interested interns to speak to elementary schools on society's programs.

David Public Relations. Varied tasks in addition to writing press releases, assisting in media relations, media pitching and client contact work. Flexible hours. Two days a week. $5 an hour. Several recent interns have been hired following internships at this agency.

Presbyterian Hospital. Very strong writing skills a must. Writing test at interview. Writing news releases and articles for hospital publications. Special event planning. $7 an hour for 220 hours per semester. Flexible days and hours.

Assemblywoman Jane Smith. This $500

stipend internship is in a state legislator's district office. It involves constituent correspondence, research, assisting with public functions and other PR tasks. A close-up look at government and politics.

WRT Corp. General public affairs internship includes press releases, special projects, research for media campaigns, press relations and writing articles for publications. Paid $6.40 an hour for a minimum of two days a week each semester and summer.

Advertising or Marketing

Jansen Associates. Long-time local agency has a mix of accounts. Four internships are offered each semester: two in account services, media and traffic. Media intern must understand terms in planning or buying media. Also, this intern will do some competitive analysis. Account intern will be assigned to different groups. Unpaid.

Dyer & Associates. Position in traffic control or vendor services. Involves production control. Work with all people and parts of ad agency so good place to learn agency business.

County Daily Report. Area's largest newspaper has internship in promotion department. Pay is $6.00 an hour for 16-20 hours per week. Prefer two full days. Promotional copy writing and some press releases and publicity. Intern will learn about planning and holding special events such as 10K run, bicycle races, home shows, circus, etc. Production of brochures and work on employee communications.

Golden Publishing Company. Company publishes weekly newspapers for several areas. This is an advertising sales internship, and intern will complete a two-week training program at start. Interact with circulation and production departments. After training intern will assist sales representatives in calls and eventually will have own service area. Commission given. Job potential good.

Marketing By Design. Copy writing, media planning, coordinate campaigns and creative planning. Some graphics work possible, if intern has skills and interests. Mac experience helpful.

Broadcasting and Television

MD Corp. Major aircraft manufacturer has internships for those with good video production skills. Will perform utility duty on commercial and industrial productions to assist camera, tape operators and technical and engineering operations. Assist in stage/ studio setup.

Carter Presentations. Internships are open each semester in this company producing commercial and corporate videos for clients in several fields. Can start as production assistants and work up to handle equipment, etc. as non-union shop. Unpaid but more than 50 percent of present crew former interns.

County Department of Education. Hands-on production site. Will be involved with both studio and remote video productions, ¾- and ½-inch audio and video editing. Approximately 15 shows under production at all times. Open seven days a week so will take weekend and evening interns.

South City Cable Company. Local cable station for two communities can take interns in two areas: (1) video production interns to run camera, edit tape. Must be available to cover night city council meetings. (2) Intern with good writing skills to produce and write new shows. Opportunity to be on camera. Flexible hours.

Browns Broadcasting. Major network-affiliated TV station has varied production assistant internships in both news and non-news positions. News includes work in sports, weather, research, assignment desk, etc. Non-news includes assistance with new Kids Show, publicity and promotion tasks, broadcast standards office, assistant to editorial producer and work with locally originated programs.

Look for Special Job Descriptions

Comments like "not a good match" on an intern's final evaluation generally imply that the intern lacked skills or qualifications. If you don't feel comfortable with assignments when you first start and/or the work is too complex to understand, you need to speak with your supervisor. Moving to another assignment or transferring to another site might be a possibility.

Supervisors hate to fire interns. Instead, for various reasons, they'll assign less-demanding, more-routine work simply to let the intern complete the hours necessary for credit.

Avoid these situations by paying close attention to the job description. You need a clear, detailed job description that you can easily understand. If one isn't available and you're on your own in finding a site, you may have to confer with your prospective site supervisor. You may need to prepare specific objectives that will be part of your work description.

The job outline can be very simple when only one or two projects are under consideration. For example, one intern wrote an annual report for a company as the only project listed in the description of a PR internship. Let's select a site from the list above to see how a job description translates to assignments.

The listing for Presbyterian Hospital said: "Very strong writing skills a must. Writing test at interview. Writing news releases and articles for various hospital publications. Special event planning. $7 an hour for 220 hours per semester. Flexible days and hours."

Judy von der Nuell is a member of the public relations staff of this hospital in charge of publications. A major part of the internship description is for the intern to complete articles for "Innerviews," a hospital publication issued quarterly. (See Chapter 4 for complete details of this internship.) As the intern's supervisor, Judy uses a three-step model to show objectives, tasks and evidence of competency (Appendix B has information on competency-based internships):

1. State a clear objective for the major tasks that an intern will do.
Objective: Write an article on an approved topic for a hospital publication.
2. State specific activities that the intern must do to meet this objective.
Activities: Discuss with the supervisor possible topics and subjects. Research books and articles on the topic. Outline articles. Discuss with the supervisor a list of questions to ask hospital personnel as sources for the article. Conduct interviews. Write the article.
3. Describe, analyze and evaluate the end product or evidence of researching the objective.
Supervisor responsibility: Edit the completed article and check it for accuracy. Check to see if writing standards have been achieved.

Seeking That Special Site

If you have the services of a faculty internship coordinator or faculty adviser in your department or school, site hunting should be easier. You may be able to review the pages of a directory or compilation of sites used by your department's interns in the past. You can also get good leads from faculty in touch with alumni or with contacts at companies and media organizations that have hosted recent interns.

If there is no formal internship program at your school and little or no faculty assistance, you're on your own. The process of finding a suitable site may take longer, but help may still be available. Check to see whether your campus has a cooperative education or experiential learning office. Although they may not place interns directly into sites, they have files, directories and computer printouts listing internships by major, location, agency, etc. Some of these lists show openings in humanities and liberal arts as well as business and marketing. You may qualify for some of these openings.

While you're looking on campus, also consider on-campus offices and facilities for internship leads. You may want to intern in the university's sports information office, public affairs office, art gallery, museum or personnel office or at the campus newspaper or radio station.

One intern set up her own paid internship with an anthropology museum on a university campus. The director of the museum was pleased to budget for future interns after reviewing the progress of the intern's work during the year. Projects this intern completed included a new brochure, press releases, radio spots, handouts for tours, an annual report and advertisements of tours in the campus daily newspaper. The $9-an-hour internship attracted several applicants the following year.

Directories and guides to internships can be a good source of internship leads. You can find them in the job placement, counseling and financial aid offices and libraries at many campuses. (See Appendix A for a listing of current sources.) Don't place limitations on your search. You can use guides for majors in humanities, social sciences, business and management as well as in communications to locate internships. Some business guides show advertising and PR internships.

Many companies will accept well-qualified communications majors for internships in positions usually reserved for marketing or business majors. They're looking for young people with good communications skills, enthusiasm, an interest in the company and a willingness to learn regardless of major.

Organizations Can Help You

In looking for site leads, a number of

organizations can assist you (see Appendix A). Both local and national chapter members can help with referrals to markets in many states. Some groups have handouts for preparing résumés, provide interviewing strategies, show sample cover letters, etc. If you're heading for an urban area, they may have information on housing. They also have networking services like the National Press Photographers Association to give job leads when internships are finished.

Minority organizations can also be helpful (see Appendix A). The demand for more minority professionals continues in all areas of communications, especially in journalism and public relations. Profiles of some minority professionals in Chapter 8 reveal how much help organizational networking can be for internships and jobs.

Jesse Hornbuckle knows. A black photographer formerly with the *Dallas Times Herald* and now freelancing in Dallas, Hornbuckle can give at least two instances in which taking advantage of networking to meet professionals paid off:

I attended a college-sponsored job fair and was signed up with people from the *Times Herald* when I noticed the *Los Angeles Times* representative just sitting there. I interviewed with him on the spot, and a *Times* internship resulted. This was an especially valuable internship since it introduced me to the feature side of photojournalism.

My second valuable contact resulted from my membership in the National Association of Black Journalists. This led to my initial interview with the Dallas paper. I urge all prospective interns to join both local and national chapters of organizations. Be sure to attend all meetings, including national conventions.

> *Another place to seek a site is at a job fair.*

Hornbuckle, who did internships at the *Times* and *Times Herald*, also worked part time shooting sports photos for the *San Antonio Light*. He stresses the need to be well prepared with "your personal sales pieces," which are your portfolio of college newspaper photos and freelancing assignments. He adds: "You need to aggressively show and sell your skills to win an internship. Then you must get some very good quality news and feature pieces from your internship to sell yourself for a job."

Writing Your Résumé for Initial Interviews

Of course, the cornerstone of your preparations is an effective résumé, which will accompany your cover letter. Both of these introductory pieces must represent your best efforts at securing an interview at prospective sites. For your résumé and initial interviews, you should develop about a page of data on work and training.

> *Résumés and cover letters are your introduction to prospective internship sites.*

The résumé is most often structured around headings. Experts recommend opening with a block style of name, address, phone number (plus a message number, if needed) and a few lines detailing your skills. This is one place you can spotlight such things as fluency in a second language, computer skills you have mastered or your ability to use a camera.

Additional headings could include education, work experience, college activities including awards and honors, and professional memberships.

Reverse chronological order is the rule for listing items in a section. Thus, under work experience your most recent and rele-

vant job would appear first. Miscellaneous jobs, especially summer employment regardless of how unrelated to your present career goals, show initiative. Don't leave them off your first résumé. Personnel people like to see what contacts with the public you have had.

Your résumé must be typed or prepared on a word processor and carefully proofread. Make sure your writing is concise and direct and clearly presents the background information without going into unnecessary detail.

Although items such as college courses may fill out a short résumé, this is not the best way to show off what you have learned in these courses. For example, you might add, "As a member of a team in a media planning class, completed a plan for a national campaign to introduce a new chocolate bar." Or, "Wrote and had published three press releases about a non-profit organization as a public relations class project." Or, "Wrote headlines and completed all page layouts for a monthly campus laboratory newspaper."

Some Tips

- Ask a classmate or two to critique your résumé, looking for corrections and ways to better emphasize your experience. If an item is unclear, rewrite it.
- Some students become quite creative and develop very original approaches. However, a more conservative approach may be necessary for many companies and sites.
- Don't include your age, height, weight, marital status or a photo. You also don't need to list references. You can simply say they are available upon request. A professor you have worked with closely will be more likely to give you an honest recommendation. A dean may appear impressive on paper, but he or she may not know you well enough.
- Use action verbs: *managed, wrote, edited, produced, coordinated, designed, created.*

■ A two- or three-sentence description of a job should focus on tasks completed. For instance, telling what specific assignments you carried out to make a job fair successful is more useful than generally stating that you worked on a company project.

Experts don't agree on a standard résumé format or even what to include and what to leave out. Many examples of résumés can be found in career-oriented publications in college or city bookstores (see Appendix A).

B Do You Meet All Requirements?

efore you get too involved in a complex application form for an internship, check the fine print. Carefully read sections on who qualifies and who doesn't to save you and the company valuable time. Check the following:

✓ Does the program require a junior when you are a senior?
✓ Do you have an up-to-date form? This year's deadline may be much earlier.
✓ Do you meet residency requirements? For example, a number of newspapers take only interns from their region or state.
✓ Are there financial requirements? It may be an internship through a work-study program in which the students participating must be financially needy.
✓ Are you required to register for credit?
✓ Does the internship require a specific major? A firm may specify that only technical majors should apply.

C over Letter Pointers

A cover letter accompanies and enlarges on your résumé. If you were in Mexico for 15 months between your junior and senior years in college, an explanation in the cover letter clears up why you took longer than four years to get your degree.

Experts recommend that the cover letter be brief and to the point. And correct. You're seeking an appointment for an internship interview, so it's critical that you know the accurate spelling of the name and title of the person who will interview you. You may have to call the company to check on correct spelling or verify the name of the department.

Directing the cover letter to the right person can be critical in getting an interview. Sometimes this person can be a human relations representative or personnel manager. Trying to get an interview with a supervisor first and bypassing the human relations person can kill your chances of ever getting in the door.

You should note any special connection between your recent experiences and the company or its clients. For example, a student intern mentioned in her cover letter that she worked for a local travel agent. The advertising agency at which she was applying had just announced in the local newspaper that it had won a large travel agency account, so this was a plus for her.

Too many "surprises" in your cover letter may lessen your chances of obtaining an interview. For instance, you can explain during an interview why your GPA is lower than you would like rather than clutter your letter with it.

See Appendix A for books with sample cover letters.

Personal Portfolios

Portfolios can be very useful, so putting together your own personal portfolio is important. You should start collecting materials from your classes and early jobs, adding to and subtracting from these materials as you progress. You may accumulate good samples during your internship.

Creative and art interns find the portfolio the best way to display their work. You may have only class samples of advertising layouts, sketches and drawings, but they should go into your portfolio.

> *Your personal portfolio of your work demonstrates your communications skills.*

If you're a journalism intern, you should prepare clips from your previous campus daily or local newspaper work, including news, features and other articles you've written. You should include your clippings even though you may have sent other copies of them earlier along with your application. Material is easily misplaced.

If you're applying for a PR internship, you also might have clips to show. Your portfolio should hold any newsletters, press releases, fliers, brochures and other publicity materials illustrative of previous jobs or class work.

Not all applicants have portfolio products to show off at an internship interview. Agency account and media interns frequently have little to include even after completing an internship. You need to do what you can to demonstrate your communications skills. If you don't have many writing or art or creative class projects to show, you may have to settle for letters, memos and reports as writing samples. For some who finish internships, letters of recommendation, references and a journal or final report may constitute the principal portfolio pieces.

If you complete a radio or television internship, you may have a videotape or audiotape of a show you produced at the station. Or you may have been a member of a team that produced a show. Broadcast journalism students produce video résumés so viewers can check out their interviewing and reporting talents. You may have tapes from classes to show at an initial interview.

A point to note as a reminder: Watch for all opportunities to prepare a video résumé or gather samples of your work on productions during your internship. It's much easier to gather this as you go along rather than after the internship is over.

Maintain a diary or personal journal regardless of whether or not it's required for credit or even if you're interning on a noncredit basis. The journal can be a day-by-day report of activities at your internship including notations about new equipment or computer software you learn to use. And whatever you call it—a portfolio or reader or notebook—you need a place to hold your letters and memos as well as notes and communications from your supervisor.

This will greatly simplify the process of revising your résumé when you start the hunt for a job. Of course, you'll want to include your internship on your revised résumé. In addition to adding the internship, you can refer to your journal when writing a cover letter. Or you may wish to select some of the internship products to show a personnel director at a job interview when you're asked to explain what you accomplished as an intern.

Examples of internship products for your portfolio could include press releases, annual reports, newsletters, brochures, readership surveys, media plans, marketing reports, magazine articles, newspaper clippings, graphic layouts, advertising copy, technical reports, scripts, slide presentations, videotapes, audiotapes and fund-raising proposals.

The Ultimate in Testing

You may place in your portfolio large projects or writing assignments graded by instructors. But if you were lucky enough to get "tested" along the lines of the following example, you certainly would want to write about your experiences (how you got the internship) and show off your article.

Maureen Hughes is now Director of Public Affairs for Children's Hospital. Formerly as Public Relations Director for St. Luke's Hospital in Pasadena, Calif., she administered writing tests to internship and job applicants.

Hughes has been well aware of the problems PR interns have with writing skills. After attending a panel on hospital PR internships where she picked up on the idea, she started giving a writing test in the form of an assignment to intern and job applicants. She explains how this operates:

Several PR people have followed this exercise. You have all internship applicants write a news release announcing their arrival. It seems to work out well as a way to weed out many with poor writing ability.

I added this kind of test to screen applicants for the recent full-time job as assistant PR person in my office. We ran newspaper ads and called a large group of nearby colleges. We received 155 applicants. The writing test exercise helped to narrow the field eventually down to five people. It took close to six months to fill this job.

I assigned a 700- to 1000-word article on glaucoma to each of the five finalists. I gave them a one-week deadline. There is a good supply of material on glaucoma in books and pamphlets. I know the subject well as I had to do a recent piece on it. The assignment was to prepare the article for one of our hospital publications.

One applicant refused to do the assignment. One missed the deadline so was eliminated. Another person proved to be a very weak writer. Two prepared excellent articles and I hired the one I thought was best for the job.

Know How to Interview

You should interview at several sites, if possible. This will help you develop interviewing skills for later full-time positions. Faculty coordinators say that as you interview you learn more about your goals for the internship. A number of books outline general interviewing strategies (see Appendix A).

You may have to ask questions of your interviewer to determine whether you are really interested in the position. In addition, some information would be helpful regardless of site. If pay is minimal or none, find out if there are any company scholarships for which you would qualify or any stipends to cover your expenses. You can ask about reimbursement for gas money. If you use your car for company business, you should find out what forms and procedures must be followed to pay your expenses.

What about insurance? If you're not covered by the company, find out what kind of personal insurance the company recommends for you. Some interns who are registered for credit have insurance or a secondary policy written by university insurance carriers that is similar to coverage afforded athletes and others taking off-campus field work. Check with your school.

Find out whether the agency or company can assist you in locating housing if you are at an internship away from home. Summer housing sometimes is available in dorms at colleges or private schools. Or recent hires at a newspaper or radio or television station may have suggestions on where to look for an apartment.

Also ask about any special orientation there may be for interns or whether there are interns in other fields at the company. Meeting them may help you learn more about the community.

Be Professional in Your Actions

You may be a good intern prospect and win several offers. If so, you need to have the time to carefully analyze the internships at each company or organization. If you're pressed to make an immediate decision on an internship offer, be open and honest and explain the circumstances. You may be able to get an extension of time to make the decision.

Accepting one internship and then turning it down later for a "better" offer may have a negative effect on both your reputation and that of your college. It may cause the company to lose other qualified applicants.

It's best to take your time and weigh all possibilities carefully. Then, in addition to writing an acceptance letter, write thank-you letters to any other companies you interviewed with. You may be dealing with them in the future or you may be applying for a job at one later.

Relax. No need to worry about what questions you'll be asked at an interview. At least that's the opinion of Bill Montana, who won an internship at an office of Foote, Cone & Belding, a major advertising agency. Montana passed two interviews to get his media planning internship, which led to a full-time position as an assistant media planner. His story and advice:

I was first interviewed by the Director of Personnel. Then I met with the media team for an agency client, Denny's Restaurant. This group included a media director, an assistant media director and two media planners.

Much to my disappointment I was not asked to compute a cost per thousand or answer a single technical question about media or advertising. I had prepared many hours the previous night by going over my media planning class textbook.

Questions were limited to those about life on campus these days, why I wanted a career in advertising, and what traveling I had done. Easy questions, nothing one should lose sleep over like I did.

My advice is to be excited about getting into the advertising business. They are looking for ambitious and dedicated workers.

Other Steps to Take

Other preparatory steps will probably be necessary before you actually begin work at your internship. You may need to complete forms to chart your progress and, if credit is to be granted, register for the appropriate class. Forms also may be necessary at your site. You may have to meet with personnel directors or department managers. Make note of the following points to help you achieve the most success:

- Meet as many co-workers at your site as possible. Employees can help interns in many ways. Some may even give you assignments later if your own supervisor has less work for you.

- Attend any special workshops or meetings because you are part of the team. You may make valuable contacts from meeting personnel from other areas of the company. When invited to employee functions, try to attend.

- Ask lots of questions. Some of the answers may apply only to the company where you're working, but others may apply to organizations of a similar nature.

- Be a self-starter, one who can move into action with minimal assistance. By initiating projects, you become more valuable to the firm. However, you do need to get your supervisor's approval before you start any project.

- Seek opportunities to sit in on company meetings. You can learn some of the details of corporate life and get insights into company operations.

■ Learn to handle constructive criticism from your supervisor and others. One purpose of an internship is to give you the chance to make mistakes and learn from them before entering full-time work. Gain the respect of people in the organization for your willingness to work hard and accept suggestions for improvements in your work.

The following profile illustrates directly how one can develop communications and networking skills to achieve success in increasingly challenging jobs in this field. *These skills cross all areas of communications.*

Barbara Metz, who entered college as a journalism major after work on her high school newspaper, tells her story:

I became a public relations major as a sophomore in college. However, I continued working part time for a community newspaper during my first two years of college. Two internships practically fell into my lap so I took them.

The first, at a small local PR agency, allowed me to do promotional work for a teachers' association. This added stories to my clip book to go along with articles written in high school. My second internship in county government was recommended to me by a professor in the department who handled job placement. This experience gave me a good look at public relations, resulted in newsletter pieces published and allowed me to write news and features for local papers on the county's medical unit.

There was not much supervision at either place. I guess this means my work was of a fairly professional quality as there was no editing either. My clip book was getting filled also with articles I wrote for the campus daily.

I developed a good professional résumé. I continued my activity in WICI [Women in Communications, Inc.]. Through networking with this organization I made contact with a woman who was manager of promotions for a large California daily. She gave me a lead for contact with a promotion manager for *Editor & Publisher*, the newspaper trade magazine in New York. In the meantime, I married and my husband and I moved to New York.

My New York contact led me to meet a woman who was in charge of promotion for one of the largest newspapers in New Jersey. I think my résumé and portfolio impressed her and I started my first job on her staff.

I got along very well with her and she had confidence in my skills. Plenty of learning went on in this job. I wrote all the copy for newspaper promotions, produced newsletters for circulation people, learned to do slide shows for presentations, worked on projects for the newspaper's program for teachers, and had news releases closely edited, which helped me grow.

After two years of excellent training, I returned to California and had a job within two weeks with an advertising agency employing about 40 people. The agency had real estate clients, and my work, principally in public relations, was to write and edit an eight-page tabloid for the Mission Viejo Co. Since this was a high-quality expensive publication, I got to do photo planning, layout, type specification work and tasks with the printers. The agency helped me to learn more about media relations and especially how to work with real estate editors.

Eventually the company left the agency. The Mission Viejo Co. started its own public relations department, and I got the job of editing their publications. There is a peculiar relationship between clients and an agency. The client thinks that you are not going all out, even when you are doing your best work. They are never satisfied. So it was a much better experience for me working for the company.

During my eight years with the Mission Viejo Co. I learned a lot about publicity and public relations in increasingly responsible positions. There was much promotional activity and community relations work—special events such as golf, tennis and swimming events.

My salary went up as I eventually became manager of corporate affairs for the parent company. I did all of the company president's presentations including very expensive multimedia shows, slide shows, etc. I became proficient in managing all kinds of audiovisual presentations. I flew with the president on many of these trips, wrote all of his speeches and handled media relations for numerous charity events that involved the company.

As the economy tightened and real estate activity dropped off, the company cut back sharply on its public relations staff. I decided it was time to leave so I contracted a head hunter. Within two weeks I was at work again, this time as Director of Public Relations for a large ad agency. This was a new experience for me since the agency was highly marketing oriented.

I learned marketing research in a very sophisticated environment. This was an excellent job, leading me to learn more about marketing to go along with my other skills.

I have noticed that agencies like this one frequently will hire their public relations staff from local newspaper writers and editors. These people, with usually two to five years experience, have valuable contacts. I sometimes regret that I did not get more newspaper experience.

Barbara Metz now owns her own advertising and public relations agency in San Diego, Calif.

For Thought and Discussion

1. Should students receive college credit for all internships regardless of pay policy? How do you justify credit when standards and work assignments vary so much in the different areas of communications internships? How many internships should be allowed for credit and why?

2. If a student can find an internship, why not allow the student and the employer to work out pay and hours as long as they follow general campus guidelines?

3. Take an internship other than the hospital publication example used in the chapter to demonstrate the three-step model of objectives and tasks. State objectives clearly, indicate tasks to meet these goals and describe fully the product or evidence of competency.

4. Outline a strategy for obtaining an internship in a desired field. Include all steps.

5. Here are two questions that you might ask an interviewer who is questioning you as the applicant for an internship: What are the primary results you would like to see me produce? What particular tasks will I have to do? Some questions would be posed when the topic came up in the interview. List 12 general questions in addition to these two that you would ask about the job or working conditions.

6. Find and talk to a student who has recently completed an internship. Ask questions about the preparations that he or she did for the internship. Make a list of the answers as well as questions he or she might ask of the supervisor before the internship began if the opportunity arose to do it again.

CHAPTER 3

INTERNSHIPS ON NEWSPAPERS

DIANA GRIEGO, a California State University, Fullerton, graduate and former newspaper intern, was only 26 years old when she was named in *Time* magazine as the winner of two journalism awards: the George Polk Award for national reporting and a coveted Pulitzer Prize.

Griego was the lead writer of a three-person reporting team whose investigation into the issue of missing children produced a series of stories that earned the *Denver Post* the most coveted of all the Pulitzer Prizes—the Pulitzer Prize for Meritorious Public Service. It was Griego who inspired the series by turning a routine story into the quest for something more. She was skeptical about the missing-persons statistics she uncovered while researching a feature story about microdot identification implants for children's teeth. She conferred with her editor.

"Something isn't right here," she recalled thinking at the time.

Given the green light to pursue it further, Griego worked on the big story in her spare time, squeezing in calls between other assignments. A month later, she turned in an article that was to be the foundation of the prize-winning series published from May to November. Fellow *Post* reporter Louis Kilzer was assigned to join her, and together they wrote the main story that appeared on Mother's Day, May 12, 1985, along with sidebars by Griego.

These initial stories sparked dozens of others in the months to follow as the pair, joined by a third reporter, Norman Udevitz, covered the resulting congressional hearings on the subject. They also exposed a fund-raising film that was exploiting for profit the national hysteria over missing children. Along the way, more than 20 staff members contributed to the series—from photographers and reporters to editors—following Griego's lead.

Griego had earned the outstanding freshman award at her university in 1978. She interrupted her sophomore year to do volunteer work for an orphanage in Mexico, where she spent 21 months helping to care for 60 children. When she returned to Fuller-

34

ton, she enrolled in education courses. But she couldn't shake her interest in journalism and decided to get some experience.

During the fall semester, she introduced herself to Jay Berman, the campus daily newspaper adviser, asking him if he could use another reporter. Berman recalls that it wasn't long before Griego was a top-flight reporter.

"Her writing skills were of a quality that you do not see every year," he said. "She always knew what she was doing and was very sure of herself."

Griego continues the story:

I took a job on a nearby weekly newspaper. This gave me some good additional clips besides those from the campus newspaper. I was ready to apply for a credit internship.

My paid academic internship was during a spring semester at the *Los Angeles Times*. Working two days—Tuesdays and Thursdays—I was immediately given police and court beat assignments after a brief training period. The internship was very successful. I had very good supervision and was treated as a general assignment reporter. My real break came after my internship when I was hired full time for the summer.

The importance of the full-time summer work is very obvious. I had lots of stories published on page 1 of the Metro section and had two articles on the front page. By the end of the summer I had filed more than 100 byline stories. I was also able to use my Spanish language skills.

I am sure that the variety of clips from college and the small weekly and *Times* experience were major factors in my becoming a general assignment reporter at the *Denver Post*. [At the time of her hiring in 1985, she was the only Metro reporter at the *Post* fluent in Spanish.]

I would like to add that a bit of advice from my instructor in my Investigative Reporting class really paid off. He said that if something doesn't sound right or if the pieces don't fit it's probably a good story. That notion guided me when my first inquiries into missing children statistics produced figures that could not be substantiated.

The diligent work habits of this former intern surely were enhanced by her outstanding journalism skills to make this series of

> *Internships can lead to full-time summer jobs.*

events a real-life success story. Griego was a page 1 columnist for the Metro section of the *Orange County Register* for five years. She now writes a column for the *Sacramento Bee*. Other examples from colleges across the country show that those students who are dedicated to journalism can and have found similar payoffs in the form of good internships and, subsequently, good jobs.

Newspaper Internships Are Unique

A newspaper internship is unique in several ways. Foremost is the opportunity it offers you to produce a wide range of writing samples, from news, features and sports; to columns and critical reviews; and even to an interpretative or in-depth story series.

> *Few other kinds of internships can offer a match for the published professional writing samples that newspaper interns can produce. Such samples are vital evidence of the proficiency needed in any position that requires reporting and writing skills.*

Another advantage of newspaper internships is their ubiquity. Most cities in the United States, regardless of size, have a newspaper in town or nearby. This situation is in direct contrast with the field of advertising, where internship possibilities are limited chiefly to large markets in urban areas.

College students often get part-time jobs

and internships on local papers, frequently as freshmen or sophomores. Your first experience may lead to the assignment of working on a part-time basis for a bigger newspaper in your home town. Or it may not be far for you to travel to a city with a larger newspaper.

Because through the years internships have become so well developed on some newspapers, the chances are good for you to have a valuable, worthwhile experience. Journalism educators have worked with newspaper publishers and editors to publicize internship programs throughout the country. The special relationships that exist between educators and editors simply don't exist between internship coordinators and top-level managers in other fields.

The Dow Jones–sponsored Newspaper Fund has greatly helped in this relationship. The Fund is one of several organizations that report the results of surveys and studies showing trends in journalism education. Some trends are related to internships. For example, a recent study showed that 80 percent of people hired for their first newspaper jobs had listed experience on campus newspapers on their résumés. And more than 60 percent of the group had served as newspaper interns.

The Newspaper Fund is an excellent source of internship and job information. Several programs under Fund sponsorship lead to internships for juniors and seniors. Special minority internships also are offered each year. (See Appendix A for more information.)

The Newspaper Fund sponsors programs, workshops and institutes for journalism teachers and for students at the high school level. It also keeps statistics on the first jobs of graduates from journalism schools and departments who are hired in other communications fields. One study showed that for people chosen for media-related jobs, 70 percent reported having completed at least one internship.

W Journalism Leads

What was a series of directories published for years by *Writer's Digest* is now for sale on bookstore shelves by Peterson's Guides. *Internships 1995* is one of the most recent and includes lists of both paid and unpaid newspaper internships. Other communications careers are introduced as well as many internships open to any college major.

Another company publishes a career directory series, updating the information every two or three years. Six directories, including one each on newspapers, magazines and book publishing, provide sections on jobs and internships (see Appendix A).

Today, if you are going for either an internship or a job on a newspaper, you will face sophisticated screening procedures. Editors no longer merely look at résumés and writing samples. If you are seeking a general assignment reporting position, you must pass tests designed to measure grammar, punctuation, word usage and other writing skills. Some questions may deal with current events, ethical situations facing reporters or how to handle certain reporting situations. (See Appendix A for sample test questions.)

C opyediting and Business Reporting

Recent trends show a decline in the number of journalism or news-editorial majors at some colleges. Nonetheless, competition has increased for available newspaper jobs and internships. But in two newspaper areas, copyediting and business reporting, interns are often sought. In these two specialized areas you will find the level of competition to be less intense.

> *Competition for internships in copyediting and business reporting may be less intense.*

David A. Zaczyk, a copyediting intern, filed a final report on his experiences on a six-day-a-week daily. These excerpts show the variety of responsibilities and experiences he had in his internship as well as how interested editors can help make the internship more successful.

Writing headlines at 6 a.m. was part of my routine. The schedule was necessary because of a very crowded day of classes. However, this was good timing for an evening newspaper.

Besides counting heads, my days consisted of taking stories off the wire and condensing them into two- and three-sentence paragraphs for the "briefs" section. One thing is certain: after reading just a small percentage of wire stories, my knowledge of the goings-on in the world increased tenfold.

Occasionally, I would edit stories from reporters. However, much of that copy was written for a column—almost every reporter had a column. Editing often meant double-checking the spelling of names. One of the other three copy editors grabbed most of the news stories that came in.

During the last third of my internship I was able to move into more creative work, that of making up the pages. This proved difficult but enjoyable. I was given a quick but comprehensive lesson in photo cropping and sizing. The other editors gave a lot of helpful suggestions and advice that I followed.

When I first started I was thrown into the thick of things, having to cover for four weeks of vacations. But when the vacations were over we seemed to have time on our hands. This gave us time for a higher quality of editing, I believe.

Not all days were routine. During the three months of my stay, we had stories on a bank robbery with police chase, two murders, the elections and a tornado. Breaking stories and the opportunity to work on stories of significance made my internship more worthwhile.

I worked under the supervision of two editors: Don Sheets, news editor, and Jim Neal, copy editor. Jim took it upon himself to teach me the art of thinking and working under deadline pressure. I followed his instructions to the letter and learned a lot. Near the end of the internship they gave me free rein to layout Page Two each day. And I got a good letter of recommendation.

Two things combined will maximize your learning from an internship: to be in a situation in which you receive highly qualified supervision, and to have a job description that allows you to get real-world assignments. This is true whether the newspaper internship is in copyediting; writing news, features or sports; or working with the business or entertainment staffs. The internship then becomes a big step along the path to a newspaper career.

According to a Virginia editor who recruits for two newspapers, two major pitfalls along this path are bypassing the opportunity to write for the campus newspaper and waiting until your senior year to begin looking for an internship opportunity. Writing at every available chance is important advice, too. When you contribute articles to the college newspaper as a freshman or sophomore, you are already placing yourself closer to a newspaper career. Even a story written as a volunteer will add a valuable clip to your portfolio.

Stringers can get part-time writing opportunities. Stringers are writers who are paid for their newspaper work on a per-inch or per-event basis. High school and college students frequently cover weekend high school or college sports events, supplementing understaffed sports departments and providing necessary local coverage. Stringers may also get news and feature assignments. A good stringer is alert to such opportunities. Personality sketches or local features can add significantly to the mix of good writing samples you need when you are seeking an internship or job.

What's the Best Academic Background?

Editors of small to medium-sized newspapers prefer their interns to be journalism majors because of the likelihood that journalism students will have writing experience and strong writing and editing skills. However, regardless of major, if you have a keen interest in people and current events and also have good writing skills, you can be a candidate for a reporting internship.

In fact, many larger newspapers look for good academic backgrounds in liberal arts, political science or English. Interns with general knowledge can specialize in areas in which there is a growing demand. For example, a second major or a minor in economics or business or a graduate business degree can be the right ticket to an internship or job as a business reporter or writer.

> *Many larger newspapers look for a good academic background in liberal arts, political science or English, not just in journalism.*

Two Ball State University grads who completed business reporting internships are good examples. Chris Jensen, now managing editor of *Do-It-Yourself Retailing*, a trade publication for the hardware industry, won an internship offered by the business section of the *Indianapolis Star*. He got the lead from a member of the journalism faculty who was working as an internship coordinator. Jensen, who had a bachelor's degree in English and graduated in 1988 with a master's in journalism, both from Ball State, describes his experiences:

My summer internship with the *Star* was a 20-hours-per-week paid job. As a graduate student, I did not need credit since I had already completed department requirements.

In 15 weeks I had 23 byline clips, mostly from writing update stories once a week for the Tuesday business section. Often, there were 20- to 25-inch stories. An example would be the update of a company that was sold in the past year. Information on new directions the company was taking would be included along with interviews of key officers. Also, I wrote many business briefs and stories on appointments of personnel. A major assignment was a cover story for the section on the oil industry in Indiana.

Jensen now supervises two interns in the summer at his own publication. They write a great deal, especially while working on a special trade show tabloid that appears each August for the hardware industry.

Jensen strongly believes that university credit should be granted only when interns are engaged in a lot of writing and reporting assignments. There needs to be a good indication or definition of what the internship does for the intern, he says, and he believes that credit shouldn't go to a student who is involved chiefly in editorial clerical duties.

Another Ball State graduate, Tim Andrews, works for the Dow Jones Financial Services in New York City. He completed a double major in journalism and economics. Since 1987 he has been managing editor of the company's *Professional Investor's Report*.

Andrews completed four internships, including one in high school with a newspaper in Columbus, Ind. His major internship with Dow Jones was a part of the Newspaper Fund's copyediting program. He attended a two-week training program at New York University before the actual internship.

His 10-week internship was actually with AP/Dow Jones, a joint venture news wire in New York, and his chief tasks were rewriting and formatting. He helped to choose and edit stories to be transmitted via wire to Asia. For example, as part of his editing he was asked to reduce longer features to short hard news stories.

Job hunting for Andrews resulted in his following a trail back to his internship. During a spring break, he sent out about 50 résumés but none to Dow Jones. Later, a blind ad in *Editor & Publisher*, the newspaper trade magazine, led him back to Dow Jones where he was hired for the company's news service located on a different floor of the same building in New York where he did his internship. His advice to those seeking business reporting jobs:

I strongly recommend a double major such as mine because journalism and economics lead directly to business reporting. I have recognized the importance of business classes.

Certainly my advanced copyediting class in journalism was a very key course, but one needs to have a basic understanding of how business works. You need to be interested in different things, since business reporting is really not just one thing.

Business is becoming an especially broad area. For example, what are the issues today in the environment that have an impact on business? When I hire anyone to replace any of the 10 reporters currently working for me, I look for people with a broad general knowledge of the field.

Planning for an Internship

Know Your Skills

An early step in internship planning is to evaluate your skills carefully. You may want to confer with an instructor or faculty adviser on which newspapers you should consider. Some universities assign interns to sites based on evaluations from faculty with whom the intern has had course work. This can lead to a frank appraisal of qualifications and the chance for success at a particular newspaper. You want to feel comfortable in your internship and be able to meet deadlines. Sometimes a smaller community newspaper or a small daily or weekly can offer many opportunities for you to grow.

Watch for Internship Announcements and Deadlines

The next step is to watch for announcements of summer intern programs from a variety of newspapers throughout the country. Most schools and departments of journalism and communications post these announcements. Some arrive through a placement office. Most appear in November and December with deadlines in December, January and February for applications for the following summer's internships. Some require a formal application. Many will state restrictions such as "only juniors accepted" or "only residents of [a particular state or region] may apply."

Obviously, the deadline is critical. Start early if you must complete an application that includes a test, requires letters from several references or involves the time-consuming process of getting grades and transcripts from the Office of the Registrar. Professors who have to write letters of recommendation need information from you and time to complete them. They are busy people and will expect you to respect their schedules.

Target Your Internship

The next step is to target local and regional newspapers at which you have an interest in applying. Directories (see Appendix A) can give you information on deadlines, tell you whether or not applications are required and list the kinds of internships that are available, such as news, features or sports. Be aware that deadlines in some directories change annually. A call may be necessary to verify information. At any rate, getting your material in earlier than the deadline can allow you to call or write at deadline time to be sure your application has arrived.

> *Don't forget the possibility of interning at a smaller newspaper, where you might have more opportunities to work in several departments or in an area in which you have a special interest.*

The United States has approximately 1,600 dailies and 7,500 weeklies, enough to give you some choices of internships. Don't overlook the smaller newspapers because they often offer the advantage of allowing an intern to work in several departments rather than being confined to just one area. Interns on small papers also are more likely to be given the chance to work in a special interest area such as entertainment reviewing. And finally, competition for an internship can be considerably less intense at a smaller paper.

Application Procedures

Most newspapers will require only a cover letter, an updated résumé and clips (see Appendix A for names of books with résumé and cover letter samples). Reproduce your clips so that they appear sharp and clear on white paper. Clips should include, of course, your best writing. However, you may have to select from various sources, including volunteer newsletters. All clips should be dated and identified with the name of the publication where they appeared.

Application specifications vary. Some may require only five clips, and others will ask for your best 10 or 12. For a general assignment reporting internship, you should submit a variety of types of stories, always including hard news and feature stories.

Specialized Areas on Newspapers

The career path on newspapers today is no longer restricted to the traditional route from reporter to copy editor to editor. News-

Too Many Offers?

In seeking an internship at several places, you might get lucky and get a couple of offers. Which to take? You may need additional time to make the right decision.

Faculty coordinators say that because of early deadlines at some sites, you might be in the enviable position of getting some early offers. Since interviewing is good experience, they recommend that you write a letter requesting more time to consider the offer.

However, if pressed for time you may have to call other sites requesting an interview soon. Inform the contact person that you have an offer and want to make a decision soon. Also, you need to know how seriously your application is being considered and when a decision will be forthcoming.

You might be the Number One choice at a site, and you don't want to lose a sure internship. Seeking more time in a careful manner is good advice. Later, you may be seeking a job at one of these places, so you don't want to jeopardize your chances by creating ill feelings with personnel there. Rejecting an offer might be necessary, of course, especially if you are confident of getting an internship and have the skills to make you competitive. Take the time to weigh all options to make the correct choice.

paper changes have included the development of specialized areas, many of which often seek interns. In addition to previously discussed copyediting and business reporting, good opportunities for interns exist in the areas of

- graphics (discussed below)
- photography (see Chapter 7)
- promotions (see Chapter 5)

- specialized supplements for advertising events (see Chapter 5)
- entertainment news and critical reviews
- internal communications such as employee newsletters (see Chapter 5)

Let's say that for an editorial internship you prefer working in a section of the paper in which you'll have a chance to write a lot of features and soft news. If you're certain that such an opportunity exists on a paper, you may need support to have your application seriously considered.

The first step would be to adapt your résumé to the position. Your expertise in this area should be documented by your clips. You will need letters of reference, hopefully at least one from a professor, recognizing your talent and urging your placement as an intern in features. You may be able to use previous references. Editors where you have worked would be particularly useful. Alumni from your school who are familiar with your writing may be a good source of support.

Location and Pay

Internships close to campus sometimes can be arranged around your class schedule during a semester or quarter. In fact, some newspapers call these types of assignments academic internships. They are part time when classes are in session. Some offer pay and some don't, often depending on the size of the newspaper.

The question of pay should be clarified early. It's important for planning. If the internship is unpaid because the newspaper is small or has a limited budget for interns, maybe your faculty adviser can arrange for the newspaper to pay your tuition, mileage or other expenses or give you a scholarship. Arrangements should be made in advance of the time you begin your internship.

Your Internship Assignment

Your exact assignment as an intern may not be determined until after you arrive at the paper. Several factors may determine this. The needs of the newspaper must come first. If someone is on vacation, your internship may involve some part of that person's duties.

> *The needs of the newspaper will come first in defining the responsibilities of your internship assignment.*

Other factors may be the needs of a particular department or the department in which your supervisor works. Some adjustments may be possible after you have been there for a while. In any case, you need to show interest and enthusiasm about all of your work.

Some well-organized newspaper internships call for a program of rotation among departments. The program presented below, operated by a Texas daily, also illustrates the range of topics that may be assigned to reporting interns and might be applicable to many medium-sized to large newspapers. The newspaper publishes daily morning, evening and Sunday editions. (An editor at the newspaper requested that the paper not be identified because currently they have as many internship applicants as they can handle.) This paper follows a 12-week outline for three interns starting at different times; thus, only one intern is at the same assignment during a given week: (1) Introduction to general assignment reporting, (2) day police (meaning, that intern is assigned to the police beat for a week), (3) city, (4) county, (5) copydesk, (6) a second week on the copydesk, (7) night police, (8) courts, (9) farm and fine arts, (10) regional, (11) general assignment and (12) options (the option to return to the beat of your choice).

Here's an edited version of the newspaper's instructions to newly arrived interns:

Welcome. We and many journalism faculty members believe that this is the best internship program in Texas. If you are willing to put forth the effort this summer and if we can fulfill our teaching obligation, you will leave here a better journalist.

We ask only that you learn. If you'll take the time to ask questions concerning problems and situations you have not seen in the classroom, then we will take the time to answer.

For the next 12 weeks you are an employee. You'll be given responsibilities, duties and some plain old chores. You will be expected to respond professionally under all circumstances. Here are some guidelines:

Intern Schedule—The schedule should be followed for the next 12 weeks. Each of you will be assigned to work with a beat reporter during all but two or three weeks of your tenure here.

Some beats, particularly county and courts, will be relatively inactive for unpredictable periods during the summer. If this should happen while you are assigned to one of these beats, you may be given general assignment work, or be given additional time on other beats, or be told to pursue enterprise work. You should be at all times alert for ideas that will lead to enterprise stories.

Although your internship technically will have been completed after 12 weeks, you may continue to work through the remainder of the summer.

Note that the last week of your schedule is labeled "options," which means that you may go back to the beat of your choice for a week. However, you are required to develop a major pre-planned story during this week.

Work Schedule—You will work Monday through Friday, barring special assignments or emergency situations (which have an annoying way of cropping up at the least convenient times). Working hours will match those of the staffer covering the beat to which you are assigned. During any weeks in which you are not assigned to a beat, you will work general assignment on either the dayside or nightside crew. You will work five consecutive days during these periods,

but they may not be Monday through Friday.

Payday—Pay is $250 per week. Pay periods encompass two weeks. Each intern will be issued a time card every two weeks. This card must be kept up to date and must be signed. Work an eight-hour day when possible. Each work week must be held to 40 hours.

Writing Coach—We employ a writing coach whose work is independent of the usual newsroom structure. At some point the coach may ask you (or you may ask him or her) to discuss your writing. These discussions are strictly between you and the writing coach. The comments have no bearing on any rating that you will receive.

Other Duties—When you are in the newsroom and not occupied (and frequently when you are occupied), you will be expected to handle routine non-beat material as do all staffers. This may include obits, regional calls, rewrites, press conferences and a wide variety of breaking news situations. In such cases you are not being singled out because you are an intern, but because you are a member of the staff and are needed to put out that day's product. You will not routinely be used as a summer replacement for vacationing employees. Should a major breaking story occur, every effort will be made to involve you, if not in a reporting role at least in an observing role.

Dress Code—You are asked to dress professionally. Slacks are always acceptable for women, and sport shirts are satisfactory for men except for time on the court beat. Levi's and tennis shoes are worn by some reporters but in truth do little to ease the barriers with a person being interviewed. They definitely do not create an air of professionalism.

Lunch Breaks—Generally they are one hour when on a beat or general assignments, one-half hour when on the copydesk. On some beats you will have to catch lunch when you can find the time. You may use the coffee shop (open on weekdays) when you desire. We have no formal coffee breaks. However, you should never bring a drink to your desk because of the damage that could be caused if liquid is spilled on your computer.

Evaluations—In addition to information that may be requested by your university concerning your performance, you will be given a verbal assessment of your work at the end of the summer. This will include strong points as well as areas in which it is felt you need improvement. At the end of the summer, we request that each intern provide a CANDID written appraisal of the internship program. The comments we receive from you can help us build and improve our program.

As an intern you, like a new employee, may be a bit hesitant to ask questions and clarify procedures. The guidelines serve well to acquaint you not only with the rules to follow for a particular paper but also to give you an idea of what to expect on your first job. Some programs have many rules and requirements, which will vary from paper to paper.

Our next example from a medium-sized daily expresses preference for minority students. The internships are chiefly in the summer although some interns stay much longer. Mark Vasche, an editor with a Northern California daily, describes his program:

We seek internship applicants from throughout the country. Announcements are mailed to more than 60 colleges and to a number of organizations in touch with minority candidates. In recent years we have had increased competition. We get more than 150 applications for the six internships available. Many who apply are not qualified.

Pay is about $350 a week. Of the six internships last summer, three were for general assignment reporting, and one each in copyediting, sports and business. In other years we have had openings for interns in photo, graphics and features.

The majority of our interns are juniors or seniors, but some are June graduates doing a summer internship after graduation. We reject those with two or three internships, favoring those who need the internship work experience. If all other criteria are equal, we would take the intern who is getting college credit.

Interns sometimes stay longer than just the summer, if they are out of school. Three out of four are journalism majors or journalism or communications school graduates. The deadline for applying is usually about February 1, but minority students are invited to apply at any time.

Some large newspapers give interns experience working for a zoned or community news edition of their publication. These editions are really separate newspapers that appear once or twice a week and have their own regional news staffs. Working as a community news intern, you might complete general reporting assignments, including police and court beats, and you also might write features. Internships sometimes may be available in sports, business or copyediting. This is a unique opportunity for you to cover a small community yet be working for a large newspaper.

> *Don't reject an internship solely because it doesn't pay; you'll benefit from many other aspects of the work and experience.*

A big hurdle blocking the path of many college students seeking internships and entry-level newspaper jobs is the lack of adequate compensation. Pay for beginning reporters is low on many small daily and weekly newspapers. These wages, along with those paid to entry-level workers in radio stations and at advertising agencies, are among the lowest in communications-related businesses.

The argument for improved pay on smaller newspapers is based on production. Unlike entry-level radio station or ad agency personnel who handle many clerical duties, beginning reporters can produce news and features that make their way into print. Some say that as a beginner or intern you are contributing effectively to the newspaper and therefore should receive adequate compensation.

Nevertheless, in a poor economic climate intern applicants would do well to consider all aspects of the internship before rejecting it solely because of lack of pay. Some editors or supervisors will pay an intern after a specific period when the intern has shown that he or she can contribute significantly.

Three Important Steps to an Internship

If you are a prospective newspaper intern, you should follow the three steps below in planning for your internship.

First, you should find out as much as possible about the quality of internship experiences at a given newspaper. Alumni, including recent graduates, can help you:

- They can tell you about their work. Interview them.
- If they have written reports, read those carefully. Reports may have answers to these helpful questions: What was the nature of assignments? What were the kinds of stories published and how many did the intern write? How much time did the intern spend in training? What supervision was available, and was it helpful?
- Find out what kind of experience the alum had. The experiences of different interns at the same paper can vary, and much depends on the intern's skills. One intern may not be as successful as another in seeking out work and suggesting assignments.
- Find out which section the alum worked for. Internship assignments for different sections of the same newspaper may vary because of the workload of the staff and time commitments on the part of supervising editors.

The second step involves getting the attention of several newspapers.

- Studies show that when you interview at several potential sites you can greatly enhance your chances for a quality internship.
- After meeting the deadline for submission of your application, you need to

follow up by calling. You may need to find out if you qualify for consideration; otherwise, you need to find other sites quickly.

- Check internship lists and directories carefully to be sure that you are covering all potential newspaper sites in your area of interest. Some interns live with relatives or friends in or near an urban area so that they can consider more newspapers.

If you live in a rural area and don't have the resources to move to a larger city, don't be discouraged. Smaller daily and weekly newspapers nearby may offer the advantage of much less competition for an internship. One journalism intern solved her problem of commuting 200 miles to work by interning on a three-day-a-week schedule, staying in a motel only two nights a week and then driving home after work.

Your third step is to prepare for the internship interview.

- This, of course, may mean updating your résumé even if you sent it a few months previously. You may need to aim your résumé more directly at internships. Add any new skills or work experiences.
- Double check the job description of the internship for which you are applying.
- Read over any published information on the internship, looking for details about hours required, length of the internship, skills required, supervision offered, etc.
- Make a list of questions to ask at the initial interview. Pertinent questions will show your interest in the internship. Also, this list gives you information you can refer to when you need to make a decision.

Toward the end of the interview, you can discuss some secondary questions or points about starting date, person to report to and total length of the internship. If pay isn't a critical factor, you can bring that up also at the end of the questions.

If you have had any experiences on your college newspaper that have prepared you for this internship, you may wish to discuss these. This is another good way to show that you have a serious interest in a newspaper internship.

Your Background Matters

Some former interns report that writing samples gathered through a newspaper internship are highly valued when seeking an entry-level job in other areas, such as public relations. The wide variety of newspaper clips usually produced working on a daily can be combined with media experience to count heavily in favor of an applicant for a PR agency job. This is true because many PR graduates have only limited published writing samples.

On the other hand, if you're targeting a newspaper career, don't conclude that this works in reverse. If you have only a PR internship on your résumé, it may become a negative factor for you. Editors often view such people as less dedicated to the newspaper business. In addition, don't expect publicity release writing samples to be a good representation of your abilities. Remember that newspaper editors often reject this kind of material.

Sandra Allen, who was editor-in-chief of her community college newspaper and a copy editor on the daily at the four-year university she attended, believes that her background was the reason she got an internship on a six-day-a-week newspaper near her home. Probably her maturity (she was about to reach her 30th birthday at this time) was also a factor in the decision of editors to offer an internship to her.

Allen reports some initial concerns typical of many interns as her internship got underway:

I had done well in my university journalism classes, but I could see that this internship assignment was going to be different. A number of questions quickly surfaced. Could I handle city council meetings that lasted to midnight and then go back and immediately write the story? What if I missed something crucial? Could I skirt libel the way my newswriting instructor taught me? How about handling attribution? What about angry politicians? And what about nice politicians who try to sweet-talk you into slanting a story their way?

It was not long before I got a major story. Some storms had affected the flood channels and dams. It was a page 1 story! What an ego boost!

This was a story that tested my own resourcefulness since all of the other reporters were too busy to help me with phone numbers of sources. I tracked down a city engineer and a county flood control manager who loaned me a map which we printed along with my story.

Of course, you have the basics to write an inverted pyramid news story. But an internship teaches you much more. You learn by experience in selecting questions to ask and of whom to ask them. No teacher is holding your hand or telling you the right way to go to track down sources. Editors, although very busy, were helpful.

During my months as an intern I handled mostly general assignment work. I covered public meetings, speeches, parades, cops, courts, and wrote features. It was a wonderful experience. I honestly believe that I learned things in the real newspaper world that were never possible in classes or a lab.

But the very best part—that which made most of it memorable—was when the city editor said, "You did good. Your stories are good, to-the-point, and we appreciate having you around."

After her graduation from college, Allen worked two years for the same newspaper where she did her internship as a general assignment reporter. Later, she became a feature editor for a nearby daily owned by Freedom Newspapers.

What You Can Expect at Your Internship

Another former intern, Jeannette Avent, produced some relevant observations when she sketched out notes on her assignments over several two-week periods as part of her required internship reports. Here is her version of what an intern can expect on a small to medium-sized daily.

Date: 3/7—I'm getting the hang of covering school board meetings, which is not to say I'm getting into a rut. I don't want to let them become routine. I am starting to know the "players" better and to have a little background about the school district. Finally finishing the recycling story. It was really a massive undertaking. I know it's my fault that I feel that I have to know everything there is to know about a subject. It's a case of over reporting. In this instance though, I felt the background information I got from interviewing and calling helped me to write the story from a well-informed point of view.

I did my first obit. People have such fascinating lives that I did not feel morbid about it at all. I tried a new format on the school board story, i.e., to write about the main point of the meeting and then summarize everything else under "In other action."

The managing editor assigned me a special story for a fitness section that the paper is promoting. He explained what he wanted and gave me a due date. The city editor also assigned me to do the "Man in the Street" feature on an ongoing basis. I'll be going to libraries, parks and shopping centers to interview people on a particular subject and take their picture for the Saturday paper.

Date: 3/16—During the past two weeks I did a good variety of stories ranging from the school board meeting to a light news feature on how a guy quit smoking to a story on hydrostatic weighing which required much research and reporting to get a handle on it.

I took a wire story on the Pro-Peace March and localized it. The only problem was that the wire service story kept changing all day. I kept following it until deadline and updated the story.

Date: 4/1—The school board meetings and the Man-on-the-Street interviews continue to be a staple of my work. Although not predictable, they were familiar and structured so that I had an established base to work from each week.

The lottery story was a significant new direction. It required that I ask three basic questions of eight different school districts and come up with a synthesized story that compared apples

to apples. It was a real challenge to digest the information. As my newswriting instructor said, boil it down to some understandable information.

From a news conference I learned that reporters don't always work under ideal conditions. I had to chase down a group of reporters who were interviewing the expert in a corner of the dining room being set up for a luncheon. I also got my first feedback call from the public on a story I did. It was positive.

Writing Skills Are a Major Concern

Writing improvement should be a major concern to prospective interns and to college students in general. When evaluating interns, site supervisors report that poor writing skills are the number one problem today. Studies have shown that both daily and weekly editors have found more than a third of the journalism graduates they employ or interview are lacking in basic grammar and writing skills. Interns are criticized for errors in spelling, punctuation and grammar usage on résumés and cover letters. However, some say that university efforts to improve writing skills are showing some gains.

> *Newspaper editors say that more than a third of journalism graduates they employ are lacking in basic grammar and writing skills. Don't be one of them!*

It's no surprise then that many newspapers require prospective interns to take writing and editing tests. Editors believe that since your writing samples may be heavily edited, testing will give a more accurate picture of your future writing performance. Test elements ranked by editors in a study by Prof. Louis Gwin (see box and Appendix A) showed that the editors placed the same emphasis on spelling and grammar as they had in earlier studies.

Spelling and Grammar Rated As Important

In a study of what skills editors think are important in potential interns and employees, spelling and grammar were at the top of the list:

1.	Spelling	99%
2.	Grammar	95%
3.	Leads	80%
4.	Fact ordering	79%
5.	Editing	70%
6.	Attribution	53%
7.	Creativity	50%
8.	Current events	37%
9.	Libel	32%
10.	Ethics	15%

Internships in Newspaper Graphics

If you are a person with an eye for detail in both art and journalism, you should look into the growing opportunities available in newspaper graphics. Internships in this specialty are open to majors in journalism, communications, photography or photojournalism, art design, graphic arts, art and related fields.

A number of major newspapers now offer paid and unpaid internships in their art or graphics departments. Some of these programs are comparatively new. Still other newspapers may be interested in initiating an internship program, as one senior discovered.

Doug Arellanes, a book arts major at the University of California at Santa Barbara, had a background in reporting and editing on the campus daily newspaper. In the summer of 1989, while serving as managing editor on

his college paper, he acted on a lead from a friend and applied for and won a job as messenger for the Orange County edition of the *Los Angeles Times.* Arellanes describes what happened next:

While I was doing faxing and other clerical chores, I noticed that there were good internships in this *Times* office in reporting and writing and editing. But there were no interns working in graphics.

This led me to spend some time researching and developing a five-page proposal outlining what I perceived to be some of the advantages of offering a newspaper graphics internship. I waited until February for action to be taken on my letter. But finally I was accepted as a graphics intern still associated with the Orange County edition. I worked during the following summer.

As an intern I was treated just like any employee, given some excellent training and allowed to perform many kinds of graphics functions. Handling basic bar graphs, locator maps and spot news graphics for developing stories became routine after a while. I also worked on some very substantial projects.

For example, toward the end of my internship I was given three weeks to put together the graphics package to accompany some in-depth features on the pressures faced by air traffic controllers at a major airport.

The task was to put together nine frames to illustrate the high-stress activity of controllers in a random 20-minute period at the airport. Each frame showed what the controller actually sees in a 10-mile radius. The color graphics gave impact to the story.

I believe that some art skills are important for this job, but you need to be more of a journalist than an artist. Good journalism skills are a key to success. You can pick up *Editor & Publisher* magazine and scan the ads to see some of the good opportunities developing in this field.

In particular markets, some editors maintain that newspaper graphics internships are very competitive. Others say that plenty of opportunities exist, especially for minorities and those who are well qualified. The Society of Newspaper Design (SND), based in Reston, Va., serves as a clearinghouse for publication of an annual list of newspapers seeking graphic interns (see Appendix A).

Jeff Glick, graphics director of *U.S. News & World Report*, is well qualified to point out some of the steps you should follow to reach participating newspapers. Glick decided to seek an internship between his junior and senior years in college. His background in journalism included experience on the campus newspaper with art as his college major. He checked both city and college libraries to locate names of attractive newspapers. He was aided through his student membership in SND, which gave him additional leads. Finally, he mailed out packages of his work to numerous newspapers.

Glick's package included three kinds of samples: (1) about 10 to 15 clips from the campus newspaper to show his writing ability, (2) photocopies of college newspaper pages he had designed, and (3) examples of his graphics work. In the latter group, he included some basic pieces such as maps.

Two other graphic illustrations were highlights of his package. One was about a traffic accident that occurred near campus, and the other showed the movements of a hurricane through the area.

> *Examples of any graphics work you have done will get the attention of interviewers.*

Glick got a 40 percent rate of response from his mailings. Some newspapers asked him for additional application information, and others called him for phone interviews. He settled on a three-month internship with the art director of the *Dallas Morning News*. He received three units of academic credit from his school, Central Florida University. He says about his internship: "This experience opened my eyes to real daily deadlines and taught me a considerable amount about

graphics. Most of my time was spent on completing graphics assignments. Such an internship shows the importance not only of art talent but also of news sense and journalistic skills."

Glick later worked a year at the *Dallas Morning News* before accepting his present position with *U.S. News & World Report*.

Some applicants for graphics internships are photo majors (see Chapter 7 for information on photojournalism internships). Often, photo and graphics internships for daily newspapers are listed on the same application form.

Steve Rice, a former newspaper photographer and now assistant managing editor/graphics for the *Miami Herald*, says that the ideal graphic internship applicant should have good computer skills including experience with programs such as Illustrator, QuarkXPress, and Photoshop. The *Herald* employs three or four interns a semester and pays them the same as editorial interns. Rice also says good art skills are important because of their usefulness in production tasks. Samples of news and feature writing for the campus daily can make the candidate more competitive.

Color catches the eye and attracts viewers and readers to the outstanding graphics on television and in publications. Newspapers, in efforts to hold older readers and attract younger ones, are increasingly using color and graphics. Internships and jobs in the design area should increase for those with good creative skills.

For Thought and Discussion

1. Acquiring skills in several ways, Diana Griego became a reporter and columnist on three major newspapers. Discuss four examples and explain how these skills in and out of college helped the *Sacramento Bee* columnist.

2. List and discuss three reasons why you think graduates and former interns rank internships on newspapers higher than other communications fields.

3. What are some of the advantages of completing internships on small community newspapers (dailies or weeklies) as opposed to large metropolitan papers?

4. Discuss at least four ways that students can prepare themselves to get the best possible internships.

5. Look at some of your writing samples and discuss how well you have applied at least six of the test elements in Prof. Gwin's study. Which do you think are most important?

6. Internships buy time for students to test their strengths and to try out the kind of work they have chosen. A study by Women in Communications, Inc. (WICI) has recommended that colleges and universities have mandatory credit intern programs. Today, most are on an elective credit basis. As an elective, many students miss the benefit and are not as well prepared to enter the competitive job market. Griego said that she was sure that the variety of clips from college and the *Times* internship was a major factor in her becoming a reporter at the *Denver Post*. Name three other former interns from this chapter and explain how their internships helped them start their careers.

4

INTERNSHIPS WITH MAGAZINES AND OTHER PUBLICATIONS

An Overview

Magazine Versus Newspaper Internships

Internships on magazines and other "slick" publications have a few things in common with newspaper internships. For one, some top print journalists in college are able to parlay a magazine internship into a job such as an entry-level editorial position on a major magazine. Also, as is the case with newspapers, employers on magazines look for campus publication experience. Your choice of major is not as important as the completion of relevant skills courses: art, graphics, publications production, feature writing, copyediting, magazine article writing, etc. In fact, graduates with a variety of majors get jobs on magazines.

If you become a magazine intern you share with those on newspapers the opportunity to develop good writing and editing experiences and publication samples. The chance to produce news briefs and short column items or contribute to an occasional major article is better on small local and regional magazines. Major magazines often start interns at the bottom where chores are likely to be more related to clerical tasks and research duties than to writing itself.

> *Interns on magazines and newspapers share the opportunity to develop good writing experiences and publication samples.*

Most major magazines are published in New York City, where the necessary connection to the advertising business is convenient. In addition to being the headquarters for publishers, New York is also home to many industry-related associations, seminars and networking events of interest to those seeking magazine careers. Therefore, whereas newspaper interns work on some of the smallest newspapers in rural areas of the country, assignments for magazine interns are usually limited to larger cities. They are also very competitive whenever available.

Staff sizes differ. Some magazines have limited editorial positions, and thus, limited job openings because freelancers produce much of the editorial content. You may have to compete with experienced writers to get published.

Frequently, the magazine intern is an editorial assistant working directly for the editors. All of the adages about starting at the bottom and paying your dues certainly apply to this field. Assigned tasks can become quite routine even though you may be a hard-working intern and show unusual initiative and energy. Nevertheless, it's possible for you to find a way around such roadblocks. A bright magazine intern who is willing to make a thorough study of a prospective magazine site can come up with the idea for a viable article and get the writing assignment.

Opportunities in Different Areas of Publishing

In your search for a magazine internship, keep in mind that magazines and publications vary greatly in focus. Watch for publishing opportunities in different areas of the field. You may hear of internships on regional, trade and consumer magazines. With desktop publishing and other computer innovations, some attractive publications are appearing in these sectors. Don't overlook their ability to offer exceptional training opportunities.

Many corporations produce outstanding publications. These can be directed internally to employees or be aimed at customers, stockholders or other groups. City and government agencies use interns to help produce such products as annual reports and special newsletters. Hospitals often turn out award-winning publications.

Many kinds of organizations in a community can give you publication experience as efforts are made to reach senior citizens, consumers, tourists or other groups with print messages. Completing assignments for these organizations can be every bit as educational as working on a regular magazine. You can experience firsthand every aspect of publication from planning through production.

These sites are often listed "public relations" or "marketing" rather than "magazines." But like a campus magazine that attracts student writers with all kinds of academic majors, these publications have opportunities open to anyone with the interest in and dedication to writing.

What Interns and Editors Have to Say

The best way to examine magazine internships closely is to look at them through the eyes of former interns and editors. Jane Westin, editor, and June Palmer, managing editor, produce a 200- to 300-page regional magazine every month. This is how they describe their ongoing internship program:

We offer internships in three areas: in sales, in art, which requires strong graphics and layout skills, and in editorial. [See Chapter 6 for details on sales internships.]

We have a couple of editorial interns each semester. They start with assignments for the "briefs" section. The short articles they write can deal with many different subjects. We assign some and rely on the interns to suggest others.

Copyediting and proofing skills are a must. We really have no time to do basic training in journalism. A magazine writing class is helpful. Regardless of major or classes taken, a strong interest in the magazine field is needed. We are mostly interested in interns who want a career on magazines.

We look at the intern's progress as a ladder with movements up the steps depending on the intern's ability to come up with solid article ideas. *Seeking out assignments rather than waiting to be told what to do is important.* It's a very busy place much of the time. Since the interns are unpaid, we allow very flexible hours around the student's college and work schedule. Most interns work a minimum of 150 to 250 hours [during their internship], some longer. They usually are with us for the entire semester or entire summer.

Many interns eventually get paid for articles and major assignments they complete. Some write these near the end or after the internship hours are completed. Several interns have maintained a long-term freelance relationship with us. One intern got a paid trip to Scotland to research and write a piece on travel there for our magazine. Pay is at established freelance rates.

Because we have such a small staff, interns can count on getting some pieces published for their files. Recent interns have written articles about child adoption, hot air balloons and their travels, and a historical piece on a local art museum. For a shorter feature, one intern interviewed a woman attempting to raise funds for a hospice center for the terminally ill by organizing a special community event. Another intern did a health profile on a person opening a new blood testing center in a nearby city.

> "Copyediting and proofing skills are a must. We really have no time to do basic training in journalism."

A former intern at the same regional magazine, Mary Archer, discusses the assignments she completed. A journalism graduate, Archer also offers some advice to future interns:

The magazine is in a regional lifestyle format and has only three editors. Since there are no staff writers, freelancers and interns produce most of the copy.

I worked mostly on Tuesdays and Thursdays around my schedule of university classes. Although the position is unpaid initially, after you write two brief feature articles they accept, you will be paid about $150 for each future feature you write.

You must volunteer for work as it is a busy place. It is easy to get overlooked, if you do not speak up and ask for assignments. The M.E. [managing editor], who is the intern supervisor, tells you about the magazine and introduces you to editorial and art employees.

The editors answer any questions you have, but you need to be aggressive to get assignments. The greatest input I received was after I turned in my stories. All three editors would read them, and if changes were necessary, they would return them to me to make adjustments. I found this very educational. The suggested changes always improved my writing and helped me to spot errors in my own work later. Also, I learned that editors don't always know what they want until they read something they *don't* want.

I was fortunate to get a feature assignment my first week. The magazine does a story each year on weekend getaways. It took six weeks to research. I was given some guidance on where to look and then I was on my own.

This was an excellent assignment to test my research skills. I made more than 250 phone calls to resorts and sifted through 150 resort brochures. I was treated to a weekend at a four-star resort to do some firsthand research. I learned how to handle PR people and how to read between the lines in the brochures. Writing the article took three days.

My second big assignment was to do a weekend getaway story with a Christmas theme. It took two weeks to gather all the facts and a day to write.

While waiting for phone calls to be returned, I wrote a couple of short pieces on new products for a column. And I did my share of proofreading. My supervisor said she liked to give me assignments because she knew they would be written on time.

After my internship ended, I was asked to freelance for the magazine. I have completed two stories and have the green light for three others.

My basic journalism reporting and writing classes gave me the foundation for this internship, but copyediting and feature article writing were the ones that helped the most. *My advice: be assertive enough to get good assignments and then be prepared to come up with your own ideas and own approaches without instruction.* Do not be afraid to get around and meet all members of the staff, even those in sales. You never know who might help you with a story. Also, it gives you a better feeling to know what others do on the magazine. Internships are the final polish to a degree.

> "Be assertive enough to get good assignments and then be prepared to come up with your own ideas and own approaches without instruction."

Initiative and resourcefulness can also pay big dividends for interns working for magazines with larger audiences, even some with international readerships. However, the prospective intern must first get hired. Beth Bower, manager of publications and editor of an international magazine for speakers, explains the application process and describes how assignments can be earned at her publication:

Internships are offered year round, but an applicant needs to tell us what quarter or semester he or she is available. We want a cover letter, résumé and writing samples. These samples can be varied as to type, but work on campus publications is what we want to see. Our interns have most often completed college daily newspaper experience, with good grades in writing and editing classes. A copyediting course usually is required.

The interview includes time for a test based largely on spelling, word usage and grammar. The test is in the form of an actual story from our magazine but reprinted with a number of planted errors. The intern must spot the errors that a copy editor would correct. We need clear and concise writers who have the skills to interpret sometimes complex language and material to the reader. Basic computer skills are required.

Once hired, the intern will be asked to complete assignments for our newsletters, special publications written for club members and officers. Editing this material is good preparation for more advanced assignments. The intern can play a role in determining topics, too.

Much depends on the dedication and interest of the interns. The opportunity is there to develop ideas and prepare articles for our maga-

zine. However, there is competition for space, some from established freelance writers in this field.

Interns have written personality profiles of major people in the field. Some of these interviews have been conducted by phone.

The internships are unpaid although frequently an intern will stay on an extra semester or summer to assist and be paid an hourly wage. Publication in an international magazine like ours can be of great help in getting a clip or two to aid in the search for a publications job.

The basic requirements for an internship are echoed at an even more specialized publication. A veteran managing editor who has worked with a number of interns tells about his publication's program:

The colleges participating in our internship program are generally on a semester schedule. So we take interns in the fall, spring or summer but not every semester. A cover letter, résumé and relevant writing samples must be in our hands before an interview.

Since we are a major car magazine, interest in automobiles is, of course, helpful but not a requirement. We have had men and women interns, and three of our most recent interns have been hired full time and are doing very well. They are all energetic people with good skills and a strong interest in doing a good job. They are not afraid of tackling new assignments or of helping out anywhere the workload is heaviest.

As far as skills go, we think some kind of editing course beyond just working on the campus daily is a requirement. The tasks assigned most interns—proofing, writing, editing—require good English skills. "A" and "B" marks in writing courses are essential.

Because of the recent sale of our magazines, the budget was tightened enough to temporarily eliminate pay for our interns. However, we do pay freelance rates to interns who will write book and article reviews and handle some non-writing assignments. Some interns have been paid for testing cars.

We strongly believe that good interns can make valuable contributions to our magazine. Most have interesting, varied backgrounds and have had experiences that qualify them as candidates for entry-level magazine jobs. We love to work with interns, and all of our editors feel that we contribute to their education.

Richard Homan, a recent intern who was hired at an automotive magazine shortly after his internship there, wrote of his experiences in a report required by his university's credit internship program:

> "Hands-on experience during my six-week internship did more for me than any college course."

If an internship is supposed to be a starting point or springboard for a career, my internship at the magazine fulfilled the requirements better than I ever could have imagined. Springboard? It was more like being shot out of an inspirational cannon.

The initial interview for the internship went well. Both the person who would become my supervisor and the executive editor asked me some casual questions. It was a relaxed atmosphere. Then based on the recommendation of my faculty internship coordinator, they hired me as an intern.

I worked at the magazine about 18 hours a week. This was about right; none of my studies suffered, and I managed to keep track of what was going on at the magazine while I wasn't there. I always felt that I was part of the team.

I was welcomed immediately by the people working at the magazine. No one acted superior. On the first day, one of the editors took me to lunch. I have formed excellent friendships with people and believe that I am on good terms with most of the staff. As one of the younger staff members told me, "It's like a family. We have arguments where we want to kill each other, but next week everything is great again."

My workload was varied. I was proofreading galleys, editing copy, writing copy, delivering cars to be serviced, going to press conferences, writing letters and reviewing books and articles. I rarely felt (or was made to feel) like a fifth wheel. Assignments were light at the beginning when I think they did not know how much I could handle. In a short time, I was very busy.

My supervisor gave me the impression that

she had confidence in me. Always willing to help, if needed, she had praise for my work. She made a point of explaining the significance of the work.

Varied writing assignments soon came my way. I began with a piece about wall posters being offered by *Automotive Quarterly Magazine*, then covered a seminar on car paints. Craig Breedlove's announcement that he intended to break the land speed record and a book on the history of the Greyhound Corporation were the basis of two other brief articles.

Hands-on experience during my six-week internship did more for me than any college course. You must have the drive to want to write and produce in print. You must learn the language, pick up the style and learn to discipline yourself. A glorious internship can be the result!

Workloads and Schedules

Not all internships run so smoothly. Joe Douglas, serving as an intern on a similar magazine, said that only about half his time involved copyediting columns and features. Instead, he was consumed by what he termed "grunt work": phone research, library work and running errands. He blames the lack of meaningful assignments on timing, explaining that an assistant editor warned him at the beginning of his internship that there would be some dead time ahead.

Workloads on magazines vary greatly. After deadlines are met and the publication goes to press, it takes an aggressive intern to seek out new assignments in the lull that can follow. Participation in some long-term assignments can help.

It is important to pay attention to the preferences noted by some newspaper and magazine internship sites for a particular sequence of work hours. Sequences can be the key to receiving better assignments or even to getting more attention and feedback on work accomplished. Some sites ask for full-time interns only, which usually means that the intern must work a summer schedule when classes aren't in session. Other sites prefer a schedule of Monday, Wednesday and Friday or a scheduled Tuesday and Thursday in the summer or during a school semester. You must often juggle class schedules to accommodate the needs of the work site. For instance, you might be asked to work two days in a row so that you can finish a project immediately.

Publications Require Motivated Students

Magazine site supervisors report that most problems related to scheduling are minor. Instead, they point to the quality of the intern's work as their most troublesome concern. They find that even when students come to them with almost identical résumés, writing samples and faculty recommendations, they still can't predict the quality of an intern's performance.

Some supervisors believe that some interns are simply not motivated to work on publications. They don't have sharp enough writing skills and may not be interested in learning different tasks. In short, they ought to be directed to other careers outside of communications.

Unqualified interns result in too much trial-and-error time, according to a few supervisors. Of course, an intern may be terminated after a month or so of ineffective or unsatisfactory performance. However, because many supervisors are reluctant to do this, they may assign more simple tasks to fill out the intern's hours. Ultimately, the intern will report that he or she was trapped at a poor internship site.

Some faculty coordinators believe that even though less than 10 percent of interns get negative evaluations, supervisors have to expect a "bad" intern now and then. They point out that students may be entering publication work for the first time. They may be unaware of the pressures of deadlines and may create some of their own pressure. Interns are naturally apprehensive about a new job where they may be asked to deal with unfamiliar experiences. Learning a complex set of style rules for a publication or getting acquainted with other kinds of new terminology and procedures can create

tension. Much of this fades away as work progresses, but for some the tension may make it difficult to do a good job.

Internship Leads in the Magazine Field

If you're looking for internships and job possibilities in the magazine field, be alert to these leads:

■ If you have any kind of job experience, you may have taken a step toward a publication internship. Two examples: If you have a computer background, an internship with a technical magazine could be a possibility; and some fashion publications seek interns with retail sales experience.

■ If you like the magazine or publishing business, you need to remember that at the entry level for many magazines you will be asked to perform various tasks. Duties such as fact checking, proofreading, phone verification and answering reader inquiries may appear minor, but they are important. Advancement is earned with achievement. Getting your foot in the door by handling basic assignments leads to experience, and that can be the key to getting a start in the field.

■ Many major magazine internships are available during the summer; however, a lot of publications look for qualified interns during the regular school year. Editors often will work out flexible schedules around university quarters or semesters. These internships, although more difficult to find, are less competitive.

The most prestigious magazine internship program in the country is sponsored each summer in New York by the American Society of Magazine Editors (ASME). Starting with orientation in June, the 10-week program assigns interns to consumer and trade magazines, chiefly in the New York area.

> *Don't ignore seemingly unrelated experience. Computer skills can lead to an internship with a technical magazine; retail sales experience may be the ticket to working with fashion publications.*

To say that this program is highly competitive would be an understatement. In the first place, it is open only to juniors who will return to college after the summer internship. And only one student can apply from each university. In 28 years more than 1,136 students and 178 magazines have participated in the program.

According to Marlene Kahan, executive director of ASME, most applicants in recent years have been journalism majors with campus publication experience and with a previous summer newspaper job. The magazine, where the student interns, pays a stipend of about $300 a week. Students can receive college credit, but many don't.

Amy Scheuler, a 1988 University of Missouri magazine journalism graduate, is probably typical of those students selected for the ASME intern program. With a GPA of 3.8, she had won several scholarships. Scheuler, seeking a career at a consumer or trade publication, was not chosen from the first round of applicants at ASME. She was selected as an alternate and then named an intern when an opening occurred. She did her ASME internship at *Sales & Marketing Management* magazine in New York in 1987. She reports:

I believe that one outstanding feature of the ASME program is living and working in New York City. We lived in dorms at New York University. Mixing with other interns as well as getting acquainted with magazine people was great.

The internship puts a perspective on a magazine career. Earlier, I had experience on a weekly magazine at Missouri and wrote news and features for the newspaper there. Although I had

not yet taken a copyediting class [which she completed during her senior year], I did not find this a problem since I did little actual editing. Dealing with the content of the magazine was no problem.

My chief tasks were in survey research. One project was to determine the compensation of marketing executives. In addition, some interviews resulted in brief articles. Getting to see the total magazine staff in action and working with them was a great opportunity!

Y ASME Interns: Their GPA and What They Study

You must be a junior to take part in the ASME intern program. A better-than-average GPA will also help. Of a recent ASME group selected, nine participants had GPAs of 3.0 to 3.5 on a four-point scale, and 11 had 3.6 or higher. However, 14 did not disclose their GPAs on their résumés.

Of the 36 interns who prepared résumés for ASME following their graduation, 21 listed themselves as journalism or communications graduates, with an additional seven having double majors including journalism. The most popular second field of study was history. Eight were non-journalism majors with degrees in economics, art and design, and English. Many of the journalism and communications majors had minors in marketing, economics, a foreign language, history and sociology.

Scheuler said that one of the editors with whom she had worked later left for a position with another magazine. He subsequently offered her a position at the new magazine. However, she declined, saying that she found living in New York to be too expensive. She took a job designing newsletters and brochures for a university in St. Louis.

As a junior, Michael Strand moved

across the country for a magazine internship. That move paid off a year later with a job offer when he graduated. Strand believes that his undergraduate experiences prepared him to be a magazine intern. A Washington State University graduate with a major in communications and minor in English, Strand was editor of his campus daily newspaper, directing a staff of 50. He was student life editor of a 640-page yearbook and a stringer for a nearby radio station.

Strand says he was treated well as an intern at Whittle Communications, which published a number of national magazines. He comments:

Whittle was not new to me as I had regularly read *Campus Voice*, a Whittle magazine distributed in college dorms. The summer internship ran 40 hours a week, which allowed me time to learn all aspects of magazine production.

I wrote articles for one of Whittle's largest magazines, *New Parent Advisor*. Its circulation is about 5 million. A typical assignment for me was to write a sidebar on child care centers. The best way, I think, to get assignments is to continually let editors know that you are interested and can contribute.

Strand maintained communication throughout his senior year with editors at Whittle. According to Sandra Stricklin, former Whittle internship coordinator, Strand was hired because he kept in close touch to watch for magazine openings, had an excellent evaluation on his summer internship and showed a keen interest in publications. Whittle eliminated its formal internship program in the early '90s.

> *Keeping in touch with a former intern site can pay off in job opportunities later.*

Many internships and training programs are listed in the career directory volume for magazines published by the Gale Research Co. (see Appendix A). Lists of paid and unpaid internships are located in the back of the directory. In addition to a good supply of career advice from professionals, the directory has publishing company job information and lists of consumer and trade magazines. Some of the latter group have internships available for students with specialized skills and/or interests, including graphics, design and production.

The Business Press Educational Foundation (see Appendix A) placed some 30 journalism majors in paid business press internships across the nation in the summer of 1993. Applications from non-graduating seniors and juniors showed interests in magazine internships in areas such as accounting, advertising, agriculture, computers, construction, environmental cleanup, fashion, finance, food industry, health care and sports.

 Typical Magazine Internship Application

Let's examine a typical application for an internship on a magazine. Questions often concern your career plans; reading habits, including magazines; and your views on the potential audience of the magazine. It's important to answer all questions fully. If critiques of articles are required, you should use the maximum length available so that you can explain your comments fully.

In this sample the applicant is asked to answer some basic questions and then indicate the preferred time for the internship. Note that the deadlines in this example are later than those imposed by many magazines.

Making sure to include all relevant experience, please describe why you would be an asset to the magazine's editorial staff. What do you expect to learn from this internship? Length: one or two double-spaced, typed pages.

Read one issue of our magazine published in the last year and critique one major feature listed in the table of contents. Clearly note the title of the piece critiqued. Be specific in your comments and/or criticisms. Length: three to four double-spaced, typed pages.

Please attach one recommendation from a professor or professional supervisor who has recently worked with you.

You may include a résumé and up to four samples of your written work. Attach all of this material together and mail prior to the deadline.

Please rank in numerical order the internship quarter you prefer to work.

Internship Period	Application Deadline
Sept. 5 to Dec. 2	August 19
Dec. 5 to March 3	November 7
March 6 to June 2	February 6
June 5 to Sept. 1	May 8

Complete any application in detail, commenting as fully as possible on relevant college and work experience. Because competition is keen, you should highlight your interests in magazines and any publication or magazine work you have done.

> *Don't be discouraged. There are always openings for qualified people with energy, enthusiasm and an interest in publishing.*

Former interns and those who have just been hired for their first jobs urge seniors to fight feelings of discouragement. They say there are openings for qualified people with energy, enthusiasm and a strong interest in the publishing business. They point out that many interns do get hired. For employers, an internship is an ideal way to get a good look at a person working under business and deadline conditions without any commitment to hire. A proven performer who already knows the way a publication operates may be a better candidate for a job than someone just showing up with a résumé and unfamiliar references.

Internship Opportunities May Grow in the Future

A bright spot on the horizon is the optimism throughout the communications industry for magazine publishing based on three trends during the '80s:

First, after VCRs and personal computers exploded onto the communication scene, prime-time television ratings declined. Audience habits have changed. VCRs permit the consumer to erase commercials. This translates as a loss to advertisers who are looking more closely at magazines and other media as a more effective way to reach their audiences.

A second trend is the growth of magazines overall. Magazine circulation is growing faster than the population. Increasingly, there is concern about the magazine habits of "Baby Boomers," the largest segment of the population sought by advertisers.

Third, hundreds of specialized magazines were started in the '80s. More consumer magazines now aim effectively at new demographic patterns and interests of consumers.

Also, the magazine business operates efficiently, making it a stable field to enter. As more magazine job opportunities appear, more internships will become available for you. A faculty internship coordinator describes his perception of the paths students can take to the magazine industry:

Many small magazines and publications need interns as editorial assistants. Of course, students need to be qualified and look for fairly good-sized urban media markets. The major is not important if the student has some college (or professional) publications experience and is interested in this field.

Another point that students often overlook is the tremendous amount of crossover within the job sector of the communications field. For example, let's say that you cannot get a magazine internship. You might complete a newspaper internship and even work on a newspaper for a year. You will find that your experience on the newspaper will qualify you for a magazine job.

The point is that any kind of writing and publication experience—an internship or a job— will assist you to eventually reach your goal of a magazine career. It happens all the time.

Does this kind of crossover really happen? The next illustration describes circumstances in which an advertising major wished to intern as an editorial employee for a magazine.

Duties at a Magazine Internship

Darcy Johnson found her own fall semester internship, which led to a job as an editorial assistant at a consumer home magazine. Anne Smith, Johnson's supervisor, filed the following job description with a university internship coordinator:

Interns will assist in all editorial functions connected with front-of-the-magazine departments. They will work 15 hours per week. While reporting directly to me, they may also occasionally assist other editors who contribute to this section. Duties include these tasks: fact checking, story research and some writing for the "Update" column; maintaining the department index; sending out tear sheets to writers and sources; compiling buying guide information; reading publications for story ideas; miscellaneous copying and filing and general clerical tasks.

Here's what Johnson had to say about her experience in this internship and how she characterized her duties:

I am grateful that my faculty coordinator did not push me into an advertising agency for my internship. Although advertising was my major, I had developed a strong interest in writing so I wanted to work on a magazine. I believe that my good GPA (3.38), my work on the college yearbook during my freshman and sophomore years, serving as an account executive for the campus

daily newspaper advertising department, and two summers in telemarketing with a computer company gave me good background for this internship.

Because I was not a journalism major, I had to work two days on a trial basis before I was hired as an intern in the editorial department. I worked every Tuesday and Thursday and a few Friday afternoons for $5 an hour. It was about a 60-mile drive from my home, but the company has a "flex" hour system so that if you wished, for example, you could work from noon to 8 p.m.

Anne Smith, the department's editor and my supervisor, the first day I was there gave me a tour and over lunch discussed with me what I would do. She made me feel very welcome by sending a memo to all of the staff explaining who I was and when I would be in. She also said in the memo that all task requests should go to her so I would not be stuck with the same repetitive jobs or have the entire staff hounding me to work.

I had an "in box" in Anne's office where she would leave my assignments. As the internship progressed, the following tasks (with percentage of my total time) were completed:

Reader Response Letters (20% of the time): Since the magazine had recently changed its design, many readers were sending letters to the editors regarding this issue. I had the responsibility of photocopying all letters and distributing those copies to the top six editors. I also had to type and send response cards to those who had written, thanking them for their comments.

Product and Material Returns (20%): The magazine photographs most of the material shown in the magazine, and when the shooting is completed someone must send the products back to the companies. I helped the "On the Market" editor, Kathy Richter, return products ranging from 40-pound rolls of carpet to miniature home-security devices. I sent back slides and transparencies to various scouters who were looking for homes that the magazine might want to feature. Again, thank-you notes usually accompanied those materials as well.

Tear Sheets (11%): I sent tear sheets of the pages where writers appeared to these contributors, along with a complimentary issue.

Article Index Binders (7%): A rather lengthy but informative project was to read every "Update" article since 1986, title it, and put tears of the articles in chronological order into a binder. This would serve as a reference book for Anne, in case anyone needed information on a subject the magazine had covered in past "Update" articles.

Roster for the Editorial and Graphics Staff (5%): This assignment forced me to learn the names of the entire staff with whom I worked. I had to find out the correct spelling of their first and last names, current addresses, phone numbers and birthdates and type an updated roster.

Fact Checking (9%): Most of the stories themselves were accurate. I mainly made calls to stores and dealers or publicists to get additional information the editors needed that wasn't included in the press releases.

Typing (10%): I entered stories from freelancers into the computer and typed the buying guide, which lists information in the back of the magazine on featured items, correspondence to contributors and, of course, plenty of addresses.

Copyediting (2%): When Anne was in Chicago, she allowed me to copyedit the stories that came through. I cut the appropriate number of lines and reworded and rewrote a few. When she returned, she used some of my suggestions for the final copy and complimented my ideas. In another incident, while reading "bluelines" I suggested a different word for a headline in the December issue and overheard the editor-in-chief approve and agree with the change. Both of those events along with Anne's positive comments kept me pumped up for even the lowest of tasks as I felt my talents were fairly recognized when given the opportunity.

Meetings (7%): I participated in all of the staff meetings that took place on days that I worked. I learned a tremendous amount about how the staff interacts and how the whole magazine fits together. My background in advertising was helpful to understand what was discussed in some of the more important business meetings about the one-year and three-year plans of the magazine and how it was being positioned to advertisers on Madison Avenue.

Photoshoot (2%): I spent one day on a photoshoot for a feature article about a craftsman's house and furniture. This was the most fun as I assisted the photographer and editor in styling the set. I was not bashful and made suggestions that I believed in and that the editor herself respected. In fact, she commented to Anne about how I surprised her with my candor.

Writing (7%): Just as I began with a writing assignment, the internship came to a close. I wrote two more articles for the "Update" section for the February and March issues. Each was very short, about 100 words, but included a byline. I especially enjoyed writing about an auction to benefit blind children. Anne and I worked together in editing the pieces and she respected my suggestions and was again complimentary about what I had written.

The magazine is a part of a communications group that publishes other magazines, most of them related to the housing industry. A managing editor tells how the intern program operates:

We assign interns to different editors who handle assignments so that the interns get work from only one person, not the entire staff. In a given semester we may have no interns at all or we may have several.

We get applications from all over the country, and usually by February I have made a choice for the summer assignments. We just ask for a résumé and cover letter, but some applicants send an analysis of articles or some comments about our magazine. We prefer 40-hour-per-week interns in the summer and pay them $5 an hour. Fall and spring semester interns are also paid and work at least 15 to 20 hours per week. The prime requirement is an interest in the home field.

Darcy Johnson has graduated and has been hired at the magazine where she did her internship. She says that her current work closely parallels what she was assigned during her internship. In addition to writing short 100-word articles about new products, she also prepares copy for the buying guide reader information section at the back of the magazine. This requires researching where readers can purchase items pictured in the magazine.

> *A former intern found that her magazine duties as an employee were about the same as those she did as an intern.*

Johnson spends time scouting homes for future features. Through her own contacts and by meeting with architects and designers, she is able to spot special homes of interest to readers. She attends housing events. She has this advice for interns interested in magazines: You need strong writing skills, an interest in the content of the magazine and a willingness to work hard with editors and other staff members.

A Bridge: Magazines to Public Relations

You can find magazine-related experiences through public relations internships that involve work on publications. You can directly apply your interviewing, writing and editing skills even though the magazine content differs from that of consumer magazines. Assignments will necessitate switching to a more persuasive writing style, of course. Many slick, high-quality publications show off innovative graphic designs and showcase enterprising, creative feature writing.

Judy von der Nuell is a member of a three-person PR staff for an acute trauma hospital with 350 beds. She specializes in overseeing the publications work and describes her program:

Our hospital staff interviews interns interested in publications work first and PR work second. We pay about $8 an hour for 15 to 20 hours per week. We are looking primarily for two qualities: very good writing skills as demonstrated by above-average writing samples, and job experience where the person has been able to show initiative and self-motivation.

At our hospital there are three major publications for which the interns can write. The first, "Innerviews," appears quarterly. It is for hospital family members, employees, board members, foundation donors, etc. There is a good opportunity here for the interns to suggest ideas for features and to write them.

Four times a year we hold a luncheon for all of the "reporters" who represent different departments of the hospital. These "reporters" are appointed for the year. At the luncheon, ideas are shared and we discuss what we want the publication to cover in each issue. The interns participate in these discussions.

The second major publication available for interns to contribute articles to is "Connections," an informational and promotional medium. It reaches 100,000 households in the hospital service area. Each issue focuses on one topic (pediatrics and cardiology being recent examples) tied into service areas of the hospital.

The third publication, a weekly in-house newsletter called "Pulse," carries only brief news items. The interns can use the desktop publishing capabilities of WordPerfect and PageMaker. We conduct readership surveys annually to search out topics to cover in the future.

The interns also are assigned to write some press releases and to work with the public relations manager on these and other assignments. We like to see all of our interns take away both good experiences and solid writing samples for their portfolios.

Terri Sherwood, who completed an internship at this hospital involving two-and-a-half days of work per week, describes her experiences:

I worked January through May while taking classes at college. The spring semester did not start until early February so that gave me some good time to get acquainted with the internship before classes started.

The public relations and public affairs department of the hospital works as a closely knit team. I was accepted as a member of this team and included in staff meetings and corporate development sessions. I had supervision whenever I needed it.

While most assignments were challenging, one major article on cataracts and same-day surgery for the external magazine was the most difficult. It required that I do extensive research and interviewing in several hospital departments, and it took considerable time to write.

I received compliments from the public relations director and hospital administration staff on this article and a newspaper article on a surgery microscope which a local reporter wrote after

I arranged her visit.

Probably the most beneficial aspect of my internship was the variety of tasks assigned. Since my main interest is publications, I most enjoyed the magazine article writing and the preparation of brochures.

Assignments for the first three months of my internship and the approximate percentages of time spent on each:

Patient surveys (35.5%)—Collecting comments and distributing them to appropriate departments; sending letters and requested information to respondees.

Publications (21%)—Research, interviews and writing articles for employee and external magazines.

Brochures (12%)—Copy and coordination of artwork and printing for "Respiratory Rehabilitation"; copy for "Medical Technology Training" recruitment.

News releases (11%)—Copy and distribution for about 10 releases on a variety of community education lectures and screenings.

Pitch letter (7%)—Copy for letter and fact sheet to media on surgery microscope. Coordination of visit by reporter to observe surgery.

Corporate development planning (6%)—Meetings with marketing and public relations staffs to develop goals and objectives for hospital marketing.

Special events (5%)—Assisting with hospital's 25th anniversary; planning for Volunteer Recognition Week.

Display boards (1.5%)—Preparation of boards clippings, brochures, magazines for Board of Directors.

Fact sheet (1%)—Copy for Chemical Dependency Center fact sheet to distribute to parents.

Opportunities in Technical Writing and Editing

Another publications area that can offer good internship and job opportunities for qualified people is technical writing and editing. Although defense cutbacks during the early '90s sharply reduced the number of both internships and jobs, there are still many technically oriented companies requiring how-to-do booklets, manuals and various other publications.

Sheila Harlow, a technical editor for the past 10 years, points out that students seeking internships in this field have varied undergraduate majors and interests. She thinks you must have good basic English language skills as well as very strong writing skills. Well-developed computer skills are also necessary to get off to a good start in this complex business. She says that although it is helpful to have an interest in general science in college, an engineering degree or training in technical fields is not a requirement.

Harlow, herself a former journalism major in college, says some interns arrive with computer science degrees and a definite interest in technical fields. But many others are majors or graduates in liberal arts or communications who have been turned on to the field through university publications work.

Harlow, who completed two internships herself while in college, reports that her last two interns were both English majors. In explaining what technical editing interns do, Harlow stresses that much of the initial work requires that interns correct grammar, punctuation and style errors and rewrite material to be sure that what is written is what is intended. A copyediting course is helpful background. She comments:

People who have corrected work of engineers know that this is not an easy task. Many of the assignments are what we call clean-up work. A document may need editing as well as corrections. For example, [a computer] spellcheck may say that a word is misspelled, but it is up to the intern to enter the correctly spelled word.

Editing may involve a lot of style corrections and rewriting materials from engineers into understandable language. This may call for the intern to clarify information through interviews with engineers and programmers.

Depending on skills and experience, interns may edit other writers' documents. But generally interns are busy cleaning up much of the elementary work, particularly in editing. More complex tasks, such as rearranging the order of sections in a document, would not be assigned to a beginning intern here. However, internships in the technical area can vary with company requirements and needs. At this company interns are more gradually given complex assignments, depending on their backgrounds and overall skill level.

Following an internship, opportunities are good for interns to get employment here or with other companies offering technical writing and editing positions. This is very good experience relevant to all kinds of publications and magazine work. Also, except for a time of hiring freezes or cutbacks, this is a very excellent field for job seekers as frequently there are not that many qualified people available when positions do open. *An internship can be a very big factor in getting an interview for an opening.*

> *Experience in technical writing and editing can be relevant to all kinds of publications and magazine work.*

Doug Richards, a communications major with a journalism emphasis and a computer science minor, completed a technical editing internship. He describes how he handled one project for a small company:

A summer internship allowed me to work three days a week there and two days at my regular job. I was paid $7 an hour twice a month without tax deductions. My employer called it "contract labor."

The company had developed a software package for IBM-compatible microcomputers called Intelligent Test, which was to be used in the field of circuit board testing. Writing this manual required three skills: (1) a working knowledge of the field of printed circuit board design and testing, including all the jargon; (2) an understanding of IBM-compatible microcomputers and their MS-DOS operating system; and (3) the ability to write effectively. (NOTE: If the owner of the company, my supervisor, had the latter ability, which he certainly did not, I might not have had an internship.)

I entered the internship with only the latter

two skills; I had to pick up the printed board circuit knowledge as I went along. My only task was to write the manual for the Intelligent Test.

The first two weeks of the internship were really devoted to getting ready to go. First, I had to learn how to use WordStar 2000, the best word processor available at the company. Then, of course, I needed to learn how to use the Intelligent Test program in order to explain to others how to use it.

Once I started, about 90 percent of my time was evenly divided between using the test to find out what the program did and writing the manual. The other 10 percent was spent performing various MS-DOS disk housekeeping functions and waiting for printouts.

A problem was that supervision (when I needed to understand an unfamiliar concept or hard-to-understand passage) was not always readily available. It was a bit frustrating at times to attempt to write a manual explaining something that I did not fully understand myself.

However, it was just one project, a 67-page technical manual, and the work was well received. In technical writing especially, one must possess technical knowledge without requiring the reader to have the same level of knowledge. This makes it interesting.

Questions and Answers About Interviewing

Here are some questions and answers regarding tips on interviewing for publishing internships. The questions are from students attending a career session in New York; the answers are from Mary Campbell, human resources director for a large publishing company in New York. The company publishes several magazines and has a long-established intern program.

Q. What type of preparation should you do before interviewing for an internship?

A. You should follow three basic rules. First, bring two copies of your résumé to the interview. This holds true even if you have mailed a résumé with your cover letter to get this interview. I see lots of résumés and may not know where yours is at the moment. It will cause me to ask needless questions unless your résumé is handy. If you are an art candidate, have your portfolio available to see.

A second rule is to know something about the magazine that you want to work on. You should be aware of the kinds of articles and general content. Then you can ask specific questions about the magazine.

A third rule is to find out something about the job description of the internship and be able to ask questions about that. I want to hear from you to see if you are really interested in this business or just here to fill some college course requirement.

Q. What about dress and tips on what you should do or not do during the interview?

A. For one thing, do not chew gum during an interview. I had a person come in chewing gum last week. It's a bad habit. And don't ask me if you can smoke. I cannot stand cigarette smoke. Clothes can be too casual. Probably for an interview with a company in a major city you will want to wear professional clothes.

> *Learn as much as you can about a site before interviewing.*

Good eye contact at all times is important, and concentrate on all of the questions. You may not know all the answers but at least show interest. Language is very important as this is a communications position and good oral and written skills are a must. A string of "you knows" during your conversation can be distracting to say the least.

Q. What kind of questions can I expect during the interview?

A. Lots of different kinds. I am not very big on questions like "What do you want to be in five years?" or "Where will you be working a year from now?" I am sure that you can expect some tough questions from some interviewers. For example, you may be asked, "What are your liabilities?" If you answer that your mother says you are always late or friends say you are not always concentrating, you may lose the internship right there. To answer the question, you do not need to list specific faults. Rather, you can say you would like to be more aggressive or that sometimes you work too hard. You can make a positive statement about your faults.

You may wish to ask what schedule you would be working, but this probably should have been clarified in the cover letter. In other words, when you send your résumé and cover letter you should specifically mention the hours you would be able to work. We try to schedule interns around school schedules, and I am responsible for this.

The other day we interviewed an older woman, liked her, and gave her a 20-minute tour through our offices. We were about to offer her an internship when she said that she would need three weeks off in a month to go on a vacation to Europe. She just wasted our time because we do not give interns any vacations.

You should be prepared to answer questions like these: "Why do you want to work on this magazine? Why are you seeking a career on magazines or publications? What kinds of skills do you have for this job?"

To get some of your points across, you may have to take charge of an interview after an answer. You want to sell yourself and let people know why you are qualified for this internship.

Q. What about skills? What skills are necessary?

A. Strong writing skills are going to be looked upon as very favorable. It does not matter whether or not you are interviewing for a writing position. Even in sales or production, you must communicate well. Examples of how your writing has improved are good.

Being able to type is absolutely essential. If you cannot type at least 45 words a minute you are not yet ready for a job in either book or magazine publishing. Having typing skills does not mean that you are going to be a secretary. Of course, as an entry-level and new employee you may be asked to spell a secretary at some time. But more to the point is this: Many believe that without good minimal typing skills, you will be too slow on the word processor or computer to turn out work in a timely fashion. You are going to have a problem holding down a job.

Q. How can one prepare for interviewing?

A. Go to your college library or the career section of your favorite bookstore and check books on jobs and careers. There are specific books on job interviewing. There you will find out about all kinds of questions you should be ready to answer. Interviewing is subjective, although I try to be objective about it. You are going to make a favorable presentation and impression if you just plan ahead carefully.

Q. How do you find out when a decision will be made?

A. That's a good question to ask in your interview. We may have to interview a few more people before we can decide. You should not expect us to call you. If I say that a decision will be made by Tuesday of next week, you can call after Tuesday.

Q. If I do not know about the pay, should I ask or wait until I get the internship?

A. It's better to ask. While we pay a minimum wage, some publishers may pay more or may not pay at all. You may have a chance to choose between several publishing companies, so it's good to know if this one or that one does pay.

Q. How does the interview conclude?

A. You want to be sure that all of the questions you prepared are answered. Tell the interviewer that you do want the internship, if that is the case, and that you will appreciate hearing soon. Thank him or her for the time that has been spent interviewing you. And with a firm handshake, you are finished.

For Thought and Discussion

1. Based on Chapters 1 through 4, discuss five internships on publications and magazines and comment on how effective learning activities and evaluation procedures can be applied.

2. Discuss the pros and cons of working on a smaller regional magazine for an internship and a large-circulation magazine.

3. Choose a magazine article and select a portion to serve as a model quiz. Plant 15 spelling, punctuation, grammar and word usage errors in various parts of the article excerpt and make up an answer key. Give the test to a classmate while you take the test or tests prepared by other classmates.

4. Discuss three trends from the '80s that may have a positive effect on increasing internship opportunities on publications.

5. Give a half-dozen pointers for someone planning to interview for an internship opening with a magazine.

6. Assume you are the personnel director for a company interviewing internship applicants. Develop a dozen questions that would help you to get to know the candidate. Brainstorm in class about how to give answers to the following questions that will present you in the most positive light: What is the last novel you read? Which magazines do you subscribe to or read regularly? What is the best vacation you ever took?

CHAPTER 5

PUBLIC RELATIONS: OPPORTUNITIES FOR VARIED INTERNSHIPS

AS A GROWING SPECIALIZATION, public relations offers the biggest variety of internships in the entire communications industry. There is literally something for everyone, and this is especially true for undergraduates eager to test their wings.

Many PR internships are competitive, with majors in business and liberal arts applying for them. However, graduate and undergraduate students in public relations, journalism and communications are the largest group seeking these internships. The field also attracts many women and minorities. A survey by the Newspaper Fund showed that some 1,840, or 21.8 percent, of all journalism or communications graduates in a recent year were hired in public relations, and most of these graduates were women.

Varied job descriptions appear on PR internship listings across the country. If, for example, you want to work primarily on publications or print production, many opportunities exist beyond those listed in the previous chapters on newspapers and maga-

zines. A good PR internship gives you the opportunity to produce excellent writing samples through in-house publications and placement of articles in newspapers and other mass media outlets.

On the other hand, if you have good "people" skills and want to be involved more in special event work and less in writing, this opportunity may also exist in public relations. A wide range of experiences at non-profit internship sites is available in many cities. Also, public relations and marketing organizations such as shopping malls and agencies that need help with special event planning will want your kind of skills.

If you intern at an agency, no matter how large or small, you may be given a chance to meet clients and aid in formulating objectives and plans for programs. Working as an assistant to an account executive or to an account coordinator in an agency is a common internship route and one that can involve many tasks.

As sites grow in terms of the numbers of available PR internships, the competition also increases. In larger companies and organizations, more complex tasks may be assigned. It follows that higher-level internship skills may be in demand.

These are just a few of the many sites where PR interns have successfully completed better-than-average internships and where some very significant assignments and projects have been accomplished:

- *A large corporation* may offer internships in several areas. An automobile manufacturer may list internal and external (public affairs) departments where paid internships would be available from time to time.
- *Hospitals* have public relations or public affairs departments where there are various publications to which interns can contribute. A large medical center or acute trauma hospital may have several PR staff members.
- *City, county and state governmental agencies* frequently have paid internships in their public information offices or in employee communications departments. The fact that a site has never used interns before shouldn't limit you. Many students have uncovered PR departments that have evolved into permanent internship opportunities.

> *Don't let the fact that a site has never used interns before stop you. Many students have uncovered PR departments that have evolved into permanent internship opportunities.*

How Do You Begin?

- Get some experience by volunteering to work with a non-profit organization, perhaps a few hours a week around your school schedule. This is an opportunity to observe professionals in action and get an inside look at the field. Do this as early as possible in college.
- Use your networking contacts from your volunteer work or other school or community contacts to seek a part-time job in the field. This can be a valuable résumé addition. If nothing in public relations is available, look for jobs in advertising, marketing or sales. Just a job with minimum typing/computer skills or even a receptionist position may lead to something bigger later.
- Allow time for an internship during the summer of your senior year or end of your junior year. Many steps are involved; months of planning and checking are required. Some summer interns begin application steps the previous summer.

Policies in effect at many public relations and other communications sites such as newspapers and magazines require that personnel or human resource people, internship contact people or even site supervisors interview several internship applicants. All of the application and interviewing time can take a number of months. It's a good idea to find out when a decision will be made at a site so that you will have a time in mind should you be interviewing at other possible places.

Be sure you have the public relations skills required. This is critical for success. Most PR internships arranged through colleges have job descriptions that indicate the specific tasks you will be doing. Some smaller agencies have general descriptions so that specific tasks for an intern are not clearly defined. It's best to be prepared to ask any questions about your assignments at the initial interview so that you have information to compare internship sites fairly when you are making a final decision.

In a difficult job market you may have to have completed more than one internship before you can be seriously considered for a full-time position. *Public relations provides some of the best networking opportunities in communications*. You should keep in mind during your first internship that you need to make contacts that will be useful in your search for another internship or a job.

Finding Your Own Site

You may have to look beyond various titles to search out elusive internship leads. PR internships are hidden behind an array of titles, such as marketing, community relations, public affairs and consumer affairs. Search through directories or use personal or faculty contacts to discover opportunities.

Examples of positions that interns have found on their own include working as

✓ an assistant to the local representative for a state assemblywoman
✓ an aide to the publicity director for a local amusement park
✓ assistant to the marketing director for a shopping mall
✓ a member of the community relations staff for a chapter of the Boy Scouts Council
✓ an assistant to the employee who prepares brochures and other publications for waste management projects for a county public works agency
✓ an aide to a chamber of commerce official on a city's anniversary publicity project
✓ a volunteer helping to promote a local museum

Your own supervisor may recommend contacts for a second internship. Take advantage of all opportunities to attend luncheons and meetings where you can meet professionals. A second internship may be easier to find than you think because site supervisors are often looking for an intern who has some

experience.

To illustrate the importance of networking, consider the experiences of two women as they progressed through their internships and other work experiences toward successful careers. Both are examples of graduates with PR majors. Teri Johnson completed her bachelor of arts degree from an accredited program in 1984. She has worked for a major PR agency and now has her own business license as an independent PR consultant. She describes her three internships:

I completed two basic reporting and writing classes as a freshman. I thought I was ready for an unpaid, no-credit internship with a chapter of the American Lung Association and this turned out to be true. This first work experience helped me build confidence and test my writing skills.

Probably the biggest advantage I can recall, however, was the contacts I made through this internship. The organization had a communications committee to advise on publicity and public relations matters. Members were among the top public relations pros from all over the county, some of whom were graduates of my own university. Immediately, two of these busy professionals offered to critique my writing and advise me. They also invited me to sit in on their monthly luncheon meetings. I learned so much from observing how public relations professionals think.

Through a contact on this committee, I was able to get a second non-credit internship two years later. It was a paid part-time position where I continued to learn even though it was a small agency. I was grateful for this chance to sharpen my writing skills.

A speaker who lectured in one of my public relations classes led me to my third internship. She announced that she would make a paid, 20-hour-per-week internship available to a senior the following semester. After completing public relations writing classes, I was selected for this internship, which was really a three-day-a-week job lasting throughout my senior year. The firm was Burson-Marsteller, a highly respected public relations agency, and the university gave me internship credit for this work.

Upon graduation, I moved into a full-time position there as an assistant account executive. I was promoted to account executive in six months and worked there for two years.

Now I work as an independent public relations consultant, seeking out my own clients and working on various projects. I charge an hourly rate and make much more money than I would at an agency. Why the change? I wanted to broaden the scope of my work and expand my opportunities in the public relations field.

In the second example, Nancy Camp places less emphasis on networking, but the experiences she chronicles are important because they illustrate a phenomenon of the PR job market—the employment of "late arrivals" to college and the workplace. For instance, women in their late 20s, 30s or 40s are entering colleges and universities for the first time in record numbers. They find that public relations is a field in which their maturity and skills are welcome. These people are prime candidates for PR internships.

Camp completed her four years of college while in her 30s, majoring in public relations. During her senior year through a competition she won a summer internship in the public affairs department of General Telephone. She comments:

This was a full-time, summer, $5-an-hour internship where I learned a good deal, improved my writing and worked on a number of tasks peculiar to a utility company. Although I worked directly for only one supervisor, I did work for and made friends with a number of other members of the public affairs staff. These people asked me to lunch to meet other public relations people and genuinely were concerned and interested in my future plans.

I worked on numerous projects, both short-range and long-range. Some of my work was on the small inserts which are mailed with utility bills. Everyone seemed pleased with my work. The director of public affairs recommended me for a second internship with a major public relations agency.

All of the challenging assignments of this second paid internship, which followed my graduation, prepared me well for my first job. I was soon employed full time with a smaller public relations agency which had as clients many food industry companies. After working there two years I felt I was ready for my next job, this time at a major international public relations agency, Fleishman-Hillard. After several promotions, I am now a vice president there supervising many accounts.

Hugh Millen, communications specialist for General Telephone, was the supervisor at Camp's original internship. He has these comments:

This is a good example of hiring as an intern a well-prepared woman who had good writing skills and the maturity to handle increasing responsibilities. It serves as a good role model for other "late arrivals" in similar need of work experience during or after college.

We look for skilled older graduates to fill our internship slots. Such interns are dependable, show up on time and are eager to search out ways to learn the business.

Since we hire full-time personnel in the public affairs department only after they have completed three to five years' experience in the field, running a good internship program is a way we can help recent graduates. We have nothing against young interns, but often 21- and 22-year-olds have some bad habits. They are often not as reliable.

Internships With Non-Profit Organizations

Another major advantage the PR field offers you is its huge non-profit sector. This is a good place for beginners. Even as a freshman or sophomore in college, you will find many entry-level tasks that you are prepared to complete. Special event and fund-raising activities will enhance your ability to work with people successfully. Many talented PR professionals got their start in the business by working on fund-raising projects. Even if you decide later to enter another area of communications, this experience will be very beneficial and make a useful addition to your résumé.

Interns can get involved in fund-raising and other tasks at non-profit organizations.

Public relations coordinators with non-profit organizations frequently serve as outstanding site supervisors for interns. Suzanne Menuier is one of these supervisors. Herself a former intern at the American Heart Association, Menuier is now a fund-raiser and public relations coordinator for a Heart Association chapter. She describes her duties and the participation of interns in her chapter's activities:

Probably about 65 percent of my job involves fund-raising activities such as Dance for Heart, Jump Rope for Heart, Bike Challenge, etc. The other 35 percent involves writing news releases, editing a newsletter, making media contacts, sending out PSAs [public service announcements] and coordinating community work on projects like CPR training.

The Jump Rope campaign requires students to get pledges of money from friends, relatives and neighbors. This year about $40,000 has been raised, largely through the assistance of interns.

I could list numerous examples of how the individual initiative of an intern has brought him or her success. For example, in setting up a program for us at a nearby elementary school, one of my interns discovered that a student recently died from a serious illness but not heart disease. However, she was able to persuade school personnel to hold a jump rope event in the student's name. She contacted area media and wrote press releases. The campaign netted $2,000 for the Heart Association.

Menuier says that she likes to spend time with interns, helping them with the development of their skills. She requires her interns to write and rewrite press releases until they are usable. This is a necessary skill, she says.

Because she can only pay her interns a stipend, ranging from $300 to $750, she tries

to advertise for interns early because most PR internships in her area pay an hourly wage. She insists on a good résumé, cover letter and writing samples. She personally interviews each applicant. Usually about five or six students apply because there are two colleges with communications programs nearby. She adds: "I want to find out right away in the interviews if they have an interest in fund-raising activities. I will be spending a lot of time with them, evaluating their writing and helping with other skills. I need interns who show an interest and willingness to work."

You might be able to develop your own proposal for an internship with a non-profit group. You would need a genuine interest in helping to fight a crippling disease or in promoting some kind of campaign for a

A Non-Profit PR Internships

A directory from a university public relations internship program gives a sample of the many non-profit organizations in this field:

AIDS Service Foundation
Alzheimer's Disease/Related Disorders Association
American Cancer Society
American Diabetes Association
American Heart Association
American Lung Association
American Red Cross
Blind Children's Learning Center
Boy Scouts of America Council
Cancer Coping Center
Catholic Community Agencies
Children's Home Society of America
Development Disability Center
Mothers Against Drunk Driving
Olive Crest Center for Abused Children
Senior Meals and Services
State Burn Association

similar organization. You would require some assistance, perhaps using some of the background information acquired in a PR class. A potential supervisor could help you design some projects and assignments that you could manage.

To make this approach practical, a key factor would be that someone with PR expertise would be willing to supervise your work. This might be a part-time consultant or an experienced PR practitioner willing to help you complete a campaign and learn some of the fundamentals of the business.

The critical importance of good supervision is illustrated by this story from a faculty coordinator who recalls how he attempted to assist one of his college's PR majors find an internship for the summer near her home in North Dakota. She was accepted by the executive director of a non-profit chapter who had a laundry list of PR tasks to do when she arrived at work.

> *An unqualified supervisor can derail the best internship plans.*

Unfortunately, three problems eliminated this assignment from being a good learning experience. First, the director had no public relations knowledge so he could not help the student with writing and other tasks. Second, he had no time to assist her because he was so busy with his own duties. And finally, there was no budget to produce brochures and other projects that required financing.

A PR professor at a major university expresses caution about arranging your own internship:

We know that there are many organizations, large and small, needing public relations help. Signing up an intern is not the answer. There must be a qualified public relations supervisor who has the know-how and time to direct an intern. He or she does not have to be on the staff but can be a qualified professional willing to supervise.

We get calls almost weekly from both profit and non-profit groups seeking to borrow equipment to produce a videotape or slide show for public relations purposes. Even if we loaned equipment, which we do not, it is very unlikely there is a person qualified enough to assist an intern through such a project.

People mean well, but no budget and no supervision spell disaster for an intern! These examples give a bad name to internships or what are very loosely called internships.

Other Areas in Public Relations

It is important to note that completing an internship in the non-profit sector does not mean that you are only qualified to work in this PR subfield. Many graduates with internships with non-profit organizations shift into other PR jobs. Many men and women who won their first job in the non-profit sector move in a year or two into "profit" public relations. Movement in this huge field of communications is very common, especially for those with a few years of PR experience.

There are many aspects of the PR field to consider when you look at the broad range of positions that, by the way, can add substantially to any internship list. Public relations launched its remarkable growth in the 1960s and 1970s, and by the '80s it achieved its highest employment numbers. Conservative estimates point to between 200,000 and 250,000 people nationally working in some part of the PR field. Much depends, of course, on defining the word public relations.

Public Relations: The Ugly Definition

When looking for internships and jobs, students and recent graduates need to avoid getting hooked on the term "public relations" as a lead for employment. As used in newspaper classified ads, "public relations opening" may refer merely to a person conducting surveys of shoppers in a mall or to someone needed to make telemarketing calls in his or her home.

In particular, be wary of the terms "intern" or "trainee" in ads, which are used to catch unsuspecting students. Small agencies will advertise that "interns" can learn the PR business by serving a non-paid "internship" or work in exchange for getting educational information.

Of course, sometimes little education occurs. The outcome of most of these situations is that graduates with no university affiliation work at no pay doing clerical tasks such as answering phones, photocopying and faxing. After a few months when they leave, a new group can be enticed to take their places. (Excerpts from a *Daily Variety* article in Appendix B point to illegal practices regarding the use of interns in film and television.)

Today's public relations textbooks do not limit PR subfields to agency, corporate and non-profit. Instead, the list has expanded to include a large number of career positions, including:

- Non-profit
- Corporate
- All sizes of PR agencies including large national and international and small local firms
- Companies offering various kinds of financial services and investor relations

- Hospitals and health management organizations and associations
- Public and private university and college offices in public relations and public affairs, sports publicity, art and theater promotions, etc.
- Travel and tourism industries and convention bureaus and hotels
- Public and private cultural organizations, such as museums
- Specialized areas including those in the high-technology field and computer software companies
- Sports and entertainment, which illustrate the overlapping of the areas of publicity, promotion and public relations

Public relations jobs reach into many other businesses. For example, PR education-related positions extend beyond those in public colleges to school districts. Many reports, handbooks, brochures and other publicity materials are produced by personnel in districts of all sizes. Jayma Engle-Cherney was able to use her production and graphics skills working in the office of a high school district. She describes her internship in these words:

> "I had heard 'horror' stories of interns who were stuck with mailing labels and stuffing envelopes. I was so wrong!"

I was really dreading my internship, which is required by my school for graduation. I had heard of "horror" stories of a few interns who were stuck with mailing labels and stuffing envelopes. I was so wrong!

My internship was in the information services office of the high school district. I was especially lucky in that Erin, my supervisor, and I got along so well. We discovered that we even had mutual friends!

I wrote several press releases and some features about students getting awards, scholarships and other related topics. Much of my time was spent in writing and editing a special handbook. I also did layout and paste-up. Erin and I went to the printer for proofreading. Yes, we did put on some mailing labels too.

Three times a year the district publishes a newsletter to parents, students and community leaders. I had to select photos from yearbook files (or take them myself) and make contacts with school people to be sure that information reached us on time. I also did the layout and paste-up work for these publications.

Although I was not paid for my internship, I was hired for a part-time position there when the internship was completed.

Sometimes a student's educational path toward a PR career follows more of a journalism route. Gary Sherwin is a case in point. Sherwin never took a single PR course. In fact, he was a staff writer for his campus daily newspaper and did his internship on a metropolitan daily.

Now Sherwin does public relations, promotion and advertising work for the Fort Worth, Tex., Convention and Visitors Bureau. His title, Director of Marketing Communications, illustrates the overlap of duties often found in marketing and public relations.

Sherwin got his start in journalism by working on his high school newspaper and joining a scholastic press association where he had contact with other high school journalists. He describes his high school and college experiences:

I was accepted for a kind of non-credit internship while in high school. After writing some features and a column for a weekly newspaper near home, I was able to develop a five-minute radio show for a small station, profiling the same people mentioned in my column.

I followed a telecommunications major in college although I would stick to journalism, if I could do it over. However, I took newswriting and reporting classes and worked a couple semesters on the campus daily.

As my sophomore year in college ended, my faculty adviser recommended me for a part-time job on the local daily Scripps-Howard newspaper. City council and school board meetings were covered. I also wrote a column, "Going Like 60," for senior citizens which became popular. I remained active in campus journalism programs and attended several Sigma Delta Chi national conventions and regional conferences.

Faculty members urged me to apply for what the newspaper termed an academic internship—two days a week during the spring semester—at a nearby metropolitan daily's community section. They said that my clips from the campus paper and the Scripps-Howard daily would qualify me, and they were correct.

This large daily internship paid enormous dividends and, I am sure, was largely responsible for my rapid career development in the public relations field. The internship allowed me to write for both the business and education pages with some excellent feature assignments.

The writing samples got me my first two public relations jobs. One was with a transportation office working as an assistant in the public affairs office for the county for 25 hours per week during my senior year.

I had some interesting experiences in applying for and getting my first full-time job following graduation in 1983. It was the position of director of public relations for a small medical and surgery center.

During my interview for this job, several doctors on the surgery center board questioned me about my writing samples. They wondered how at such a young age I had been able to write so many articles for a large daily newspaper. After I got the job, my supervisor told me that I was the only candidate of the finalists with very strong writing samples. He said that some of the doctors were blown away by the amount of writing I had accomplished.

After six months I was hired for a position with a convention bureau and stayed there for two years. I moved with my boss to Fort Worth at an increase in salary. I like my present work, which involves a lot of both internal and external public relations. I get to work with travel writers and other groups at a demanding but enjoyable pace. But I still use my writing skills, which I believe got me where I am.

A Director of Marketing Communications and former intern believes that his writing skills got him where he is today.

Public Relations Agencies

A good place to look for a PR internship is with PR agencies, which range in size from large national and international companies to one- or two-person operations. Chief tasks for interns at small PR agencies include writing, meeting clients, pitching stories to the media and providing ideas for projects.

John Dennis says that a small agency has more of a "family" atmosphere to offer an intern. He now owns his own agency after working for nine years with Basso and Associates, a medium-sized public relations and advertising agency. Noting that "PR" stands for more than press releases, he says that interns can help in a variety of ways:

I enjoy working with interns and have hired a few after they finish their internships and graduate from college. The intern who is willing to work can get a complete picture of how public relations works, dealing with clients from all walks of life.

I am not as concerned as some managers or owners with top writing skills. I want the intern to work in public relations as a career and be willing to put in the long hours it takes to learn the business.

My interns contribute ideas at client meetings. I take them to all business meetings so they can see all aspects of the work. Many small agencies cannot pay a salary, but they should offer a stipend to cover expenses and mileage costs.

It is important to consider that a smaller PR agency may give the intern a more varied assortment of tasks than those assigned to interns at larger firms. However, a large agency, possibly requiring more-specialized tasks, also is more apt to pay the intern. Usually, more entry-level openings exist at bigger agencies. However, competition for internships can be tougher at these agencies.

One larger agency, Hill & Knowlton, offers specialized internships. Ron Miller, a manager, describes them this way:

Our internships are primarily writing for a news bureau with one of our major accounts. We look for good writers. Since internships are paid, we get a number of applicants.

We prefer those with campus newspaper experience or published writing samples. Some colleges do not require the public relations students to work on the campus newspaper. But we tend to hire interns who have had this university writing experience.

We get a very close look at the interns while they work with us. Those with superior writing skills may be hired here, but we refer many more good interns to agencies where we know there are openings.

Prospective interns who have special interests or expertise should remember that at a large agency you will be better able to use your highly focused skills. Agencies specialize in financial public relations, industrial and technological marketing communications, food marketing and specialized media relations.

Smaller agencies can provide a variety of tasks and a "family" atmosphere, whereas larger agencies may allow you to use more-specialized skills.

Writing business news about a major client was the principal task for Bruce Wadman, who completed an internship between his junior and senior years in New York City with Bozell & Jacobs, one of the country's largest PR firms. He said that aside from allowing him to visit a large city, the internship brought to life many of the principles he had been learning in classes.

I wrote articles about a client who sells copier machines, getting information from the results of surveys conducted by Bozell & Jacobs. Survey forms had been sent out to dealers nationwide. I checked the returned forms for newsworthy items and called dealers for more details.

The agency people were terrific to me and were willing to help with my writing. They were very easy to work with. I made a few mistakes, but the agency personnel took it all in stride.

This experience sharpened my grasp of public relations techniques. Some clients can be difficult and I learned how important the relationship is between client and agency. All in all it was a great experience.

Working with specialized clients at a much smaller agency were among the tasks handled by intern Carol Arns, a senior. Although it did not pay her a salary, her internship did lead directly to full-time employment upon graduation. She comments in the report she filed:

I assisted in developing and writing a public relations proposal for a new bank, which was the major assignment in my internship. I was invited by the agency president to accompany him as he presented his bid for their business to the bank's board of directors. We did not win the account, but the insight into the process was invaluable to me.

I helped in coordinating grand opening plans for a new luxury motor hotel, and I wrote some press releases on the event. Some articles also followed my attendance at client meetings related to the opening of a new residential housing development. I designed invitations, participated in brainstorming ideas for creative tie-ins, and planned and completed most of the publicity for a new restaurant opening.

As noted above, public relations as an industry has grown rapidly. Formal guidelines leading to the accreditation of PR programs at journalism and communications schools across the country were not developed until the mid-1970s.

Earlier, and still to some extent today, professionals entered public relations from other media jobs, especially from newspapers. Some will argue that reporting experience and contacts developed while working on a daily newspaper form the best background for a PR applicant. Many of today's managers and high-level PR agency personnel earned their communications experience from the journalism side. Thus, it isn't surprising to find that when they are evaluating applicants for internships and jobs, they place a premium on any kind of newspaper writing experience. Good writing skills seem to be almost essential for most PR positions.

Clarify the Job Requirements

Aside from the emphasis on producing good writing, PR internships may require you to have a number of skills from related fields. It's very important for you as a prospective intern to clarify your understanding of job description requirements such as graphics and computer skills. For example, as a prospective intern you may assume that "graphics skills" means having completed a graphics class or two and having a general understanding of how graphics are used in producing a newsletter. To another person it may mean that you need excellent production and paste-up skills, not unlike those of an art major or minor. Or the agency might be saying that "all we need is someone with desktop publishing skills and we will train them." Whatever the case may be, you as a prospective intern have the responsibility to find out what is meant by "graphics skills" or similar terms.

Some site supervisors indicate that they will train interns with basic computer knowledge. You must ask in a letter or in person at an interview whether minimal skills will be sufficient. It's best to find out about rigid skill requirements early, before either you or the manager from the prospective site wastes too much time.

Skills can be discussed at an interview. If you possess a particular skill, clearly note it on your résumé. Otherwise, you may never get called in for an interview. For example, an internship in a state assembly member's office or with the field representative for a member of Congress may have as a general requirement good writing and organizational skills. However, if you have a minor in political science, emphasize that information on your résumé in order to get an edge needed for what might be a competitive internship.

Various experiences carefully described on your résumé are always useful. Don't forget to list your courses in marketing or business management that may be of special interest. Take a look at résumé samples to see how you can get maximal value from such entries (see Appendix A or visit a bookstore or library for books on résumés).

Corporate Interns Face Competition

Many PR professors rank corporate PR internships as the most prestigious. To qualify for these internships, you must have a high GPA and some previous work experience. Maturity, good interpersonal skills and a strong work ethic are key ingredients for the corporate-bound intern to possess. Since the communications department in these companies usually numbers several people, there is a possibility that a job may open while the intern is there. A well-performing intern with good all-round skills should have a definite advantage over other applicants.

Such a scenario favors the idea of extending an internship over a longer period. Interning for a company for a full semester or an entire year, as opposed to only a few

months in the summer, extends the period during which such an opportunity could occur.

Another possibility would be for you to take a leave of absence from university classes for a semester or year, perhaps between your junior and senior years. Such an arrangement might increase the chances of interning with a company in a larger market away from home.

Usually, a fairly large number of specialists, working on both internal and external communications projects, form corporate PR staffs. It's not uncommon for hiring to require a three- to five-year experience level. However, an alert intern will be watching for possible entry-level openings in other parts of the company. Should a job be posted and you have a strong recommendation from your supervisor and if you are otherwise qualified, you would be a strong candidate for the job.

This proved true for Linda Burns, who completed a four-month summer internship with Aerojet General Corp. She earned $6.50 an hour for 20 hours per week in employee communications. Her supervisor, Dan Coleman, comments:

I discussed Linda's application for this internship with her writing and public relations professors. She checked out fine. Her chief tasks were in writing and editing material for the monthly employee newsletter, assisting in providing audiovisual support for communications projects, and working on new employee orientation materials for the company.

When I left the company a few months after Linda's internship was completed, she was immediately hired for my full-time position. I think that my strong recommendation was a big factor in her selection.

Hourly pay for interns is higher in corporate communications. Robin White got almost $10 an hour for a 40-hour-per-week internship during the final semester of her senior year. She earned three units of credit for her internship and was able to complete one evening class as well. Her internship at Hewlett-Packard shows how PR skills can be used in company settings that call for sales and marketing-related tasks. Her final report had these highlights:

My major responsibilities included some public relations assignments and jobs that required common business sense. The office had more than 500 employees with a majority being field engineers (FEs) in sales. I helped the FEs in research and in gathering information for a possible sale.

As a result of this work, I had direct interpersonal communication with both the FEs and our customers. I enjoyed the one-to-one interaction and always felt that I was contributing to the company.

I found out that it is important to be flexible and think of better ways of getting the job done. My supervisor was very encouraging and helpful. He invited me to brainstorming sessions with other employees.

At one of these sessions early in my internship, a colleague said: "Here at H-P it is baptism by fire so you had better be ready and willing to jump in." Let me add that this was true wisdom.

The internship was a humbling experience. My life as a student had always been structured, and I was in control. In the business world I found out that the control is not always yours alone. At H-P we worked as a team, not alone. If a mistake was made, we were all responsible. It was different for me, but I enjoyed it.

As shown in the previous example, as a PR intern you may find some assignments that slide into the sales and marketing areas. When working for the communications department of a major company, your tasks may be more product-oriented or you may be dealing directly with marketing. These positions may require less writing and public relations activities.

> *PR interns may find that some assignments merge skills and duties from the areas of marketing, advertising and public relations.*

Another internship by a senior illustrates the merging of marketing, advertising and public relations principles, this time in high-tech communications. A PR major, Mike Henrickson describes his internship at Conrac Corp., a technical communications firm:

My supervisor, the marketing services manager, had a "let-the-intern-do-it" style, allowing me to digest and understand some rather technical subject matter without pressure. However, he did help, if I had technical questions.

Most of my time was in writing feature articles, news releases, product bulletins, direct-marketing letters and ad copy for various publications. I was published in various trade magazines.

I finally learned to ask more questions at the beginning of assignments. Not getting sufficient facts led me to spend more time rewriting than I should have.

Although I received slightly above minimum pay for three eight-hour days per week for a semester, I did get an all-expense paid trip to Las Vegas to assist in a trade show. I did absolutely no clerical work as I had access to a secretary.

It was not difficult to understand the technical nature of the material once it was explained. Graphics, editing and technical writing classes would have helped as background for this internship.

I did have a few spelling problems. But, all in all, I learned definite skills applicable to my new job. The primary one was to be able to meet the challenge of simplifying the abstract so that it could be understood. I enjoyed this aspect of the work the most.

Henrickson credits his internship with helping to cover a gap in his education and training so that he could become more knowledgeable in technical communications. He now holds a job similar to his internship. It also involves a combination of product marketing and public relations.

More Opportunities to Write

Public relations internships at media offices offer the intern many opportunities to write.

■ They can focus on writing up promotional and PR special event activities for newspapers, television and radio stations.

■ Promotion and marketing departments at newspapers produce publications for employees.

■ Special advertising sections on newspapers spotlight auto shows, mall and store openings, and community events and celebrations. Interns can help editors write articles, prepare headlines and lay out pages.

Although this is a good way to acquire writing samples, these internships are difficult to find. You need to search them out through personnel and advertising departments.

Let's say that you write usable press releases published in a community newspaper. You clip these out of the paper yourself. If you are already interning, your agency may subscribe to a clipping service, but you must save these published writing samples.

On the other hand, daily newspapers may for various reasons rewrite your press release or hand it to a reporter to do more research on the topic. In this case, it's no longer your story. In fact, you probably won't recognize it, so you can't clip it and call it your own without proper explanation.

> *Since your press release may go into an editor's wastebasket, internship supervisors suggest you keep a copy of all of your work, published or not.*

Your press release may only go into some editor's wastebasket, so internship supervisors suggest you keep a copy of all of your work. Attach a brief report on what happened to a particular assignment. For example, you might put in your portfolio an original news release completed on assignment. Also, include the actual story published from the release even though it may have been rewritten. Be sure to date and indicate the name of the newspaper printing the clipping.

In this way you are showing that you wish to focus on your own work, separating it from writing that is not yours. These steps are preferable to simply showing clips without any explanation. Interviewers often ask, "How many of these stories were completely written by you? How much of the work was rewritten?"

Measuring writing effectiveness is very important to those who interview prospective interns. If you don't have many published writing samples, there are still ways to show off what you have accomplished. Nancy Fletcher, vice president of the consumer accounts department of an office of Fleishman-Hilliard, discusses her ranking system for writing samples:

Prospective interns bring us three levels of writing samples. The top level includes those from previous work or internships. For example, an intern currently applying has samples to show from a previous internship with a smaller public relations agency.

The second level is also important. It would include clips from campus newspapers or from other college publications. Maybe you also have a story or two written when you were a volunteer for an organization.

The third and lowest ranking level of samples would be stories written simply as class assignments in reporting or public relations writing classes. Some may have comments by instructors in the margin. Possibly this is all you have to show. That's okay, as we want to see your work.

I may give a test in addition to looking at some writing. I may give you facts for a release. I would stop you in 15 minutes to see what has been accomplished.

More important than writing samples is having completed one or two prior internships or having some good work experience. I had two very good internships myself, and there is no question that they helped me greatly in advancing my career.

Not all PR internships go smoothly. Problems can develop at the student's end or at the employer's end of an internship. A faculty coordinator describes a case that gives some perspective:

There is a small percentage of internships where Murphy's Law might apply. The intern's supervisor—the manager of marketing/ communications for the company—was very busy and the intern wanted more attention at first. He gave her several tasks to do but when they were finished, he said that they were not what he wanted. She admitted that she should have asked more questions for clarification.

Her first story for a company publication was a bit technical. The intern was not sure of her facts. This probably caused more tension between her and her supervisor.

The intern said that she learned a valuable lesson, which was to always ask questions when you are not sure. Her interview subject was not pleased to see her a second time for information that she should have gathered on her first interview.

The intern was disappointed at the end of her internship. She said that she was led to believe that she would get a job there, if she did a good job. Her supervisor said that it was a matter of economics; another $7-an-hour intern would replace her and the company would save on benefits required, as opposed to hiring a full-time employee.

This is sometimes the way a supervisor handles the situation. The supervisor admitted later that the intern was slow and not strong in her work habits and writing skills.

It turns out that the supervisor tired of the intern early because of her lack of performance. He turned her over to his assistant, the managing editor of one of the publications, and this is where the intern got most of her assignments.

The intern reported that the two chief benefits of the internship were the valuable addi-tion to her résumé and the interaction that she had with executives and marketing professionals in the company.

However, the intern showed that she had some maturing to do. She did not refer in her final report to any criticism of her writing by the supervisors. Yet, some spelling and grammar errors cropped up in her final report. She was advised to take an additional writing class.

In hindsight, this was not a good internship fit. She should have been matched with a smaller company, perhaps one that would have made fewer demands of her writing skills.

Some Advice from an Internship Veteran

A few pieces of advice may help you in searching for an internship or PR job. The advice comes from Donn Silvis, associate professor and chairman of the Department of Communications at California State University, Dominguez Hills. A veteran of 25 years' experience in corporate communications, Silvis has been on committees screening applicants for full-time entry-level PR positions. He lists three major points to remember and elaborates on each:

1. Be familiar with the company where you are applying.

Too many applicants know little or nothing about what the company does or what their products are. They have simply not done their homework. Even checking an annual report of a company will tell you about its operations.

While you are in the waiting room of a company prior to your interview, check around for brochures or publications of the company so that you can pick up some current information. Just being able to answer some brief questions about the company can make you a stronger candidate.

2. Tailor your résumé to the job.

You need to be well acquainted with the position's description so that you will understand what skills are needed and feature these on your résumé. Be very specific in detailing these skills. Merely listing typing and computer knowledge is insufficient.

Placing on your résumé specific [computer] programs such as QuarkXPress can be picked up quickly by interviewers and help your chances. Do not simply list "photojournalism." You can tell about what kinds of photos you took when working for a non-profit organization or give examples of how you have used your photo skills.

It's necessary to list basic typing and computer skills. But this may not be enough. You need some information to move you out in front of the other candidates. For instance, if you are applying for a publicity position with a performing arts center, information on your résumé about some theater arts courses you took may make a difference. Also, be knowledgeable about recent productions there.

3. Describe your internships or work experience in detail.

Do not ever be discouraged by the number of applicants. For many internships and public relations jobs, there are many unqualified applicants. Details about your experiences, particularly related jobs, help.

To illustrate, assume that you have participated in a volunteer assignment with United Way or a similar organization. Tell what your role was. How much money did your campaign make? Descriptive comments showing a way of measuring your success are useful. But do not list any facts that cannot be verified.

Media relations can be a big part of a job. If you can show on your résumé how you worked with reporters or television people in publicizing some of the organization's big events, this can stand out.

Your previous experience including college work should be reflected in the products in your portfolio. Besides newswriting clips, you may have samples of PSAs, brochures and even letters you wrote. These should be attractively packaged in your portfolio. Even 10 to 12 class assignments

with the instructor's comments can be included.

For Thought and Discussion

1. Assume that you are the adviser of a college freshman interested in public relations as a career and desiring some professional experience. Give this person two recommendations or suggestions on how to break into the field.

2. Why did the PR supervisor believe that the company favored employing people in their 30s or older as interns as opposed to younger people?

3. One of the non-profit organizations in this chapter offered a stipend instead of an hourly wage. What experiences would an intern accepting this opportunity receive that might make it more attractive than a regularly paid PR spot?

4. Suppose that a certain non-profit organization in your city has a large list of PR tasks to be done by a student with your communications skills. In fact, the director wants to hire you for the summer and agrees to pay minimum hourly wages. The executive director of the organization, a young man with boundless energy and an excellent, outgoing personality, thinks that the two of you can pull this off even though he has little PR training. Give three reasons why this could be a bad idea.

5. What are at least three things that you can do when told to "learn something about the company where you are applying for an internship?"

6. Give two examples of descriptive comments that could be used on a person's résumé.

CHAPTER **6**

ADVERTISING INTERNSHIPS: AGENCY AND NON-AGENCY

PREDICTING THAT AN INTERNSHIP can lead to a job is a good bet in many of the communications specialties, but not in advertising. Like broadcast journalism, advertising agency work is what career counselors term a glamour business. Consequently, the field often has an abundance of qualified candidates and a shortage of entry-level jobs and internships.

Advertising agency work can be compared to a fragile boat on the high seas. Waves of full employment and new accounts can carry it high, but just as quickly a recession can sink it into the depths of lost business and layoffs. It has become axiomatic that in times of a weakening economy or bad business conditions, public relations is the first to go. But advertising personnel can feel the pressures of a business downturn just as readily.

Advertising education started in the Midwest and spread nationwide, particularly in the 1970s and '80s. More than 30 universities offer accredited advertising majors throughout the country. In the past many journalism school graduates either went to work for ad agencies directly out of college or arrived there later after acquiring some experience from jobs on newspapers or in public relations. Some of these people teach advertising classes today. Many communications or journalism schools currently offer a sequence of classes to form a specific advertising major.

College degrees from many disciplines are represented among entry-level ad agency personnel. University majors in art, business, marketing, speech, psychology and the liberal arts are found as often as those who major in advertising or communications. Graduates with MBAs appear among those hired for entry-level positions at agencies.

Therefore, the educational preparation for a person who wants to advance to a top agency position is not tied to any particular degree or work experience. For example, a major in art or graphics design may move up rapidly from an entry-level job to become an art director and a major player on the agency's creative team.

The word from the advertising community is that the Help Wanted sign is out for only the brightest, most energetic, hard-working graduates dedicated to an advertising career. And these people must work very hard to make it.

Advertising jobs and, similarly, internships cannot be found in equal numbers everywhere in the country. Ad agencies generally locate in major urban markets, with a heavy concentration on the East Coast. New York City continues to be the heart of the nation's advertising industry and the home to most major agencies. The Big Apple also is the home base for broadcasting companies, giant marketing firms and other businesses closely allied with advertising agency activities.

This explains why many seniors or college graduates are attracted to New York and other large markets for internships and jobs. Entry-level agency jobs are usually competitive and salaries are low when compared with those in other fields competing for university graduates. Salaries can increase after several months on the job, of course, but moving to another agency is often the key to getting more money. Thus, employee turnover is common in the industry.

Ad Agencies: Where the Action Is

Why is there so much interest in ad agency work? Perhaps a cliché explains it best: This is where the action is. The agency is home to professional ad men and women. This environment is where the creative juices flow toward the goal of helping businesses realize a profit. Professional communicators team up to originate the concept for the ad, design it and place it in the media.

Another answer may be traced to the college instructors who by their very presence on the faculty cultivate this agency interest. Many of them are former agency professionals, hired because of their experience.

Sometimes this glamorous image distracts students from looking for non-agency internships and jobs. For example, many companies with in-house advertising departments offer established internships that have potential for both good advertising work experience and a job later. These departments actually resemble the agencies. Internships in the marketing department of these companies and organizations will help you perform better in other jobs in the ad industry.

> *The glamorous image of ad agencies sometimes distracts students from looking for non-agency internships, which can be just as interesting and rewarding.*

The bad news is that advertising is not the easiest field in which to acquire an internship. There are several reasons:

- Organized university internship programs in advertising are not as common as in journalism, public relations or television. In many situations students must find their own sites with little or no help. This increases competition for internships.
- Some faculty coordinators say that overall the advertising industry is not receptive to the idea of internships. And when the college is located in a rural area, few if any agencies or companies are available for internships.
- Many advertising agencies do not pay interns. When they do, the pay is an hourly minimum at best. One midwestern faculty coordinator reports that whereas about 85 percent of the school's PR internships are paid, only 25 percent of the advertising interns find paid positions. Most of these are in non-agency marketing or sales

areas, according to the coordinator.

- It is estimated that the 10 largest advertising agencies handle about 40 percent of the total advertising dollar volume. These 10 agencies, employing about 40 percent of the workforce, are located in New York, Chicago, Detroit, Los Angeles and San Francisco. Internships are available in these large urban markets, but they are extremely competitive.

The good news is that internships and related work experience are highly valued in getting a job in advertising. An ad internship can be an important foot in the door, leading to valuable networking contacts. Other factors on the plus side include:

- Many small agencies need the help of an intern. Depending on how one defines "advertising agency," there are about 5,000 in the United States. Some are small, numbering from two to five people. A career directory (see Appendix A) shows that of 173 medium-sized and large agencies, about 130 are located outside of New York.
- Advertising internships are not limited to agencies. They extend into promotional and publicity writing, graphics and production work and various aspects of public relations and marketing. Clients may include department stores, grocery and restaurant chains, computer companies and marketing departments of corporations to name a few.
- Some faculty coordinators say that many non-agency sites offer excellent learning experiences that for the well-prepared intern can lead more often to a job than interning at an agency.
- Sales and marketing firms especially want to train and hire interns upon graduation. Students with good business or retail experience are sought for these internships.

Some agency personnel say that the three most important ingredients for success in getting an ad agency job are good computer skills, internship experience in an ad agency and closely related part-time work experience. Also, it certainly is a plus to elevate your typing skills and be familiar with several computer software packages. In a tight job market a temporary receptionist or clerical position may be the only position open, and this would get you into the agency.

Three Areas of Ad Internships

Advertising internships can be divided into three major areas, which range from several kinds of opportunities in agencies to supporting organizations to those in media organizations.

(1) In agencies, an intern works most often as an assistant to an account executive or to a person in charge of media planning or buying. Other agency departments that contract for internships on a more limited basis include creative, research, production and traffic.

(2) Supporting organizations include research and ratings companies, production houses, companies that produce television and radio commercials, and printing companies. Internships, which are not as common in this group, may require talent in art or graphics, good skills in computer software programs or some background or skills in print production.

(3) Advertising skills can be directly applied to media internships with radio and television stations, record companies, magazines and newspapers. Interns prepare publicity materials for newspaper marketing departments, work at sales tasks with publishing companies, participate in sales work with outdoor advertising firms and work in the direct response or direct mail advertising business.

Dave Little, whose professional background includes work with several large West Coast agencies, was the advertising sequence coordinator for the Department of Communications at California State University, Fullerton, until his recent retirement. His explanation of where interns go in his program gives one view of intern placement:

In our mandatory internship program probably the top four or five students each semester and summer win positions in the creative departments of agencies. These openings are scarce. Probably the chief reasons for selection are grades in advertising, interest in the field and previous work experience or internships in communications.

About a third to a half of the candidates end up in media or account services, the two most popular internship areas of need by agency supervisors. These interns have interviewed at several agencies, and often they must mail résumés and cover letters. They choose the sites from a directory we have.

Maybe six a semester will go to agency sites where they can use their above-average graphics, production and art skills. Some in this group will go to graphic houses. A few will intern with art directors.

Some of our nearby sites have well-established programs where interns go through departments, spending three weeks in traffic, three weeks in media, three weeks in creative, etc. The objective here is to give the intern a broad view of agency life.

The remainder of the interns, especially the larger numbers in the summer, contract with non-agency sites such as advertising sales and marketing firms. Our interns sell cable television commercials, newspaper ads, etc., and many of these sales folks hire the interns after a good performance.

Faculty coordinators warn interns to negotiate carefully. Many advertising internships are unpaid. Along with a job description you should look for information on starting and ending times and the total number of hours required.

Paid internships might require many more of your hours.

If you are able to get a paid sales or marketing internship, be sure to get in writing details on any commissions required. Also, pay may force full-time work or hours well beyond those stated for university credit. You may have to adjust your schedule of classes or reduce hours at another job.

Internships in Media Buying and Planning

Reports by media interns at medium-sized to large national agencies show significant assigned workloads. Lori Benjamin, once an intern herself and now a senior media planner, gives some tips:

You need to look carefully at all possibilities. I had good offers from smaller agencies but decided to travel a bit farther from my home to a major agency. It was a good move. After my four-month internship, I was hired and worked in media for almost two years before advancing to my present job.

You need to realize how necessary it is to complete each and every task assigned. You are constantly being evaluated. You must often take the initiative to show your skills.

Agencies look for the dedicated intern to work long hours, often at no pay. I stayed late as there were many people working overtime all the times I was there. My media class helped a lot in learning the routine.

There's not a lot of glory in being an assistant media planner. However, it does pay off eventually. Entry-level salaries in many large agencies are low, but in six months you can get a good increase.

Jeanine Jasfarina details some of her experiences as a media buying intern at an office of a major agency, Foote, Cone & Belding:

I was assigned to Mary Lynn, who supervises the department's six senior media buyers and four junior media buyers. I worked primarily with the media buying assistants. This might be termed more of an apprenticeship than an internship. From the first day, I worked side-by-side with buying assistants.

The steps in the process began with the media planners. After they do their work, the media buyers forge into action and buys are formulated. Then the ball is passed to the buying assistant. The assistant then phones the appropriate media representative and places the buyer's order. The order is then entered into the computer and a few days later the "Brandtime" [print-out of the media buy] is generated.

Then the assistant's job is just beginning. Contracts from TV and radio stations must be recorded and checked for accuracy. The smallest error could cost the client and the company thousands of dollars. If there are any discrepancies, the assistants must correct the errors. They must field calls for the buyers, make appointments and contend with an ever-growing amount of paper work.

To say there is a great amount of stress in this position is putting it mildly. However, the work does not go unnoticed. Media buying assistants are promoted to junior buying positions in a relatively short time.

I was taken under the wing of several buying assistants, and they were extremely helpful in teaching me their job. After my first week, I was checking contracts, phoning in orders and operating the computer.

Of all my tasks, probably phoning media representatives and inputting orders were my favorites. The most valuable experience was working closely with the buying assistants. I learned more about the media department and the total agency from them than I did from anyone else.

Two other media interns report on the tasks assigned at other major agencies. Dean Black worked primarily on the Orion Films account and gives this rundown as to tasks assigned and percentages of time applied to each during his internship period:

Media recommendations, 20%
Computer work, 20%
Executive summaries, 10%
Letter, memos, 10%
Weekly budget recaps, 10%
Meetings, 5%
Research, 5%
Phone work, 5%
Positioning report, 5%
Photocopying and errands, 5%
Movie screenings, 5%

Black says: "The clients require that we write a recommendation before they will consider advertising in a particular medium. Therefore, I would be given a potential magazine to analyze. Then based on the magazine's target audience, CPM [cost per thousand], total cost, quality, editorial environment, etc., I would either recommend for or against the client's use of the magazine."

Linda Jones worked on a holiday cruise company account and gave this partial list of tasks completed during her media internship at a large agency:

- Calculated the cost of newspaper insertions either by month, quarter, region or specific newspapers only.
- Requested on the computer and mailed contracts to newspaper and magazine representatives.
- Requested on the computer weekly spending updates distributed to all management and media personnel to provide them with current status on weekly spending.
- Contacted each newspaper representative by phone so that space reservations could be made.
- Sorted through various newspapers and magazine special sections, brochures and letters to list possible locations for cruise ads in the future.
- Mailed out insertion orders.
- Calculated short rates.
- Verified costs from different media to ensure correct charges.
- Provided a report indicating positioning received in all newspapers and developed a new method for processing mailing insertion orders and contracts.

Media Course Principles

Some major advertising agencies, particularly in the East, have trainee programs. These differ from advertising internships in that the trainees are usually paid some wages and the program continues for up to a year. Advertising coordinators and instructors have suggested that both trainees and interns master these 10 objectives (often covered in media planning and buying courses) before beginning work in a media department:

1. Learn the basics of media language and media math, including an understanding of cost analysis such as CPM (cost per thousand) and CPP (cost per rating point).

2. Expose yourself to personal computer and media software.

3. Develop an understanding of media and market source books such as Standard Rate and Data Service (SRDS), Simmons and Leading National Advertisers (LNA). Be able to handle insertion orders and contracts and learn how to do rate cards.

4. Know how to write a media plan, starting from an overview of marketing objectives. Be able to formulate media objectives and strategies.

5. Be able to use media tools in marketing and media analysis to gauge media data (readership and ratings) and product usage data. Have a basic understanding of reach and frequency concepts.

6. Be able to develop insight into media options through an awareness of the strengths and weaknesses of each medium and an understanding of new developments in each field.

7. Know how to work with creative and account management teams. Especially important, know how to incorporate marketing judgments into strategic media decisions.

8. Be able to determine when to stop analyzing and make conclusions on available options.

9. Review actual account histories for developing media plans. These case studies show how media skills are applied; some instructors make such studies available to students.

10. Know how to handle diverse accounts and assignments.

Jones said that these and other "real-world" assignments gave her a feeling of accomplishment. Regardless of previous experience, she believes that an intern can learn to perform the media internship tasks if he or she works hard. She comments:

I was a bit timid at first. I had not had a lot of computer training prior to my internship. I was first introduced to the basics of the Donovan Data System, one of the agency's computers. Almost all print advertising is recorded and purchased through this system along with newspaper and magazine contract information. The cruise account is 90 percent print advertising.

In addition to mastering the computer, I also learned how to use the different media publications, including the Standard Rates and Data publications. The SRDS was especially used for billing discrepancies and contract levels.

You need to be very comfortable with numbers if you plan to be a media intern.

> "You need to be very comfortable with numbers if you plan to be a media intern."

Account Management

Account management is considered the nerve center of an advertising agency. Those who work in this area are sometimes organized into teams, each of which works with specific clients and products. Responsibilities are varied because these teams coordinate the entire range of activities for any one client. Assistant Account Executive (AAE) is the entry-level title on a team in account services. AAE duties are usually similar to those that an account intern would expect to perform.

Mary Cavallaro, an advertising major, completed her account services internship with Chiat/Day, a major agency. She describes a wide range of activities:

I worked three days a week and usually nine to 10 hours a day, depending on the assignments I was given. I was not paid but received academic credits toward my major.

My originally assigned supervisor left the company shortly after I arrived. My new supervisor, Ann, was very helpful and made me feel like a useful player on the agency team. She was around if I had questions.

Overall, I received very little supervision. I was given projects that were interesting and demanding as well as important to the agency. That gave me satisfaction that I was doing well.

Limited supervision worked well for me. I was an AAE employee with my own projects and responsibilities. I had my own office, Mac computer and a secretary, if I needed one. I don't know if the lack of supervision would be appropriate for everyone. It meant, however, that I alone was responsible for the outcome of my projects.

At Chiat/Day the motto is "Good enough is not enough," and if you decide to intern there, you must give them 110 percent. In the end, however, it paid off for me because they said they want me to stay on in a paid position. We are negotiating.

I interned with the Nissan [a major client] account team. I often had to do the automotive news recaps and monthly summaries. This involved writing summaries of activities in the automotive world. My reports were distributed to the entire Nissan team at the agency.

I worked on a lengthy report on Motor Trend's car of the year award (COTY). This involved researching past competitors' use of advertising after winning the COTY. I called all the trade and consumer magazines in which past winners had advertised. I then evaluated the ad content.

I researched what the typical procedures and practices are for companies that have won the COTY. The two weeks of research resulted in a 20-page report including graphs, charts, etc., which was then added to a bigger report presented to the client.

I also worked on a product vs. competitor report. This project included research work and compiling information on the different product specifications and attributes for Nissan's competitors.

I completed two competitor incentives reports to determine what promotions our competitors were doing, how long they lasted and for whom they were targeted. I did creative research and evaluations on new incentive programs.

Next were three regional grids. These grids contained the quarterly information for all vehicles within different subclasses. I also completed a grid for ads running the next quarter and media spending for past quarters. This was very interesting because I had the chance to get familiar with different research material and the Mac Excel program. I also did some paste-up work for charts for our reports.

The biggest project was a 30-page marketing overview for a manufacturer. It took me two weeks to finish, but the results were worth the time and effort. I had to do extensive research to get information about the import and domestic automakers. This information ranged from advertising new models, changes in old models, and incentives to even plant openings and closings. In the end they decided to send my report to the client!

One thing that I learned from my advertising courses was the ad lingo. Specifically, my media planning courses helped me often. I worked with almost every research catalog that we dealt with in the class, including Simmons, SRDS and BRA/ LNA. From the internship I also acquired an understanding and working knowledge of J.D. Powers Research, Maritz Automotive Demographics and *Ward's Automotive Reports*.

I think that the writing and English classes that I took were most helpful. It was important for me to have very good writing skills. Also, I think that any class in computers would be very helpful for internships like this one. I was often expected to learn new computer programs quickly.

Although Cavallaro did not get hired at the agency, she said the experience helped her greatly in getting her first full-time position as a media planner with a smaller agency.

Opportunities at Smaller Sites

If you are searching for an account internship with an agency, consider smaller sites. If your work experience is limited and/or you believe that you need more training in advertising, you may have a better chance to get individual attention at a smaller agency. There will be plenty to do there in possibly a less hectic environment. Also, you might gain more knowledge about the total workings of an agency at a smaller one. The specialization of a larger agency may not allow you to see the interplay of all parts of the agency.

Another argument for interning at a smaller agency is that your chances for a job are more likely than at a larger agency. You will have become acquainted with personnel, learned about the accounts and established good work habits. All of this should give you an advantage should an entry-level opening occur.

This is not to say that interning with a small agency has no downside. It does. Faculty coordinators say that the worst problem develops when a small agency loses an account or two and the workload suddenly drops. There may be fewer and fewer advertising tasks available for you to do as an intern.

> If business slows, you can create some ideas and projects to promote the agency.

What can you do if business drops? You can volunteer to work with those employees seeking new business. Or as some interns have done, you can create some ideas to promote the agency. Working on the public-

ity of community events on behalf of the agency can be a good use of your time. Other interns have assisted in updating files or completing shelved projects that cannot be accomplished during peak work periods.

Keep in Touch

It's a good idea for interns to follow the advertising slogan, "Keep in Touch!"

A prospective intern was accepted in December for an agency internship the following summer. An acceptance letter said that she would be getting more details about April 1.

When the intern had not heard anything from the agency by April 15, she began to worry. So she wrote a letter to her proposed supervisor. She got no answer. After May 1 she called the agency. She was told that the supervisor had left the agency in March and that the agency would not be using any interns that summer.

To avoid being forced to hunt for a summer internship in May, simply keep in touch. Write a brief note to your proposed supervisor expressing your strong interest in working there or report your relevant progress in school. Call, if you have questions about the internship.

Setting Up Your Own Internship

Robert Arns, vice president of a 20-person agency that has accepted interns for several years, has this advice for account interns setting up their own internships:

- "Many students attend career conferences. It's a great way to meet recruiters under informal conditions. Always have an updated résumé available. It should be professionally typeset and printed.

- "If you can learn before the conference that a company you are interested in will be attending, do some homework. Research the firm through faculty, alumni, library sources, etc. You now will be ready to ask the recruiter some intelligent questions at the conference. This shows you have a genuine interest in the company. As the conference concludes, collect the business cards of representatives attending for two reasons: You will later have a contact, if needed, within the firm, and you can use the cards to write thank-you letters as a follow-up.

- "When you have your first meeting with your prospective supervisor and are asked to suggest activities for you, present some kind of idea for a significant project to work on during the internship. This may give you an excellent portfolio addition. Or it can be useful to show other personnel in the company should you get a job interview.

- "Strongly urge that you report to only one person. You can get assignments more easily and avoid getting buried with requests from several staff members. However, you do want to meet and work with other employees, if it is necessary, as the more contacts the better. Consider volunteering for any field assignments or opportunities to meet with clients.

- "Use caution in asking for too many activities. Interns often complain about an overload of assignments. If necessary, more can be added later. An internship period of 150 to 350 hours is brief in terms of work time.

- "You must be prepared to work at a much more accelerated pace than in college. In both advertising and public relations, there are times when work becomes quite frantic in the haste to meet deadlines. You will be astounded by how quickly everything happens. You will eventually get up to speed.

- "You can ask about a stipend or some form of minimum compensation. We have lost a few interns the past two summers because their parents insisted that they hold part-time jobs. It is difficult to justify an unpaid internship to parents."

Some highly structured intern programs in agencies place the intern with several supervisors, especially in account and media work. Agency officials say that this gives the intern more varied assignments and the chance to work with different personnel. Also, supervision does not burden one person.

However, for the intern one supervisor does have several advantages, especially in terms of getting enough work to do and receiving needed feedback on completed tasks. A good supervisor may encourage some kind of trade-off: The intern completes some routine tasks in exchange for hands-on experience that can lead to portfolio samples.

Some large agencies in New York and Chicago sponsor their own trainee programs, attracting college grads with numerous degrees. Because these are paid assignments, competition for openings can be fierce. Many of the trainees work in account or media. Because of the agency's investment in recruiting and training, a good percentage of the trainees get jobs.

Some large agencies have special sessions from time to time. Agency specialists will cover current topics or discuss innovations. For example, a media planner might speak to entry-level personnel and interns at a brown bag lunch meeting. Attending such gatherings can be educational and a way of meeting agency people.

Account Internship Tasks

To fully understand an account internship, it is necessary for you to look briefly at some of the tasks that will be assigned. Assignments for account executives can vary greatly from agency to agency, often depending on the specialization of the agency.

For example, a business major may feel comfortable with agencies that deal with financial institutions. Other agencies might specialize in food or automobile accounts. The variety and depth of assignments for interns can also depend on whether or not the agency is a full-service agency. If serving clients with both advertising and PR needs, the agency may involve an intern in a wider range of assignments including some copywriting.

Here is an example of an AAE internship with a lot of tasks. Kim Browns had her hands full with this internship, which ran two full days a week. She was paid $5 an hour and was able to work the hours around her spring semester classes during her senior year. She comments:

This was a small advertising and public relations firm so that even though my chief interest was in advertising, I wrote many press releases and handled some media relations work.

I was given copywriting assignments for three accounts. One was a country store. I had to do a lot of research and phone calling to get the necessary background. I would do a rough sketch of the ad and the copy. My supervisor and I evaluated the work. Then I would do any necessary revisions to improve the ad.

After the country store ran a promotional campaign, I was asked to do evaluative research involving coupons that had been used in ads. An analysis of the way customers used the coupons gave me the basic information I needed for a report showing which newspapers achieved the best results.

I learned that press clips can be an important addition to your portfolio. Several of my press releases for a construction company account were published with only minor revisions. Since the agency subscribes to a clipping service, I was able to reproduce my published clips for my file.

The agency brainstormed a promotional idea for Helen Grace Chocolates. This was tied into Halloween. My task was to find someone to wear an American Eagle costume and to get some balloons for the stunt. It took numerous phone calls to finally locate a costume to rent and arrange it all.

My most difficult task was producing a fundraising ad for the chocolate company. I had never written such an ad before. But I was finally able to produce something that satisfied me and my supervisor.

Account work involves a lot of little projects. For example, I had to find Spanish names for a housing development. Other tasks involved selecting color for ads, calling publications for rates and demographics, researching mailing lists, reserving ad space, tracking down military publications on various bases and contacting direct mail houses for project information.

Chances for a job at this agency appear slim. An accountant was just laid off and a fairly big account was lost. I was told to apply again in three months.

Working on accounts demands good communications skills. You have to learn to listen, especially during stressful times. I think because I have good communications skills I was given opportunities to interface with clients.

Traffic Internships

Traffic is another agency job open to interns. It's a good way to learn the inner workings of an agency and to meet a number of agency employees. A good traffic intern has the opportunity to be on top of everything that goes on, although some traffic interns report that the job involves numerous clerical tasks and is unrelated to anything they learned in college.

> *Working in the traffic department is a good way to learn the inner workings of an agency and to meet a number of agency employees.*

Although traffic internships are not as plentiful as those in media or account services, neither are they as competitive because interns don't often seek them out. For medium-sized and large agencies, traffic work is considered very important and a good route to follow toward an agency job.

Monetee Labeaune describes what traffic interns do. Labeaune, who was paid for her six-week summer traffic internship at Saatchi & Saatchi, had to face competition for the job because this was a major agency in a major market. She recalls:

My internship was not at all what I expected. There was very little supervision. This is really neither good nor bad as close supervision is not needed in traffic.

Each project is really under the supervision of a traffic assistant. If a problem arises, the assistant can write memos, call a meeting or do whatever is necessary to remedy the problem.

A large amount of my time was spent routing copy and art. You log in the piece, listing where it is going and why. You may take the art or copy to eight or so people and get them to "sign off" on it.

The function of the traffic department is to know the status of every piece of art and copy at all times. The copy could be in rewrite, being typed or with the client for evaluation. The purpose of traffic control is to smooth the flow of work and prevent bottlenecks at deadline time.

This was valuable agency experience. Traffic work allowed me to talk to employees and find out what they were doing and why. Seeing an art director cry because a title on a piece was wrong or listening to the frustrations at deadline is all part of the agency picture.

If any class in school was helpful it probably was graphics. Otherwise, a physical education class or being in good shape helps.

The Creative Side

The most coveted of internship assignments in advertising agencies are those in creative. Working with a creative director or team can be a real test of skills and a valuable learning process. Brainstorming ideas, creating concepts and writing headlines and copy can be a part of this experience.

Much depends, of course, on the skills of the internship applicant. Since these internships often interface with art departments and art directors, some previous experience in art or production can be helpful. Thus, a

good route to creative is to have previous production, paste-up or computer graphics experience. Working in a medium-sized agency, the intern designing print pieces can eventually ask for an opportunity to prepare copy, too. Some supervisors ask interns for suggested improvements in copy.

Good journalism skills can give an intern a decided advantage. Many projects involve a large amount of writing, not just headlines or body copy. Preparing different versions of the same product information can give an intern invaluable experience and a chance for feedback.

Grayson Young, an advertising major who as a junior completed a creative internship with a major agency, discusses his experiences:

I worked eight to 12 hours a day Monday through Friday. I was paid a $500 stipend for two months' work and worked two additional weeks in August for free. Then I received $300 for three days' work as a freelance copywriter.

I worked on a team with an art department intern. We were under the supervision of two copy/art teams. They would drop off projects or creative briefs and say, "Let's see what you can come up with." When we had questions, one of our mentors was always available. Both creative teams were well aware that we were student interns there to learn.

About 70 percent of our time went to print ad work (newspapers and magazines) with the remaining time devoted to television and billboards. The newspaper ads taught me to write simple and effective copy. The storyboard for a TV commercial allowed me to display some proficiency in this area as it was very close to the final ad.

We continued to show improvement and got a lot of encouragement along the way. In fact, one of our "tissues" [rough spec drawing] got approved over that of our supervisors. They took it in stride and treated us to lunch!

My class in copywriting and ad layout was most helpful, and one needs good writing skills. But it is also very helpful to have a good understanding of American culture and to know a little bit about a lot of things (movies, literature, history, etc.) to succeed in this business.

> *One intern thinks it's helpful to have a good understanding of American culture and to know a little about a lot of things to succeed in the advertising business.*

As mentioned above, some agencies put interns on a rotation basis so that a couple of weeks might be in media, some time in account work, etc. When it comes to your turn in the creative department, you need to be ready to test your copywriting skills. Hopefully, by then you will know something about the agency's major clients and their products. A good effort here can pay off with more assignments later, if time permits.

Another route to the creative department is through an internship as an assistant art director. Good graphics and art skills are needed. Often, an art major or minor with previous work experience in typesetting and production is required. Assisting an art director at a small agency through a part-time job or internship can be a good initial step.

Along with a résumé, a portfolio showing off your class and professional experience is desirable. You might even include ads created for the campus newspaper. In fact, all available work samples in writing or art are needed because of the competition for these positions.

Senior Melinda Smith was accepted for a paid eight-week internship with N. W. Ayer & Son, working with four art directors and under the supervision of the agency's creative director. She says of her responsibilities:

I worked on layouts for direct response pieces, outdoor boards (bus cards and billboards), magazines and newspaper ads. In all cases it was necessary to be able to spec type to the exact pica for wraps or special columns.

I also helped in new business presentations by pulling scrap materials and information, assisting in the creation of slide montages, organizing

visual boards and again doing marker comps. I followed the whole process from client input and concept development to a finished slide presentation. And if we got the business, I followed through to the finished ads.

I heard tapes of people for voice-overs, helped choose music for various projects and went out on photo shoots. There were a few clerical tasks, too, such as helping to clean out the magazine library, substituting for the receptionist a few times a month and doing paste-up in the art studio.

I got an excellent view of what the art director does. Also, it was most beneficial to see the different areas of activities of an agency.

My skills at being able to spec type and layout a page came from my graphics and art classes. I had learned different printing processes as well as making proper choices of paper and designs. The best art classes were those in photo illustration, two-dimensional design and graphic processes. Most of my portfolio is developed from pieces from these classes.

I also attended a night class at Art Center, a private school. It was called figure indication, and it was beneficial for this internship. Lettering and type also seemed to be helpful background.

After her successful internship, Smith was able to attend Ayer's management training program for account executives in New York. After two jobs at smaller agencies, she is now an art director for DMB&B.

Internships in art or graphics may be more plentiful than you think. Some characteristics that will help you watch for these internships:

- Some *do not* require that you have extensive art or graphics background. You can be trained. Simple paste-up and production skills may be all that is necessary.
- You *do* need to have basic computer skills. Many agencies can build on this foundation. For example, one intern with desktop publishing skills was taught Illustrator and PageMaker programs so that she could do more effective client presentations. Good computer literacy can open many doors. Another student won a well-paid non-agency internship when she answered an ad requir-

ing QuarkXPress background. She was the only qualified candidate.

■ You may have to search harder for these art/graphics sites because they are often not publicized as much as other openings. Especially be on the alert for non-agency opportunities.

Non-Agency Internship Opportunities

A wide variety of non-agency sites are available for you to have the chance to write copy and work on creative projects. These less-competitive locations may be listed under different titles because some are in marketing or sales departments of companies. Others appear under promotion or in public relations/marketing departments.

In addition to using your creative skills, you often gain much more PR and promotional writing experience here than at an ad agency. Graduates completing internships in these areas noted the following:

■ These internships are hard to locate, so look carefully. Often the company will apply a unique title to the department such as internal communications or public affairs.

■ Since these are more business intensive, you are on the front line of the company and not hidden away in an office. Contact with clients and attending meetings to learn how sales proposals are presented can be regular assignments.

■ Varied writing assignments, especially for projects and special events assignments, can be beneficial. You may get a whole project assigned, which can result in portfolio pieces.

■ Unlike agency internships, many of these positions are paid. Since pay is already in the budget, it may not be a big step for a manager to get additional funding for a position to hire an intern full time. Thus, the internship frequently can be a job tryout.

■ Some of these positions are aimed at students who can get academic credit. The university affiliation is attractive to some companies.

An intern who was successful in this area was Dorothy Fuqua, who had been working for several years as a checker with a grocery chain. When a faculty adviser urged her to get some intern experience and offered the possibility of credit, she followed through. After contacting the grocery chain's vice president of sales and advertising, she talked with the personnel department. She was able to complete forms to ensure that she could get academic credit.

Because she was a union member, she had to get permission from both her manager and supervisor to arrange her hours. The vice president set up a 20-hour-per-week schedule for her summer internship. She describes her work:

Working closely with the department's public relations coordinator, I wrote press releases, memos, letters, correspondence inside and outside the company and pitch letters to the media. I assisted the marketing director on a variety of assignments including the grand opening of a new store.

Another assignment was assisting in the planning and promotion of a cholesterol screening program. I had to drive to three stores to check on the program. All of the work was educational for me, the supervision was excellent, and I had the opportunity to work on my own.

I will continue to work part time in the department when I go back to university classes this fall. There is a good chance for a full-time job in the department when I graduate at the end of the semester. According to my supervisor, I am the number one candidate.

Marketing Internships

If you have strong speaking and writing skills and an interest in a variety of assignments, you can benefit from a marketing internship because this involves projects calling for different skills. Communications majors can compete successfully with business and marketing students for these internships. Angela Belloli did just that.

Belloli, an advertising sequence major without any marketing or business classes, interviewed with the marketing director of an automobile polish company. When she asked if her art skills could be used, the tasks of her internship were broadened to include graphics. She explains:

Graphics was just a part of my internship. But I did handle six projects in all including designing labels for a new line, price sheets, coupon books and work on a new catalog. The work required trips to the library to get names of companies and calls to get printing bids. I learned about working with vendors.

By far my biggest project was a long-range planning assignment, working with the marketing director in setting up a trade show in Chicago. I was responsible over a six-week period for a number of tasks: contacting display and production companies, calling firms to supply flowers, carpeting, electricity, television, in-show advertising, etc.

It was a bit stressful since there were so many variables and I had no experience in this kind of work. I got many compliments and the trade show was a highlight of my internship. You need to be well organized, check periodically with your supervisor and move ahead independently so that you can get the tasks accomplished.

The marketing intern can get a full plate of activities. In some companies the marketing department many times crosses over into public relations, advertising and sales. Assignments can vary from simple consumer-oriented projects to complex ones of a technical nature, such as writing a trade magazine article.

Marketing departments may involve public contact, particularly when they are non-profit associations or community organizations. Good "people" skills are important. Your willingness to work as a team member on varied projects is necessary too.

You can use your advertising skills in marketing internships for many firms: a publisher of legal books, a label and printing firm, trade associations, banks, a home video company and direct marketing companies with travel and financial clients. These are just a few of the listings in the *1994 Direct Marketing Directory* (see Appendix A).

> *The marketing intern can get a full plate of activities, with duties sometimes crossing over into public relations, advertising and sales.*

Shopping centers and malls seek interns to work with merchant promotions, writing news releases and preparing posters and displays for special events at holidays and other times. One intern devoted her entire internship toward promoting the opening of a new mall store. She had good networking opportunities with both the store's PR and advertising agencies.

Faculty coordinators warn interns about strictly telemarketing internships that involve cold calling to consumers, described by some as "slave labor." These so-called internships, advertised as both paid and unpaid, are often open to any degree or major. This says something about how few skills are needed.

However, as part of some internship job descriptions, telemarketing can lead to sales training. Much depends on the objectives of such calls and who is to be contacted. Lori Leban, who reported that 30 percent of her internship at Sales Media, Inc., involved telemarketing, pointed out positive aspects: "A telemarketing project taught me how to become better acquainted with the products of pharmaceutical clients. I handled phone calls to field technical questions and assisted in promoting sales. A first step in working with a client is to get a complete understanding of their products, services and marketing position."

Moving from routine tasks toward more challenging and better learning opportunities depends a lot on the initiative and aggressiveness of an intern. This is true in most internships, of course, but especially so in sales and marketing. Catherine Campbell, who supervises interns in the advertising department of a large metropolitan magazine, comments:

Interns start out by learning how a magazine works. Tasks require spending time in the production department, performing some traffic and clerical duties such as organizing sales reports, typing contracts, pulling tears for advertisers, etc.

If the intern is professional in dress and actions and handles these assignments well, he or she should be moved along in the process. You must show initiative and interest and act as a professional to get some higher level duties. An intern here can become an assistant account executive with duties that parallel mine on a smaller scale. Developing good sales skills can lead to part- or full-time employment following an internship.

Media Promotions

Broadcasting stations and newspapers have marketing departments where public relations and advertising or promotional activities are planned. One intern at a TV station coordinated an employee blood drive for the Red Cross. Another, working in a marketing department internship at a newspaper, completed the layout and writing of several issues of an employee newsletter.

For still another intern, a newspaper's special event promotion, handled through marketing, provided an excellent project. Using his graphics and writing skills, he submitted several fliers to the marketing director. They were to promote a fair co-sponsored by the newspaper. He also wrote several press releases spotlighting aspects of the fair. The published fliers and stories became attractive portfolio samples.

The project allowed him freedom to meet and interview art and production people at the newspaper. He worked with artists in designing and laying out the fair program. Being responsible for several key parts of the project increased his confidence in his skills. The additions to his portfolio were extra pluses.

Direct Marketing

As the name implies, direct marketing provides sales and services directly to the consumer without a retail outlet or dealer. Advertising for direct marketing can involve any media but most often uses television commercials, telephone solicitation and the largest channel of all—the U.S. postal service.

Direct marketing uses advertising—communicated by mail, telephone, print, broadcast and electronic media—to generate a response. The responses may be inquiries or orders, and they can come in by mail, phone or fax.

As this area of advertising grows, more advertising agencies have started their own direct marketing divisions. These divisions have their own creative people, account executives and research and production personnel. However, the work does differ from that of a consumer agency.

Internship assignments in direct marketing agencies depend on the focus of the agency or department. Direct marketing interns have been employed as assistants in compiling mailing lists, marketing research, product planning, subscription fulfillment and media buying and planning.

The Direct Marketing Education Foundation does not offer summer internships in New York. Instead, the Foundation each year publishes a directory of internships throughout the country (see Appendix A). Strong faculty recommendations are required for these competitive internships. Openings are available for various communications and liberal arts majors. The majority of applicants accepted have some business or marketing course work.

Heather Burgett, a marketing major from the University of Cincinnati, participated in the program. She reported that her paid, eight-week internship with Doubleday in New York gave her experience for a couple of weeks in each department of the publishing firm.

Internships in direct marketing and related areas may appear under several headings, including "Direct Response," "Direct Mail" or "Media Mail." Some larger cities have direct marketing clubs or associations, another possible lead. Deadlines are very early for many of these summer internships, usually in January or February, so that selections can be made in March.

Mary Barnett's internship was in the international marketing department of a major company. She suggests the following recommendations to prospective interns:

This was my third internship. As a graduating senior, I was looking for something to really challenge me. I wanted pay and a job, if possible. The pay was $6.87 an hour with benefits for an internship of more than 25 hours a week. It did not lead to a job, but there were numerous pluses in terms of assignments. My previous internships helped me in getting the job.

You need all communications skills. This internship involved public relations, marketing, special event work, advertising and promotional writing, and even a slide presentation project. I used a camera to get some photos.

Take as many courses related to communications as possible. I found that graphics, marketing and management courses in business school, and writing classes were the most helpful for my internships.

Even though I sent out for the third internship more than 20 résumés and cover letters, the internship appeared from a contact at a professional meeting of IABC [International Association of Business Communicators] where I met my prospective supervisor.

In summary, my advice is to make up some business cards with your name, address and phone number on them. Take them to professional gatherings as it makes an impression. It's always good to have a copy of your résumé handy, too. Networking can lead to both internships and job contacts.

> *One marketing intern says: "You need all communications skills. This internship involved public relations, marketing, special event work, advertising and promotional writing and even a slide presentation project."*

Sales Work Leads to Jobs

Many companies have marketing and sales department internships that involve selling. These internships combine marketing and sales but more frequently involve serving as support for one or more sales representatives. As an intern you will in time accompany your supervisor on client contacts and participate in sales presentations.

Some newspapers have established paid training programs for advertising sales interns. Upon completion of their internships, a high percentage of these people have been hired where they interned. Most are summer positions because of the large amount of time required.

Many newspapers request minority applicants for these assignments. Pay can be an hourly wage, a stipend, a scholarship, or it may be a percentage of sales or commission.

After an initial training period, an ad intern on a newspaper may sell and write display ads. Increasingly, interns are selling air time on local cable channels to merchants in the area. For example, many cable channels localize advertising in an effort to reach restaurants and stores in a specific region.

As is the case with some internships in any field, not all of these sales internships are well developed, and job descriptions may not be carefully thought out. Remember, too, that not all interns are cut out for sales work. If there are a number of other support and general duties in addition to sales, the internship may be more appealing.

This list of assignments from the log of an intern working in a newspaper's advertising department shows the percentage of the intern's time spent on a variety of tasks:

Classified sales (60%)

- Assembling media kits
- Creating layouts
- Canvassing newspapers for sales leads
- Calculating rate increases
- Assisting telemarketing representatives in contacting advertisers
- Gathering info for home buying guides and the church directory
- Mailing tear sheets

Display sales (25%)

- Delivering proofs
- Making cold calls
- Researching leads for special editions
- Looking for artwork
- Distributing fliers to merchants

Art (5%)

- Designing layouts for ads

Editorial (10%)

- Verifying information for upcoming church directory
- Inputting information on directory into computer

Advertising major Kris Cole completed an internship with a publishing company producing several community newspapers. He lists several favorable outcomes:

- "You learn how advertising (including classified and real estate) fits into the total newspaper operation.
- "You are a bit scared or timid at first. But when they use some of your ads and parts of others, you are encouraged. Working with production people can be fun.
- "By accompanying sales representatives on contact trips you can learn a lot about effective sales presentations and how positive attitudes are projected.
- "You can learn to accept rejection when you are asked to sell some ads on the phone. I sold some, but this was the only part of the internship I disliked. It's not exactly a favorable outcome, but I did learn that I am not cut out to sell via cold calling on the phone.
- "A highlight was laying out pages of newspapers. This followed building some ads and doing a lot of paste-up work."

For Thought and Discussion

1. Explain why the East Coast is a better place than other parts of the country to find advertising employment.

2. "Improve your typing skills" is one recommendation by some ad agency personnel for anyone seeking ad agency work. What are three other ingredients important for job hunting in this field?

3. While most advertising graduates want to get into the creative side of the advertising business, more jobs seem to be in sales and marketing. What are three other factors that make it difficult for entry-level graduates to enter the advertising field?

4. Explain some of the tasks of a traffic intern.

5. Give three or four pieces of advice for someone setting up his or her own internship in the account area.

6. Explain how a promotional internship assignment involving several accounts can lead an AAE intern into work in these areas: public relations, art layouts, copywriting, research and fund-raising.

CHAPTER 7

INTERNSHIPS IN BROADCASTING, FILM AND PHOTOGRAPHY

PROFESSIONALS RATE INTERNSHIPS highly as a giant step toward a career in broadcasting. In no other field of communications is networking as important, and internships are a key way to establish such contacts.

The educational paths that point toward careers in radio, television, film and photography are diverse. But many professionals in these specialties either have been interns themselves or have had supervisory contact with interns at their place of work.

Competition is as keen here as it is in advertising, especially for internships at choice large and medium-sized television and radio stations. And like advertising interns, those who intern in broadcasting often are not paid. Also like advertising, students and graduates often do more than one internship in broadcasting. One reason for this trend toward multiple internships is the need to get a broad base of experience. And, of course, the more successful your internships, the more contacts available to you for job hunting.

One phenomenon does set jobs in the entertainment industry apart from all others and affects both jobs and internships in the motion picture and television industries: its temporary nature. For example, a writer may join the staff of a TV show or work on a particular film. After the film is completed or the show is canceled, the writer will move to another short-term project, perhaps with another production company. Thus, there is continual movement toward new projects that have reliable funding. As an intern you can get a variety of experiences and train at several different jobs as you move up the ladder toward tasks that require more demanding skills. However, the bottom rung is where an intern starts.

Another way that careers in these fields are distinct from others in communications is their dependency on technology. You may have to know about such equipment as a video camera, character generator, tape editing machine or even just the lenses a photographer has to choose from for any single shot. As a prospective intern in this field you might be required to have some equipment expertise or specific production skills.

> *Interns in these fields may need to have specialized production skills or specific equipment expertise.*

How much of this training should be done in college classes and how much on the job? Professionals argue this question to no avail. Much depends on the size and sophistication of the station or production company and the amount and complexity of equipment required. And if you are working in a union shop, you won't be allowed to touch or use cameras and other equipment anyway. You will find answers to questions about training and experience by carefully checking the internship job description to see specifically what skills are required on the job.

For many interns, especially those chosen to work at smaller stations and companies, some production know-how may be essential for any progress beyond the internship. A radio, television or film major may have an advantage because of previous experience on a campus radio station or local cable station. However, people with all kinds of degrees and backgrounds are at work in the entertainment business today. As in most fields, energetic, hard-working people with a strong dedication to the field are sought as interns and entry-level employees.

Competition Requires Education and Skills

A college degree is considered important for most jobs in broadcasting, film and photography. Since the proper educational route is still up for debate, it's useful to consider some of the options. Below, they are condensed into three recommendations:

(1) Many educators favor emphasizing production courses in their communications and broadcasting majors' programs. In such a program, students are still urged to take liberal arts courses. Educators and some professionals say that production skills can help interns and graduates handle required hands-on equipment and assignments. Even with minimal skills, beginners can see how their work contributes to the total production picture.

(2) Many professionals and some educators argue that production skills are not that important because they can be taught on the job, and they recognize that diverse talents are required in this industry. They think that knowledge in a number of fields can be beneficial to a well-rounded communicator. Therefore, they recommend liberal arts majors or a variety of related courses.

Speech majors become anchors or reporters for television stations. And speech, theater and drama majors end up as actors or directors of drama and comedy programming. Students planning to become writers or directors need to know about plot, character development and history. Majoring in political science and economics can be good preparation for the specialized demands of broadcast journalists today.

People who work in business or marketing often start in sales and move up through promotions to management jobs in radio and television. Internships can be particularly important here as students often have little or no previous contact with the field.

(3) Since film is a part of this field, some universities have highly specialized film degrees that are recommended for students specifically interested in the film industry. Various kinds of internship and training programs are available, several with special alumni connections. Graduate programs in this specialty have numerous prerequisites for admission.

Some of these schools have strong links with Hollywood and New York. Frequently, directors and producers are adjunct professors who encourage students to produce their own films through special classes. Networking with alumni can lead to employment. In addition to these university film programs, private schools train students for jobs in the motion picture industry.

Although the need for many talents and skills make this a giant industry with various opportunities, the numbers of people competing for a foot in the door can be awesome. Internships can lead to an important step through that door because of such competition.

You may need good typing and clerical skills because many of these entry-level assignments have mixed duties. More essential are having good work habits, being punctual and dependable, and having a strong interest in working in this business.

You also need a positive attitude. You may travel a long distance to a site that pays little or no salary or expenses. If you accept such an internship, it's best to look at it as paying your dues. Continual negative harping about your driving time, parking costs or personal problems will soon take you out of the networking chain.

For a chance at those internships that require a background of specific equipment experience, you should enroll at a college that maintains state-of-the-art laboratory facilities. After learning basic skills in classes, you will be able to apply them at once at student-operated radio stations or on closed-circuit television stations right on campus. You can also develop skills at local cable stations by doing an internship or working part time, or you can get your first crack at writing and producing a show for local cable on a freelance basis.

Community colleges are in the training picture, too. Some two-year schools have major television production facilities. You can write, produce and perform as on-the-air talent for programs that reach both campus and community audiences.

You can even get your first taste of production work in high school. Through journalism and television production classes, high school students can create local newscasts, offering both reporting and production experience. These skills can be used to get early jobs at local cable stations, jobs that become good résumé additions. These contacts can give you an understanding of what jobs are available and what skills are needed.

As a potential broadcast journalist it will be helpful to you if you focus on gaining production skills at an early age. Then you can devote more college time to liberal arts and broadcast journalism classes. This will prepare you for various broadcast journalism internships at cable or network stations.

> *Learning production skills and understanding the technology early can help you get your foot in the door.*

It may appear on the surface that competition for broadcasting jobs is so intense that internships in electronic communications are very difficult to find. However, this need not be the case, especially if as a prospective intern you start planning early. Ralph Donald, a former faculty internship coordinator at Westfield State College in Massachusetts, comments:

Internships in large markets such as Boston are available to those who are qualified and apply early. Interviewing at several potential sites can be critical toward getting the kind of experience you are seeking.

We require our students to have the skills needed before allowing them to apply at certain sites. Not all are qualified for every internship opportunity and that's another big reason to start the process promptly.

If I were a student searching for an internship, I would want to be sure in an interview or in correspondence with a potential location that a definite job description was on hand to explain what I would be doing. This can save many problems later.

Westfield State College has a structured internship program, as do a number of colleges. To give you a picture of how these programs work for interns and the role of both faculty advisers and supervisors, let's look at these requirements and steps:

■ You must complete a formal application, meet with a faculty adviser and be approved by a faculty committee for a semester-long internship. You must complete 50 hours of work at a site for each unit of elective credit.

■ To apply you must have 30 hours in your major, be at least a second-semester junior and possess either a 3.0 GPA in your major or 2.5 GPA overall. Completion of specific prerequisite courses is required before you start the internship.

■ After approval you get assistance from the faculty coordinator in setting up interviews with appropriate television stations, production companies or other suitable sites. After you find a site, the coordinator contacts the site to get a list of assignments or a job description, which is then reviewed with each prospective intern.

■ Meeting with your faculty coordinator for periodic site evaluation is another requirement. You must complete a detailed final report (following an outline) when the internship is finished.

■ The faculty coordinator meets with the supervisor for a final evaluation of your work, and the supervisor completes an evaluation form.

In this program and others, students are not allowed to visit or interview at sites until applications are approved. According to coordinators, this is necessary to screen out unqualified interns.

The Entry-Level Broadcast and Film Production Assistant

The most prevalent internships in broadcasting and film are those designated as production assistant (PA). This is also an entry-level job title, and descriptions of duties vary throughout the industry. Most PA internships have fairly simple job descriptions. Some include clerical tasks. If this work is not what you want to do, you need to look elsewhere.

As mentioned earlier, some faculty coordinators reject awarding credit for what they term "go-fer" internships. Yet in many university internship programs, PA internships in radio and television with a heavy dose of clerical duties are acceptable, even though credit for clerical positions in journalism or public relations is denied. Coordinator Donald explains that the radio and television business is different, adding that many interns are doing the identical work of entry-level personnel.

Station personnel directors and managers maintain that if you are a competent intern you can learn better about how a station operates with a mix of duties, including some support or clerical tasks. Supervisors also say that many interns are not prepared to complete production assignments and operate very expensive equipment.

> *As part of a mix of duties, clerical tasks will help you learn how a station operates and may be the fastest route to the job you want.*

According to graduates and former interns, this scenario parallels what can happen in accepting a secretarial position in an ad agency following an internship. A production secretary job with a television production company at your site may open at the time your internship is ending. If you have been a good intern with above-average recommendations, your supervisor may help you get the job. After several months of this work, you may be promoted to a regular production position if another opening occurs. Many television station employees admit that they started the same way. Some graduates start short-term positions in large-market stations on a per diem (per day) basis, which is temporary without benefits.

Some stations may impose limits on your assignments, such as:

- In a sports internship you may be only handling phones and taking scores.
- At a large-market station you may not be allowed to touch equipment or do any writing.
- You may be assigned to a PA who has very limited work for you to do. You may need to ask for something to do in another department. If possible, it's better to spot this problem when you discuss your initial job description.

Watch for contact with producers of local shows. Instead of working in a newsroom, you may get better experience assisting a show's producer. You can be rewarded with increasing responsibilities and perhaps get screen credit if you are thorough and alert in your work. Tradeoffs work sometimes: For some routine duties that you do, you may work on the set or get to talk to directors or other personnel. After a semester or two of good evaluations, some video companies move the top PA interns up to part- or full-time production jobs.

Even though one would expect to find these PA internships in larger markets such as New York and Hollywood, many of the PA tasks match up with what one finds in a smaller market. In fact, PA internships in smaller markets may allow you to move into more significant and challenging assignments, especially when a non-union station is involved.

Nevertheless, because PA internships in larger-market stations are so numerous, let's examine some of the students' experiences. Larger stations may have 30 to 40 interns on board each semester. Mary Pipes completed her internship at a CBS-affiliated TV station. She served as PA for the producer of the show "Studio 22." The show's producer, Judy Huern, was Pipes' supervisor, although Pipes also worked for Alex Nogales, executive producer. Excerpts from a final report about her internship follow:

My work schedule was Tuesdays and Thursdays from 9 to 5 for the entire semester. The highlight of my internship was the close relationship with the producers so I could see quickly the problems they faced.

Judy was a good supervisor in that she had a list of assignments ready for me when I arrived. The usual routine was to be involved in the taping of the show in the mornings and call agents and do paper work in the afternoons.

Upon arriving I had to check to see if there was food and coffee in the guest's waiting room. Usually Judy would have the coffee made and these tasks completed as she wanted me to avoid go-fer work when possible. When it was show time I would have the TelePrompTer pages ready to go. When actual taping began, I was in charge of the TelePrompTer.

I had success in meeting the guests and chatting with them until the show started. Several of my ideas for show themes and guests did materialize and both Judy and Alex said that I did a good job in this area.

Lisa Parker, also a radio-television major, completed a PA internship at the same station in the news research department. Her assignments are fairly typical of what to expect at larger stations. Parker describes some positive and negative aspects of her experiences:

I worked side by side with Lorraine, manager of the station's research department and a long-time employee there. She was a good supervisor, introduced me to many people at the station and promptly answered questions that I had.

Probably 90 percent of my work was clipping and filing newspaper stories on current topics used by reporters and producers in researching stories. I did a lot of filing by topic or person.

I often had to clarify a fact (number, size, location, dollar amount, etc.), frequently under deadline pressure. I ran files to the newsroom. A person needs to be able to relate well to people and always think clearly and logically to do this job.

On the positive side, I saw a station in operation up close. I went with a reporter on a story, watched a broadcast from the control booth and toured the company's radio station next door. I learned how fast-paced the industry is by talking to people in various jobs.

On the negative side would be the clerical tasks such as picking up the morning mail. I was dismayed to find that the only job possibility was as a news associate on a per diem basis. I did not pursue any job there nor was one offered to me.

As pointed out earlier, interns need to look alive and be aggressive in seeking out new work to do. This is particularly true with PA assignments where there is a tendency to merely observe what is going on from the sidelines. Some of this is necessary. But sitting in a back office doing homework or reading a magazine is sure to create a bad impression all around. It looks like you are bored and can find nothing better to do.

It may be that your supervisor is neglecting you because of his or her own heavy workload. If you can't suggest some meaningful tasks to do, you may have to check with another supervisor to see if there is a project you can work on. Or you may have to get permission from your supervisor to search out work in another part of the station for a few days.

Some kind of university affiliation is required for many internships on soap operas, television shows and films, as well as with production companies. You simply may need to show a letter from a faculty member verifying your student status, or you may be required to show proof of registration in an internship or related course involving credit.

Stacy Gurley says she owes her internship success to the efforts she made to im-

prove her typing skills just before beginning the assignment. Her soap opera internship was supervised by one of the show's co-producers, Gayle Marley. About half of Gurley's time was devoted to typing letters and memos, a task she said she had no intention of doing for a living. She explains one assignment dealing with the show's scripts:

I was in charge of summarizing every script and making a synopsis book for reference. Script changes were my responsibility. Another task was handling call times so I had to contact actors by phone. Some of these calls had to be made in the evening.

The remainder of the time was really not work but time viewing the taping of each show on the office monitor or visiting the set. I was in the control booth sometimes. I could observe the work of the five rotating directors. My supervisor Gayle would have the final say on how a scene looked.

Just past the halfway mark of my internship a position opened and I was suddenly offered the job. It paid $400 a week and was called a receptionist/intern with many of the same duties I had been performing as an intern. I accepted.

John Sallot, a broadcasting major with more interest in writing than production, completed an internship with a Los Angeles television company that has produced several network shows. He had to cut back on his regular summer job to work at this three-day-a-week unpaid internship. But he said it was well worth it. He comments:

About five interns work at one time and you rotate duties, working from about 10 a.m. to 5 p.m. Probably the best way to describe it is to say that there are jobs and non-jobs.

The jobs are typical PA work. You do some office work, mail runs, script deliveries and other errands. The script delivery work involves taking copies of next week's shooting script to the estimators, art directors, set builders, etc.

Probably more than 50 percent of your time falls into observing and setting up appointments for interviews. You get access to any rehearsal or taping of any show on the lot. It's exciting to see the actors, but after this wears off it is fascinating to observe the construction of the show.

You can observe directors and listen to them set up shots. I set up appointments so that I could observe editing and dubbing and sit in on production meetings.

I was able to speak to different producers, directors, writers, publicists, crew members and others. I was never turned down. If someone was busy, he or she would talk with me later. All answered questions about their jobs and how to get into the industry.

The actual work has little or nothing to do with what you learn in school. But being a television major does help in knowing the principles of production. You are better able to carry on an intelligent conversation when you are familiar with the equipment.

Sallot was called back three months after his internship to interview for an opening. He accepted the job offer and has been working in story development at the studio for the past two years.

Video Companies Have Varied Clients

Corporate video companies represent a growing area of the television business in some markets. Interns can become involved in a range of activities including production, research and writing, if their skills are good.

Various opportunities also exist in this corporate setting for photography interns who have skills matching the current activities and tasks of the company. Assignments usually include handling equipment and assisting at shoots. Work on proposals and projects can result in good internship experiences.

> *Video companies seek interns for production help with shows and may hire interns on a freelance basis later.*

Timing: An Important Key

A key to a successful internship lies in knowing when the action is going to occur. Almost all production companies and television programming go through "down times" when work for employees and interns may be limited or nonexistent. Be aggressive in any initial interview and ask questions about workloads in the months ahead.

Maybe next semester or next summer will be a better choice to go to a site where work is presently limited. It's important for you to find out before starting. An example would be a television show in Hollywood in the summer. This could be a poor choice because many TV shows experience a hiatus in summer months.

Bob Shane interned with a company specializing in producing videos and multi-image slide shows to be used as marketing tools, orientation programs for companies and special event entertainment. Shane was not paid for his internship. However, many companies in this category hire interns for freelance work during and after the internship.

Shane describes about half of his internship time as "grunt work" involving cleaning and mounting slides, setting up equipment, making dubs and checking equipment inventory. He says he was even asked a few times to pick up film and deliver slides and tapes.

His video production experience was chiefly on the set of a shoot for the Toshiba phone systems. He transferred dialogue to TelePrompTer reels for the talent, ran the TelePrompTer and helped to dress the set. The remainder of his internship was spent helping on slide shows. For this he arranged a storyboard to be used in programming the slides.

Video companies produce tapes to

market various specialized products. Jim Griffin, a telecommunications major, accepted a paid internship with a firm producing medically oriented videotapes, films and audiocassettes. The products were sold to hospitals and medical establishments. His comments:

I worked chiefly with the programming supervisor and an editor. There was plenty to do. All the employees were cordial and helpful, answering any questions I had.

Since I had completed both introductory and advanced video production classes, I had no problems at all with the basic equipment. At times when no productions were scheduled, I duplicated tapes from the tape library. Of course, there were some clerical duties associated with filling these orders.

I think the company is very concerned that an intern get plenty of production time and introductions to any new equipment. All aspects of the company's business are explained. Apparently, few interns are hired. But since the intern supervisor is in charge of production, the intern is at the center of activity and the total internship experience is valuable.

Peggy Turner used her contacts with classmates and professors to locate a noncredit internship with a new production company. Her success may have something to do with the fact that she was the company's first intern.

The company was in the process of preparing funding proposals. Turner spent the next few months assisting in the preparation of a proposal for a 13-part series on crime prevention. Her research involved contacts with police departments, insurance companies and public service agencies. She also interviewed criminal justice professors at several universities and read current periodicals and books on crimes and crime statistics.

While this proposal was awaiting action, Turner was trained as a reader because the company was receiving books and scripts for production consideration. She wrote a short synopsis for each book or script.

Turner tackled a larger project with the help of her supervisor, a former PBS station producer. Together they wrote a detailed treatment of a novel, with Turner making a list of suggestions and changes to be implemented if the story were to become a movie. Later, company officials met with the novelist's agent to negotiate screen rights to the book.

After her internship, Turner moved on to the payroll, being paid for writing each synopsis for the company. She continues to work part time for the company and is now learning more about script writing, for which the pay will be higher.

A journalism major, Turner is married with two children. She has been working toward her bachelor's degree for 12 years. This type of internship proved ideal for her because she could do most of the work at home.

Some large companies have video departments involved in a number of projects. Some maintain well-equipped studios with state-of-the-art equipment. For example, contractors who do government work have studios and laboratories with more sophisticated equipment than many television stations.

Some of these potential sites are open to interns and some are not. Defense contractors may be unable to accept interns because of security regulations. Other sites, required by company policy to pay all interns, limit the number of interns because of budget restrictions. Timing is crucial for prospective interns because a sudden increase in projects can be a green light for intern assistance.

Cable Stations: A Good Place to Get Experience

Although interns looking for hands-on production work would be welcomed by city agencies and other organizations, their best chances are with the large number of cable television stations across the country. A cable company can be an especially good site for the production beginner because supervisors often have time to give more detailed explanations of equipment and conduct training sessions.

An internship production experience with cable can lead to similar work with PBS or larger network-affiliated stations. Cable production work can pave the way for a broadcast journalism intern to take the first steps in reporting and writing. It can also lead to work with news departments of local television and radio stations.

Cable attracts interns in at least three areas:

(1) Production interns are needed for studio and location shoots where you operate cameras, character generators, tape-editing equipment, etc. For example, you may run a camera at a city council, school board or other community meeting.

(2) Some cable stations seek interns to write and produce shows for local audiences. You need good writing and organizational skills and must be able to meet people and work well with community volunteers. Motivation to set and follow deadlines is important.

(3) Many cable companies have local newscasts. If you are in broadcast journalism and have a strong interest in news and public affairs, you can contribute effectively. Some interns even work as reporters and anchors.

Cable offers several advantages to interns. Non-union cable stations need internship help and thus are willing to be flexible in scheduling work time around a student's classes. Evening and weekend work is often available. Because deadlines and the pace may not be as hectic as at a larger station, there may be more time for you to learn more tasks and improve your skills. The best production interns may get freelance or part-time paid positions after their internships.

One intern with previous non-profit

volunteer experience was able to research and write a cable program for Easter Seals, a non-profit organization. The show was designed to demonstrate what the organization does to assist individuals, and after it aired on local cable, other cable stations picked it up.

Because a cable TV station staff is usually small, interns might be encouraged to present ideas for programming. Producing your own show is a good possibility for a strong intern. Many of the supervisors were once interns themselves and want to help you quickly learn basic tasks.

Shelly Picardi says she considers her cable experience to have been a significant part of her broadcast journalism career. Her three-day-a-week unpaid internship at a community station led to a full-time job. She reports:

My supervisor demanded that I get as much done as possible during the 18 hours a week I was on hand. My first day was exciting in that the sports stories and scores that I prepared got on the air.

My assignments included writing and researching stories, shooting stories and interviews, performing as a sports anchor on the news, and editing and producing a weekly news show. I was required to do about one ENG [electronic news gathering] story a week. While in school, I had to do three a semester.

My most difficult assignment was an interview with a very big-name football player. I had to go to a nearby high school to set it up. Once we got into the interview, it was fun and it turned out well.

I covered so many sports events that I could have used the background of some kind of sports statistics class or one that dealt with techniques of coaching and sports terminology.

Being at a small station I did telephoning, research and writing, a little bit of everything. My typing skills helped a lot. And, of course, time was taken up with shoots.

I learned how to edit better and believe that my TV production classes as well as broadcast writing courses were essential background. My supervisor and co-workers said that I looked good on camera, that I had a good, strong broadcast voice and that my ENG stories were solid. When someone moved to a larger station in another market, I was offered her job and accepted it immediately. *Timing is just about everything in this business.* Although I had the chance to intern at a larger station, I am sure that the community station was the correct choice. A smaller community television station probably has more to offer in training and experience to make it in this competitive business.

> *One intern feels that a smaller community television station can offer more training and experience to help "make it in this competitive business."*

Hands-on Broadcast Experience at Larger Stations and in Distant Markets

Internship opportunities at larger stations are typified by those at a Pennsylvania PBS station. "Hands-on" truly describes much of the available work at this non-union station. As an intern you can work as a camera operator, audio technician or lighting assistant, as well as with producers and directors. Programming covers news, public affairs, entertainment, local events and many other subjects.

Usually one or two video production courses are required as an internship prerequisite. But this is not true at all stations. Hours are flexible, running from a minimum of 16 to 40 hours per week. Some assistance is given the interns who wish to leave the station with a video résumé.

A broader assortment of chores can be available at some large stations. Assignments may be arranged in remote production, post-production, editing, lighting, graphic design, set design and props, talent preparation, script writing and storyboarding.

Management of interns is handled much like at network stations, by assigning a specific person as an intern coordinator, principally to interview and talk with prospective interns.

Some broadcast journalism students have to seek out internships away from home. Both television and radio stations with news and community programming in small and medium-sized markets are good prospects for interns. These markets may be less competitive, and the personnel are likely to respond positively to a qualified intern.

This was the experience of Jaletta Albright, a communications graduate who is now a reporter with an NBC station in West Virginia. After researching stations and markets in several states, she made an informed choice and wrote a proposal to a station that then accepted her for a summer internship.

The station was located in the 114th market in the country. Albright said she decided that the station was big enough to be representative of how news coverage operates in a larger market, yet small enough to be more accessible for an intern. The station had consistently higher ratings than the two competing stations in nearby cities, she noted.

Albright's proposal was that she work intensely in the news department for 10 hours a day, five days a week, for the two and a half months of the internship. She reports:

The time included the weekend newscast when fewer staffers on board meant more work for me. I think an intern should always look for chances to fill in holes. Also, working three other days (Monday through Wednesday) allowed me to see the inner workings of a regular full-hour newscast production.

I assisted a news writer regularly on these tasks:

- archiving stories
- filing slides
- writing scripts
- running the TelePrompTer
- operating newsroom cameras

- preparing air tapes for editing
- writing stories and introductions for packages
- preparing stories from the bureau office in a nearby city
- accompanying reporters on story assignments

The station's five reporters do all their own camera work and editing, so they were appreciative of a second hand. Most were very helpful. All had two to six years' experience.

Although I never got air time myself, on a few occasions I wrote and edited a piece that was on the air. I was often given a chance to do camera work and sometimes to interview and edit.

The internship was a challenge. The lack of structure for someone working in my capacity meant that I had to be very assertive in seeking responsibilities and experience.

Billie Purugganan completed a similar broadcast journalism internship at a station in Honolulu, Hawaii. At the beginning of her unpaid internship she worked a two-day schedule Thursday evenings and a day shift on Saturdays. A Friday evening shift was added later.

Initially hired by the managing editor and assignment desk manager, she was supervised by the assistant assignment editor. She said that the supervision was very clear and specific. Some excerpts from a report she compiled outline the tasks she was assigned:

Weather—My main task was collecting weather information from news wires and forecasters and typing the script. This included any advisories for that day.

Break sheets—They are part of the script indicating to the necessary people when commercials are scheduled during the newscast. My job was to obtain this information from the programming schedule and type it on a script to be collated into the final script.

Menu—I typed the menu or rundown sheet including story slugs, reporter, and type of coverage after the producers finalized their story choices.

Closer—I wrote the last page of the script for the anchor. This closes the show with information on what comes next and when the next newscast is scheduled.

On-location assignment—I had the opportunity on Saturdays to go out with a cameraman and do a story for the 6 p.m. news. This included interviews, sound bites and writing of the story.

Briefs—I wrote these stories, which do not include video and are usually obtained by phone. I did a number of these.

Rewrites—I did this job about six times. It involved rewriting the 6 p.m. stories for the 10 p.m. news show. I had to change the angle and condense some of the stories.

I also did some newspaper clipping for the library file when all other work was completed. Probably the highlight of the internship was actually reporting with my own cameraman. Although I was not on camera, my writing was read over the air.

My video production class and all of the writing and broadcast journalism classes required in my major were helpful. Operating editing equipment and having good typing skills were necessary prerequisites. Computer and speech courses also were essential background at this site for me.

In order to have some accomplishments to show from an internship, many broadcast journalism students believe it is necessary to complete stints at two or three sites because of the competition for jobs. Even with good writing skills and on-air experience, the chances of an intern getting a story on the evening news are slim. Here, the sharp contrast between print journalism internships and those in the electronic media become obvious. A journalism intern at *Newsday* or the *Louisville Courier-Journal*, despite competition for an intern position, can come away with writing samples of interest to many potential employers. These clips may represent a variety of news and other kinds of stories published.

> *Unlike print, news samples from TV are difficult to get.*

Large-Market or Smaller-Market Station?

A broadcast journalist must look at a much smaller market to get hands-on situations and collect good examples at an internship. The opportunities to show off news-reporting skills may lead to samples for video résumés. Even though there are exceptions, the internships in large-market stations mostly are limited to research and clerical or routine tasks.

A case in point is the example of an intern assigned to a network-affiliated station in Rhode Island on a summer internship. She reported that she spent 60 percent of her time on general observation of the newsroom and the news set, 20 percent talking with station employees about their various duties and 20 percent learning to handle the floor manager's duties and other tasks associated with the evening news shift. One problem was that her assigned supervisor rarely saw her because most of the time the intern was there, the supervisor was working on another shift.

Production managers and producers who work with interns defend the tasks given to interns. They say that because interns are newcomers to television news—some may even have majors other than broadcasting— any time devoted to acquainting them with behind-the-scenes activities is valuable experience for them.

Broadcast journalist Elizabeth Almaraz knew that getting on-the-air experience in an internship was doubtful. She wanted some writing possibilities, so she interviewed at a few smaller stations, checking all job descriptions carefully for reporting and writing tasks. She accepted an internship in the newsroom of a small independent station.

Since the news staff at the station she chose was very small, Almaraz found that the way her time was divided favored her needs. She reported spending about 80 percent of her time rewriting news stories, sports and weather briefs, including researching and writing some story assignments that went on the air with only minor editing.

Her supervisor, who usually has one intern each semester, held the twin jobs of news director and news anchor, so Almaraz got to observe closely all aspects of the operation. She comments: "Michelle, my supervisor, was very helpful and supportive. She wanted to be sure that I got hands-on experience. For example, I wrote some fast-breaking stories that went right on the air. While I got very little on-air experience, both of the anchors helped me produce a résumé tape that turned out well and should be a big plus in my search for a job."

Opportunities in Radio

Sandra Gonzales, a broadcast journalism major, completed a radio newswriting internship with an all-news, CBS-owned radio station in a major market. To get this competitive internship, Gonzales had to submit a résumé, pass an interview and demonstrate in a writing test that she could take a newspaper story and create a broadcast story.

Since the internship was with a guild station, work time had to be scheduled on weekends. Gonzales worked from 4 a.m. to noon on Saturdays and Sundays for 16 hours a week and was paid $6.56 an hour.

Good computer and typing skills were necessary, Gonzales says, but she credits two college courses with teaching her the best skills: broadcast newswriting and an audio/radio production class.

Although this station hires no one directly out of college, Gonzales said the internship experience was excellent and served as an impressive addition to her résumé. She was asked to stay on past the time required for her credit internship.

Her supervisor told her that deadline pressure leaves little time to teach the basics of radio newswriting on the job. Gonzales comments:

I personally liked the limited supervision because it made me feel responsible and professional. I did retrieve the edited versions of my stories from the local script files to see what changes, if any, were made so I could learn from that.

I was expected to write three stories an hour to be read on the air. I wrote international, national and local stories. The newsroom was computerized with access to most wire services. The computer screen was split so that I could write my story on one half while getting information from the other half.

I could write around actualities [a report from the scene of an event], write wraparounds [a lead and a tag or further copy to go around a reporter's story], conduct in-studio interviews and record reporters calling in their stories.

I like to write features because I think I have a knack for them. I worked on feature assignments in order to show my creative skills.

I made a few grammatical mistakes when I did not read the story aloud but, all in all, I learned a lot, especially about equipment.

All-news radio station internships are rare and competitive. Prospective broadcast journalism interns seeking positions in the news departments of larger stations often have to do as Gonzales did, that is, show journalism writing samples as well as pass a writing and editing test. Tapes or samples of campus or local radio station work are very helpful to present at interviews.

You are more likely to be chosen for a news internship at a smaller station. There, the news director and announcer are likely to be the same person, and you can help with the writing. Air time may not be available, but if you are resourceful you may volunteer to cover local sports events or community programs and tape interviews for use later.

Other internships at radio stations are reasonably parallel to the PAs at television stations. You may be assigned to a number of clerical tasks in the programming or sales departments. These internships are usually unpaid, but a few may offer minimum wage.

Overall, radio internships can give you some excellent hands-on training. By examin-

---

T Where Jobs Are in Radio

hese are some of the jobs in programming at large and small radio stations. Many radio stations take interns as assistants.

PROGRAM DIRECTOR: All stations/all markets.

ANNOUNCERS: All stations/all markets.

CONTINUITY WRITER: Most stations/most markets.

NEWS DIRECTOR: Most stations except for stations with strong music formats and those where news is fed by network/satellite.

NEWS REPORTERS: All stations with news focus.

SPORTS DIRECTOR: Stations with strong sports format.

PROMOTIONS DIRECTOR: Most large and some medium-sized stations.

MUSIC DIRECTOR: Most stations.

NEWS, PRODUCTION ASSISTANTS: Major and large-market stations. At small-market stations, these positions are filled by interns and part-time employees.

---

ing the description below of an internship program at a radio station in a large market, you will see some of the activities available to interns.

Sample Program for Radio Interns

(NOTE: The station requested anonymity because only six interns are accepted each semester and its managers do not want to encourage more applicants than they are now seeing.)

PROGRAM OBJECTIVES

- Build skills to deal with radio station affairs on a daily basis.

- Gain a perspective of the radio industry in this market and nationally.
- Develop writing skills.
- Encourage self confidence.
- Set realistic goals and take action to prepare for a job in the radio industry.

QUALIFICATIONS

- Must be at least 18 years old and enrolled in a college broadcasting or communications program.
- Must receive some kind of academic credit for the internship.
- Must complete valid paperwork from the university at the beginning of the internship. This includes credit requirements as well as agreements regarding any station functions.
- Must be dependable, have transportation to and from the station and be available a minimum of 10 hours per week spread over two or three days.

MANDATORY MEETINGS AND FUNCTIONS

Each intern must attend

- at least two sales department meetings,
- an intern sales seminar,
- an intern programming seminar involving production,
- a programming staff meeting,
- an intern copywriting seminar, and
- two station functions (usually at night or on weekends) outside of regular internship hours. These are usually concerts, fund-raisers promoted by the station or trade shows.

POSSIBLE PROJECTS

In addition to submitting time sheets each week, the intern will participate in various departments through projects and tasks of this kind:

- Reading weekly trade publications (i.e., *Radio & Records, Billboard*).
- Assisting with monthly press releases to trade magazines regarding station activity.
- Assisting with marketing research and surveying.
- Working on the station's T-shirt promotion campaign.
- Updating commercial and promotional copy as well as writing new spots (each intern will write a minimum of five pieces of copy).
- Working with the sales department on new business leads, posting of sales percentages, tabulating daily check lists and gathering figures for reports.
- Assisting with station promotions and on-air giveaways.
- Keeping the media table stocked and updated, production studio and tapes organized, etc.

The promotions department seems to be a favorite for interns. One intern compiled a list of new promotional projects for the station after interviewing listeners who had called in requests. Another intern fielded questions about the station and gave out bumper stickers and other promotional materials at a county fair booth.

Programming is a popular radio assignment. For music stations with a historical record format, interns have researched and charted selections to find dates of their highest ratings. One intern in programming gathered local record stores sales data to make music choices to match up with national charts.

Complaints from radio interns are not unlike those from other unhappy communications students, such as rigid deadlines, low pay when a job is offered, poor schedules of working hours and little or no job security for employees. The worst abuses of interns at radio stations relate to errands from the station. One intern reported that she was humiliated when she had to go back to a restaurant a second time in one day to try to get the manager to pay his overdue advertising bill. Later, she had trouble getting her site supervisor to pay her promised reimbursement for gas money to run her car on station business.

Supervisors at small stations say that requests for interns to deliver tapes or records are only a tiny part of the job description. They add that if an intern is not able to tend to the request, an employee will be asked. The interns should be paid gas money for their cars, according to personnel at stations.

Some radio stations operate very effective sales training seminars for interns and new employees. The top-ranking internship area in terms of hiring possibilities is in sales as an assistant to an account executive. These internships should be scheduled in the summer when there would be more full-time work within a shorter period of time. When a station is delivering a good audience in its market, interns selling air time can move directly to full-time advertising positions on the sales staff.

> *Radio's top-ranking internship area as far as hiring possibilities is in sales as an assistant to an account executive.*

In summary, radio offers substantial internship opportunities. However, intern Linda McLaren warns that there is far too much to learn at a busy radio station for a semester-long internship. Nonetheless, she enjoyed her internship and comments on her duties:

I created fliers, pasted up photos and worked with the printer on the typeset copy to be sent to trade magazines. After updating the station's press list, I wrote a number of press releases which were approved by my supervisor. I sent them out accompanied by pictures promoting the station.

Writing radio commercials for an account executive was fun and I got favorable feedback. You have to be creative and learn to use the "lingo" of the listener to get your message across. It's exhilarating to hear something that you have written used on the air.

Competitive Internships at Record Companies

Internships in the entertainment industry can be as elusive as they are highly prized. Certainly this is true for the record company business. Internships at Hollywood firms in this field are highly sought by applicants with energy and enthusiasm and possessing strong clerical and oral communications skills. Much of the work relates to responding to requests by radio stations throughout the world.

Generally, interns go to publicity, promotions and marketing departments or departments handling guest and media relations. Some record companies have international departments in which skill in a second language might open a door. To get these competitive internships, network as much as you can, particularly for a second internship or a part-time job.

These internships are unpaid. Registration in some kind of credit class is required. Many graduates do a couple of internships by registering in a college in the area. Some do more than one internship in a semester as long as their credit eligibility is maintained.

Film Positions: Hard to Locate but Worth the Effort

Film internships are the most difficult to find. Some are with new companies or with small, practically unknown production houses; competitive internships are available with Hollywood and New York studios. Internship announcements appear in some periodicals.

As new production companies begin, others are going out of business. Like television, a film company starts a film hiring employees and interns. When the film project is finished, like when a television show is canceled, these people are out of work.

Source for Help

The heading "Film, Audio, and Video" in the *1995 Peterson's Internships* (see Appendix A) lists some leads for film-related internships. Some companies and associations employ interns on both a paid and unpaid basis to work as library assistants, researchers, production people, photographers, marketing and publicity representatives, etc.

A few of these sites are located out of the major film markets of Hollywood and New York. Some states are opening offices to coordinate marketing efforts of locations for television and film productions. An example would be the Maryland Film Commission office, scouting locations for film and TV productions. In the office, semester interns work in a number of positions, including marketing, photography and videotaping.

Film internships share some characteristics, including the following:

- Working on a film on location usually requires a full-time commitment. Summers, between semesters and holiday breaks may be the best times.
- Most film interns are hired as PAs and are paid on a per diem or weekly basis. PA interns usually work on several films before they move up the employment ladder.

- Long hours are standard, frequently more than 10 or 12 a day, depending on shooting schedules, weather, available daylight and other factors.
- Special skills such as stagecraft experience or a background in art can make you a stronger candidate.

Starting out with an internship for a small film company producing industrial or educational films is a good idea. Virginia Trooian developed her own film internship with a small production company owned by a graduate of the university where she was a student. Later, she worked on a children's film project for the same company. Her description is based on her experience as a PA on a management training film:

As is typical of most film work, the day started early. Crew calls were at 6 a.m. As a PA, I was basically the "go-fer" and had to arrive a little earlier to set up breakfast and make coffee.

I worked closely with the production manager. She assigned me to help the art director clean up the set or location, which involved numerous tasks. I had to bring in props, hang art, do painting, make signs and assist in the lighting.

There is much detail work around a film location. I assisted the sound men and grips, moving equipment and other items. Errands included driving to town to pick up hardware and other supplies, makeup for actors and delivering the dailies [film prints of the day's shooting].

My most valuable experience was learning how a professional film actually is made and information regarding the roles of casting and script supervision. I absorbed a great deal of information simply by observing and talking with the director, key grips and gaffers and cameramen. All of them answered any questions I had and explained their roles in the film's production.

You need to show a genuine interest in their work to get the attention of some of the professionals. You can learn a lot about the business and make this a part of your internship.

Sometimes routine assignments can be minimized by letting people know of your skills and interests before you begin your internship. For example, an intern with a company producing educational films expressed to her supervisor on arrival that she had an interest in special effects, so she was assigned to the art director during the shoot. Because she had some art background, she was able to animate a doll to represent a library fairy who shows a young boy around a library. She tackled several similar projects. Through a lead from her supervisor, she later got a paid internship on a film for another company, building miniature sets for an animated dinosaur.

> *Let people know of any particular skills or interests you have, and routine assignments might be replaced with special projects that take advantage of your expertise.*

Interns also work as grips. This involves the physical labor of setting up camera shots and lighting as well as other jobs around the sets. A grip is in the center of action and therefore in a position to observe closely the work of the director and camera operator.

The best way to get hands-on film experience is with non-union production companies making educational, trade or industrial films. Some of these companies can be found in smaller markets. Directories at libraries and other sources can provide leads.

Script analysis work and some writing assignments are available in film to qualified interns. John Reese did an internship with a small concept-oriented company producing made-for-TV specials. Reese and other interns worked directly under the supervision of the owner, a former writer and production executive. Reese comments:

Working two or three full days a week for 18 weeks on this unpaid internship, I would say that 30 percent of my time was spent on non-writing tasks, including research, and 70 percent of my time involved writing. The owner of the company gave me constructive criticism of my writing, but she often was demanding, exerting lots of pressure to produce copy within strict deadlines.

At first, my assignments were research oriented. I had to read newspaper and magazine articles for ideas on topics or concepts and summarize them in a narrative form that fit the angle of the show. These "write-ups" then were submitted to a researcher who would finish the presentation. Soon I was doing all the research as well as conceptualizing the show and writing the presentation treatment. The owner would critique my writing and concept and ask me to polish and add any ideas that she would like to see included.

Once I interviewed an FBI agent and a police vice detective to get background for a confidential topic. There is always the fear of losing an idea to a competing producer. The owner also expected me to complete assignments as quickly as possible.

You must be willing to work under pressure. You have to turn out creative writing that grabs the reader's attention for four to six pages. It's necessary to be a self-starter, work independently and be innovative in approach. Many requests for information require very "creative research" efforts.

Photo Internships Are Plentiful

As a photo intern, you may work a variety of sites with a variety of duties, including the following:

■ As a photojournalist on a small newspaper you may write features or news stories and take accompanying photos. You also may process the film and make prints.

■ On larger urban newspapers you may shoot all kinds of photo assignments from traffic accidents to society events. Some time may also go to lab work.

■ You may assist a photographer who is a support person for a news bureau or public affairs staff for a large company or corporation.

■ You may handle assignments in non-profit or profit public relations.

■ Interns also have worked for commercial photographers. The clients can be very different, from fashion settings to industrial companies. You could help set up on location.

Education in photography has evolved from the strictly training aspects of operating increasingly technical and complex equipment to higher education programs. The impetus toward photojournalism came from the success of U.S. Navy photographers during World War II. Photography was added as a sequence or specialization in many degree programs in the '60s and '70s. Today more than 100 colleges and universities throughout the country have photography emphases or sequences as part of communications arts, journalism or industrial technology programs.

Because of the need for practice in skill development and operating complex equipment both in the darkroom and in achieving that all-important picture, internships in photography are important and plentiful. Many pay a good wage. There is constant demand for interns to serve as photo assistants in different job settings.

Photojournalists pride themselves on having the latest in sophisticated equipment and being well prepared. Many students of the art demonstrate their skills early by completing internships and holding down part-time jobs on newspapers and magazines. Later they become very competitive for some of the larger well-paid internships on major dailies.

Here are some observations that outline some of the skills needed by a photojournalism intern. The comments were made by the photo editor of a 150,000-circulation daily newspaper after supervising his summer intern, Diana:

Minimally, an internship should provide an opportunity for an inside look at the profession coupled with some hands-on experience performing the tasks of that profession. Diana's experience has gone beyond that, placing her right in the thick of the business and in many ways treating her like a staff member. She met the challenge.

Several times she produced photographs that rated page one play even while shooting alongside a staff photographer. She showed a willingness to work hard and a healthy openness to criticism. She has photographed a broad spectrum, from major league baseball games to society lunches to traffic accidents.

In contrast to day-by-day brief assignments, Diana spent several days riding with an animal control officer. It allowed her to develop rapport with the subject she was photographing and gave her the chance to add some depth and a greater variety to her shots. Diana also photographed the officer at home to show a contrast with the woman behind the badge.

Diana has demonstrated excellent people skills and good work habits. She is to be applauded for an honesty of effort and for her desire to learn and succeed. However, Diana is still a beginner and, not surprisingly, her technique and craft need improvement. Her professional growth has gotten a healthy boost during the internship, and her work has shown noticeable improvement during the summer.

There are more students looking for jobs in the other communications fields, so photo internships, especially on newspapers, are available for the well-qualified photography student (see *Student Guide to Mass Media Internships*, Appendix A). However, photojournalist interns must be well grounded in basic skills and prepared to complete a variety of assignments, ranging from hard news, sports and features to full picture stories. They also should be ready to write news stories, if needed, and have some experience in writing captions and headlines, because some photo interns are asked to dummy pages.

Newspaper photography can be demanding work. Taking photos every day, despite the rewards, requires good concentration and very strong work habits. Since interns seeking positions on daily newspapers must be well qualified to be accepted, the ratio of those who later are hired for staff work is high, possibly one of the highest in the communications field.

The number of photo interns later hired for staff work is probably one of the highest in the communications field.

Photo Requests

Here is a sample of the assignments a newspaper photo intern, working on a large weekly newspaper, was asked to complete:

✓ Need three-column vertical for page 1 in Valley City with residents enjoying company of "Brandy," who is the resident dog. Get a first-class shot that shows people and pup.

✓ Valley City Park Clubhouse under construction. We need one three-column vertical print showing progress on building. Dennis, who works part time in circulation, is a member of the construction crew and has promised to get you up in the tower for a super shot, so see him.

✓ Brugge Memorial Library. We need wild art. Be creative in search of kids looking up material in the library. Look for intelligent-looking kids.

✓ Go to high school drama production room. Get several shots of dress rehearsal for Cole Porter Review. See Doug as he will help you set up.

Andrew Temple, a photo major, completed a spring photojournalism internship with a metro daily. Because his college classes were scheduled only for evenings, he was able to work days and often logged 40 hours a week. A few times he started as early as 6 a.m. He was paid for 24 hours a week and received $5.65 an hour, plus mileage and film.

Temple says his supervisor, Rick, made this a good internship. This type of internship operates by having editors assign interns to topics such as people (editorial portraits), events (community marathons), an occasional spot news event (truck crash on highway) and, most often, wild art (kids in the park or at county fair). Temple describes his experience this way:

Each time I received an assignment I would discuss it with Rick, telling him the types of photos that I had in mind. Often he would come up with angles I would not have thought to consider.

If I made a mistake or did not get the right shots, Rick would sit down and talk to me about what needed to be done to improve. Many editors ignore interns unless they need something. Perhaps they have been burned by interns in the past.

One thing I learned was to bring back at least five photographs from each shoot. I was able to photograph everything as if it were a photo story.

My most difficult assignments involved a visit to an AIDS hospice to see what kinds of pictures I could get to show how it works. It took several trips to get the confidence of the people and to win their trust. It turned out well, but I had to work on this for several weeks.

Prospective photojournalism interns can get assistance from the National Press Photographers Association, which maintains a listing of internships as well as a job information bank for members. The list for interns covers 11 regions throughout the country and includes openings for news photographer internships at TV stations as well as those on newspapers and some in graphics (see Appendix A).

In the category of non-photojournalism internships, you should look to non-profit organizations for leads as PR interns do (see Chapter 5). Some groups need photo help to complete fund-raising brochures, annual reports, publications, etc. A good photo intern may fill an immediate need because the PR coordinator for the non-profit organization might not be skilled in photography.

Since some organizations have limited needs, you might consider doing an internship that would serve multiple non-profits. If you are getting internship credit, your coordinator might permit a job description that would call for specific assignments at two or three organizations so that you would have enough work.

Also, in large or medium-sized markets, some companies might invite an intern to help on a freelance basis with needs of the public relations or public affairs staff. Some PR and advertising agencies might have one-time-only photo needs in assisting some community organizations and other clients. One intern accepted a paid internship with a real estate firm. She was able to take and process photos of homes for sale and layout a publication for printing.

A popular site for many photo interns is with a photography studio where they serve as an assistant to the principal photographer. Assignments can range from weddings to shooting products for industrial clients. Interns are usually paid, with the amount depending on how much assistance and skills the intern can deliver. Some do extensive darkroom work. Below is a list of some of the tasks that photo interns who work for commercial photographers are asked to complete:

- Take film to and from photo labs and load film for studio and location shoots.
- Develop and print black and white film and put together proof books for customers.
- Organize an image bank consisting of slides of photographers' work.
- Complete darkroom tasks such as mixing chemicals, developing and printing film, making proof sheets and drying prints.
- Assist on-location shoots by carrying and helping to set up equipment.
- Learn lighting techniques and setup for inside shoots.

Here is some advice from a veteran intern supervisor, Jim Wolf, a local origination manager for a national cable company:

Interns get caught up in using equipment and slack off when it comes to seeking out work to test other skills. I like to see interns come to our station and produce a show.

There are many opportunities available from city and county agencies, community organizations and non-profit groups that need programming. Some may have funding. A qualified intern can actually produce and direct a program. By rounding up a few friends and using other interns, a crew can be assembled. This represents a creative challenge for an intern. Showing off a completed project as part of a video résumé can go a long way in getting interviews in a very tough job market.

Interns are often sitting around, waiting for the next production to start. It's true there are equipment and scheduling problems, but an aggressive, motivated intern can overcome these problems just as they would have to do in the real world. Better articulating what they can and want to do can help to make the internship the valuable experience it should be.

For Thought and Discussion

1. What are concerns that educators have about student internships in broadcasting and television in particular and other media in general?

2. Assume that you are the faculty coordinator of an internship program at a university. In response to a call from the director of television services in a small nearby city, you have mailed information and a form for him or her to complete. When the form is returned you notice that the tasks for the intern are only operating a camera at the city council meeting, operating a character generator and answering the phone in the office. Give at least two arguments why this job description should be upgraded.

3. Employees often have to run errands or drive their cars to pick up film and other

supplies. Does the employer who pays the intern "own" that student as far as being able to ask them to do such tasks? Is the employer free to use that intern for any legitimate company task, and if so, under what conditions?

4. Based on some of the learning experiences of interns presented in this chapter, give at least three reasons why you think a radio/television/film intern should consider two or more internships regardless of academic credit.

5. You have been offered internships at a large Public Broadcasting System station and at a small nearby cable station. You have some broadcast journalism skills. Give at least three advantages of an internship at each site.

6. After reviewing the personal experiences of a number of interns, what actions can you take to assure yourself of a good experience in terms of learning and improving skills and of meeting the requirements of a good evaluation from the site. Discuss about a dozen.

CHAPTER 8

PERSONALITY PROFILES

THIS CHAPTER ILLUSTRATES how hard-working communications professionals can use their skills acquired through previous internships and jobs to reach the highest rungs of the career ladder. This chapter also emphasizes again the varied and challenging opportunities open to qualified communications graduates. You can follow the courses, internships and work experiences of these professionals and find many tips regarding your education and search for internships and jobs.

■ Linnea McKean beat out hundreds of applicants for a job she had her eyes on. She knows how you can use your communications and marketing skills not only in internships and jobs but also in marketing yourself.

■ Peggy Conlon tells how she became the successful publisher of a major national industry magazine after working in other parts of the communications industry.

■ Sophia Nieves got a helping hand from her minority contacts, including a valuable internship with the Hispanic Link News Service in Washington, D.C., which has led to her job handling media relations for one of the country's largest corporations.

■ Kevin Corke, a black sports anchor/ reporter for an ABC affiliate in Denver, credits his internship and rapport with his supervisor for his successful start in broadcast journalism.

■ Sonja Gantt, a black general assignment reporter, worked her way to one of the country's largest independent television stations, WGN in Chicago. She exemplifies what all of these professionals learned: The more internships you do, the more you learn, the more people you meet, and the better your chances are of finding rewarding work.

■ Ray Wong describes the path his career has taken from a photojournalist to the systems editor of a major newspaper. He discusses the importance of positioning yourself in each job you take for advancement to the next position.

This chapter was contributed by Edward J. Fink, Department of Communications, California State University, Fullerton.

- Jeordan Legon is a Cuban-American and general assignment reporter for a large California newspaper. He explains how his internships and professional contacts led to full-time work without his having completed his college degree.
- Ian Kawata, a Japanese-American, has begun a career in advertising. He studied broadcast production in college but through the Minority Advertising Training Program he became fascinated with—and learned the skills for—work in the advertising industry.

With Her Eyes on the Job

Current Job

LINNEA MCKEAN is the Marketing Services Supervisor for the U.S. headquarters of Cathay Pacific Airways, a British airline that flies to 41 destinations in 26 countries. She is responsible for a $2 million annual budget in a department that produces up to 5 million pieces of promotional materials each year.

December 4, 1989, was a red-letter day for Linnea McKean. While driving home with the latest issue of *Advertising Age* magazine, she recalls an intuitive feeling that the issue held something for her. "When I got home," she says, "I opened the magazine and read that Cathay Pacific Airlines was moving to Los Angeles to provide the first and only nonstop flights between Los Angeles and Hong Kong. The company was looking for a Marketing Supervisor. It was the job I wanted in the location I wanted to work. *I had to have it*."

Realizing that there would be serious competition for the job, McKean used her own public relations and marketing strategies to make herself stand out from the crowd of applicants.

I began by researching the company. I learned that Cathay Pacific was only one of three profit-making airlines operating in the U.S. that year. I created a variety of graphics that incorporated this information. I used graphics to design an eye-catching red folder that held my résumé, references and cover letter. I hoped Personnel would take note.

I later learned that because of my file I became known as the "Lady in Red"—a distinction that helped me stand out from the other 650 applicants. I was one of 30 finalists brought in for a series of interviews. And I eventually won the job!

McKean did maintain some traditional, and important, conventions: following prescribed résumé outlines, writing a cover letter with a serious tone and dressing professionally for the interview. But she also wanted to take some steps to stand out and encourage the Personnel people to remember her. She learned that the sales marketing manager, who had the final hiring decisions, liked classy cards, so she bought a gold and red thank-you card and mailed it to him after the first interview.

Because the Cathay job involved marketing strategies, McKean felt it was worth the risk to market herself creatively. Besides, she had nothing to lose—except her dream job!

Road to Success

The road to McKean's career success began in college. She received a Marketing Communications Certificate from the University of California, Irvine, and in 1988 she earned her bachelor's degree in Communications with an emphasis in Advertising and Public Relations from the California State University, Fullerton. In June of 1988 she performed an intensive four-week, non-paying internship at the Fullerton offices of Beckman Instruments, a large scientific research and development corporation. She was assigned to work in the Employee Communications division and also worked for the Marketing Communications department. It was during her internship that McKean put into practice what she had studied in school.

Plenty of Creative Work

In her internship report, McKean credits her supervisors for a lot of support and general direction. She liked their management styles and was able to think and solve on-the-job problems. With some real hands-on experience she

- created the concept, design and copy for two national direct mailers,
- wrote an article for the company magazine,
- developed a magazine readership research study and analysis,
- produced the *Designer Genes* catalog and brochure product information sheets,
- wrote Beckman news bulletins for posting on company bulletin boards,
- served as a volunteer assistant at the International Association of Business Communicators conference.

McKean was so successful in her internship work that a new position in advertising and sales promotion was created for her in the marketing department. She worked two years in this position, which called for a number of tasks, including supporting field sales at major trade shows. She designed and wrote brochures, newsletters, direct mail materials and technical data sheets for products.

It's obvious that the skills McKean developed both as an intern and as an employee of Beckman Instruments carried directly into her current work for Cathay Pacific Airways. Especially valuable were her writing tasks and marketing promotions. The writing skills she honed and the production and advertising skills she acquired are skills that she uses every day in her present position.

McKean began working for Cathay Pacific four months before the company launched its non-stop service between Los Angeles and Hong Kong. This made her initiation to the job very exciting as she worked on introducing this service to the public. Her first task was to create a full-color, 15-page brochure to promote the flights. She wrote the copy, got the photographs, designed the brochure, printed it and had it to market in just four weeks—record time for such a project. The brochure even included a die-cut in which the travel representatives could place their business cards, a production step that required additional time.

The Excitement Has Not Stopped

Today, McKean averages five promotional packages per month, for both consumer and trade travel. She is involved in every step of production, from concept through design to marketing. To be successful in this position, she needs to know all aspects of both production and promotion.

For example, she has learned how to "manage vendors." For instance, she knows what reasonable printing prices are, such as how much 80,000 brochures should cost. Because of this knowledge, she can tell if a printing vendor is overcharging. She began accumulating this knowledge in her internship when she wrote and designed brochures for Beckman Instruments, and she has continued to learn every facet of public relations, advertising and marketing as her career has progressed.

Important Skills

Some knowledge of computers is helpful to McKean. Although she contracts with freelance artists and publishers for much of her work, she needs to communicate with them about what they do, so it's important for her to know the fundamental terms and concepts of the most popular software programs. In her day-to-day work, McKean herself deals mostly with databases, such as client and mailing lists, and with word processing. She is also taking a course in a popular spreadsheet program.

McKean recommends some other skills as being vitally important:

- "Perfect your language skills. You can never take too many English classes. You'll be surprised how you can stumble across grammar questions in your daily communication.
- "You must learn to speak well. Take any necessary speech classes. Speech courses may help to improve your presentation skills.
- "Research thoroughly what you are presenting so that you know what you are talking about.
- "Get organized and stay organized. Learn to use filing systems and tracking systems.
- "Learn to budget and manage projects. Take a finance class in a business school. Then simulate a marketing communications plan on a budget of, say, $250,000 to $1 million.
- "Brush up on your people skills. Etiquette requirements are different in every corporation and culture. Know when and how to shake hands, when to clap and how to make introductions properly."

Professional Organizations

Memberships in professional organizations have also helped McKean along the way. As a student, she was a member of her school's chapter of the Public Relations Student Society of America (PRSSA). In this organization she did some public relations work for the Orange County, Calif., airport when it moved from its former to its present location. Today, McKean is a member of the International Association of Business Commu-

nicators (IABC), the Business Communications and Marketing Association (BCMA) and the Direct Marketing Association of Southern California (DMASC). These memberships help her keep current in her field and maintain professional contacts in her business.

> *Knowing where you want to be and believing you get can there will help you achieve your career goals.*

Some Advice

In passing along advice to future interns, McKean suggests the following do's and don'ts:

- **Do** seek out an internship that will give you the best opportunity to learn.
- **Do** go for the experience that will stretch your endurance skills.
- **Do** listen to your internship supervisor. Then think and do for yourself.
- **Do** consider non-paying internships. Experience counts for more than money in an internship.
- **Do** take everything seriously because you never know where it might lead you.
- **Don't** take an internship that is an easy way out or that sounds glamorous.
- **Don't** be intimidated. Feel the fear and do it anyway.
- **Don't** expect anyone to hold your hand. Don't think your internship will be a schoolroom experience.
- **Don't** forget you are trying to work on challenging projects.
- **Don't** be afraid to approach each task from the perspective of "I can" instead of "I can't."

McKean believes that "you are what you think" and that your mind plays a major role in your personal and professional development. She says to envision the completion of each project assigned. This will help you in each step toward its completion. Envision yourself five and 10 years down the road, she adds. Knowing where you want to be and believing you can get there will help you achieve your career goals.

Her Trade Is Publishing

P Current Job

PEGGY CONLON is publisher of *Broadcasting & Cable*, a leading magazine in the broadcasting industry. She holds a bachelor's degree in Communications (1973) from California State, Fullerton, and a master's degree (1980) in Communications Management from the Annenberg School of Communications at the University of Southern California. She served as a public affairs officer in the U.S. Naval Reserve from 1974 to 1981.

As publisher of a major broadcasting magazine, Peggy Conlon has reached one of the top positions in the communications business. The road she took from student to publisher reveals the importance of establishing a strong record in your chosen field. This can begin with an internship. As Conlon explains:

I did an internship at Dozier Eastman, an industrial advertising agency. I was given the task of writing public relations and marketing press releases. This opportunity to practice writing proved to be quite valuable in the publishing career I eventually pursued. Prior to my internship, a summer part-time PR agency job also helped to develop my writing skills.

After completing my internship at Dozier

Eastman, I was hired there full time in account management. The experience in sales and management also was valuable training for publishing.

Career Steps

Here are some of the major steps in Conlon's career:

- Advertising manager at the Marine and Recreation Components Division of ITT, a position held for five years.
- Hired by Electronic Engineering Co. (EECO), today part of Transico, to run the company's in-house advertising agency. Promoted soon to district manager with display advertising responsibilities.
- In 1981 moved from advertising to publishing.

Conlon says she hadn't always planned to be a publisher:

When I was in school, I only knew that I wanted to be in communications. In the late 1970s, my work in advertising for EECO brought me into contact with the publishers of electronics magazines.

I read the magazines not only to make decisions regarding what advertising space to buy, but also to stay up to date on trends in electronics, and of course to see what the competition was doing. This contact with electronics publishers got me interested in a publishing career.

One of the publishers with whom I had contact was CMP Publications. In 1981, my contacts there asked me if I would be interested in a job with *Electronic Buyers News*, one of their trade newspapers in the electronics industry. This was my opportunity to move into publishing, so I accepted. I stayed with CMP for 10 years.

During the 10-year period, Conlon received a number of promotions:

- In 1982 she became district manager of *Computer Retail News*, a trade magazine for the computer industry.
- In 1984 her title became National Sales Manager for CMP, and she moved to

New York City.

- In 1985 another promotion made her Associate Publisher.
- In 1987 Conlon became publisher for the newspaper on which she had first worked, *Electronic Buyers News*.
- Two years later she launched a new publication, *Electronic World News*, making her the publisher of two trade publications simultaneously.
- In 1992 she took over as group publisher for the electronic division of newspapers at CMP.

Initiating Changes

In November 1992 Conlon was recruited by Cahners Publishing Co., part of Reed-Elsevier Publications, the third largest magazine publisher in the United States. Through her work with CMP, she had become well acquainted with publishers. One of them, Cahners, was looking to fill the publisher position on its magazine *Broadcasting*. The company, impressed with Conlon's background and accomplishments at CMP, offered her the job. She accepted.

"During my first year as the publisher of *Broadcasting*," she says, "I was able to initiate a number of positive changes. Two changes were especially noticeable in March of 1993 when the name of the magazine became *Broadcasting & Cable* to reflect more accurately the industry that the publication represents. We replaced the advertisement on the front, which had been a feature for 62 years, with an editorial cover."

Importance of Education

Conlon comments on how several keys have opened her career and helped her rise to the task of publishing a major magazine:

> "Networking is an important key in this business."

A college education and internships are very important. I found that two courses were especially helpful: business writing and advertising in marketing. The copywriting and media buying at my internship helped me in both advertising and publishing. I was a member of the Public Relations Student Society of America (PRSSA) when I was an undergraduate. This experience gave me practical insights into public relations.

My graduate program and resulting master's degree have also helped me in my career. While I was in graduate school, I was working full time, and I was in the Naval Reserve, so I had to attend classes at night and during the summers to finish my M.A. in two years. That was a very hectic time, but the experience proved to be beneficial. It tested my motivation to get a graduate education, and it forced me to learn to manage my time effectively—an important skill in any field.

Professional memberships give me relevant information and keep me in contact with other people in the business. I'm a member of the Business Marketing Association, and I'm an at-large member of the Board of Governors of the International Radio and Television Society (IRTS). You can learn about job openings through these kinds of contacts with other publishers. Networking is an important key in this business.

Stepping Up the Ladder

Current Job

SOPHIA NIEVES is a brand public relations supervisor for the Miller Brewing Co. in Milwaukee, Wis. After a nine-month search by the company for an applicant, Nieves was selected from 10 finalists for the job.

Many small steps along the way are necessary to reach the top in any field. For communications these steps probably include an internship or two and a part-time related job. Sophia Nieves, a 31-year-old Puerto Rican, has accumulated many of these experiences.

Nieves' first internship occurred when she worked on a fashion publication after high school. She gained experience in retail sales at a department store where she later became a department manager, but her interest in journalism took her back to school:

Following two years attending a community college, I enrolled at a four-year school majoring in journalism. I recall that copyediting, although difficult, was one of my most useful classes. The professor, like some of my editors, was very tough and demanding. But she was an excellent instructor and certainly taught me important skills that I have used throughout my career.

Work on the campus daily also was beneficial. As part of my requirements, I completed 15 stories a month and one weekly column. During my junior year, a non-paid internship with a CBS-affiliated station introduced me to electronic journalism. This was an assignment desk internship with some clerical work, some of which related to getting copy to the production room.

An incident at the TV station was a highlight for me at the time as I got to use my Spanish language skills. A news producer could find no one at the station who spoke Spanish, so he asked me to interview a Mexican official for a story. I gathered the information, but someone else wrote the segment.

After her junior year, Nieves won an internship on a large newspaper that earned her some credit toward her major. Part of her pay came from the newspaper and part from a Scripps-Howard scholarship she had won. She wrote for one of the newspaper's zone editions. A number of news and feature stories added some strong pieces to her growing collection of clips. She continues:

I was treated more like a member of the staff at the newspaper internship compared with my time at television stations. I was told that I was replacing reporters on summer vacation. Cooperation on the part of both editors and other reporters in the newsroom helped me to build my confidence. I became more interested in newspaper work.

However, my next two positions were in television. Immediately after graduation, I worked for a Falcon Cable Co. station as an intern. In addition to my reporting and writing assignments for news-type shows for the local community, I was able to produce a weekly magazine interview show. The tasks included establishing a format, writing and handling all the necessary research for the shows.

Next came a real job. It was brought to my attention that the manager of a nearby ABC-affiliated station was looking for a Hispanic woman in the newsroom. Although the pay was not great, I wanted to get some additional television experience, so I accepted the job as a news desk assistant.

Chiefly, I assisted the assignment editor in directing reporters and camera crews to assignments. There was also planning and research to do for the news department. I did not feel that I was able to advance there into any writing positions, so I left. I was also disappointed in the standards of television news, so I looked for newspaper work.

My next job from the summer of 1987 to May of 1988 was with a publishing company operating a number of weeklies. As the news editor of one of the weeklies, I really got to do almost everything necessary to get the paper out. Photography, headline writing, editing, page layout, etc., all tested my skills. I produced some major stories, but there were a lot of city council and school board meetings to cover and write about, too. This was real experience I could not get in college!

Hispanic Link News Service

A handful of reporters working on a very tight budget send out a report each week from Washington, D.C., telling what is happening in Hispanic communities across the country. The Hispanic Link News Service produces three weekly opinion columns in English and Spanish and a weekly newsletter that reaches some 200 newspapers nationwide.

The agency offers unique opportunities to interns. Reporting interns have moved on to top jobs on such prestigious newspapers as the *Miami News,* New York's *Newsday,* the *Hartford Courant,* the *St. Paul Pioneer Press,* and many others. The Gannett Foundation has financed one or two full-time internships each year since 1983. Other non-paid internships also are available from time to time (see Appendix A).

In 1988 Nieves accepted an internship with the Hispanic News Link Service, renting an apartment for her one-year stay in the nation's capital. She also won a fellowship that helped to pay her expenses.

This was my best internship as assignments helped me improve my interviewing and reporting skills. Charlie, my editor, was exacting and always demanding. He made me ask a lot of questions and be well-prepared for my stories. He was the best editor I have met.

A number of news and features were distributed by the service with my bylines. Many stories required a number of sources in various Washington bureaus and agencies. I wrote several guest columns or editorials, such as one explaining the impact of the 1986 Immigration Reform and Control Act.

Nieves' advice to interns is basic: ". . . be well-prepared ahead so that you are ready to apply your good writing and editing skills. Then go for an internship. . . . You will learn reporting first hand as you get acquainted with sources in political, educational and health agencies. If you have good Spanish skills, so much the better. I was not very fluent in Spanish, but I was able to get by."

> *"My advice to interns is simply to be well-prepared ahead so that you are ready to apply your good writing and editing skills."*

Nieves' experience worked to her advantage when she applied for her current job. The Miller Brewing Co. was looking for a person with a strong journalism background to handle media contacts in a specialized market. Now entering her fifth year as a public relations supervisor with increasing responsibilities, Nieves describes her work:

While I needed a journalism background and experience to get this job, I now have staff members working under my supervision who do most of the writing required. I have a lot of details to handle instead.

Each brand has its own public relations/advertising/marketing company, so to speak. Mine is Miller Lite Beer. If a new advertising campaign starts, I have to be involved in several areas. I have to work with the media, including trade magazines, to help put it all together.

One of my assignments is to represent the company in all kinds of public relations situations. For example, about the time that Miller aired a lawyer-bashing scene in a commercial for TV, some San Francisco lawyers were shot and killed. There were a lot of media questions that I had to answer. The commercial was good, but the timing was bad.

More pleasant are my public relations and promotional as well as marketing activities associated with some of the music tours that Miller sponsors. Recently I served on the marketing and PR team that planned some events involving recording star Clint Black, who represents the company.

Traveling is a big part of my work, too. In New York City I assisted an organization in planning the judging and awards presentation for a women's sports journalism awards program. Also, I served as a producer in Mexico City for video news releases for both Spanish and English language media. This event was a soccer match where Miller was one of the sponsors.

Whatever I do, my internships have been most helpful. It's up to the student to watch for opportunities and to take advantage of them. *I know that I would never be where I am today without my internships.*

Internships: The Career Connection

Current Job

KEVIN CORKE, a black sports anchor and reporter, is with TV station KUSA TV-9, an ABC affiliate in Denver. He graduated with a degree in journalism from the University of Colorado, where he completed a credit internship.

Kevin Corke traces his success in broadcast sports directly to his internship. In 1985 he interned in the sports department at KUSA news. Although he was not hired there immediately after his internship, this experience "ignited the fire" in Corke for the broadcast news business.

"This internship really got me excited about television," he says. "I was 19 at the time. It would have been easy to turn me off, but the people at KUSA were very enthusiastic and treated me like a colleague. I couldn't help but catch their enthusiasm. They made me feel like part of their team, especially because they used most of the stories I wrote!"

Supervisor Is an Important Key

Corke credits his internship supervisor as the key to the teamwork that he experienced.

I had a close relationship with my supervisor. We talked. He asked for my input. He would come to me and ask, "What story do you think we should use for the lead tonight?" I'd say, "I think this or that story because of this or that reason." He'd say, "Okay, what do we use to follow that?" I'd say, "How about this or that?" He'd say, "I'm not sure. What do you think about this other idea?" It was this kind of rapport that really hooked me.

He wanted to know what I thought. He asked for my opinion. I'm sure he already knew what he wanted before he came to me, but the fact that he took the time to consult me meant a lot to me. It really made me feel like a valued part of the news team.

Corke believes that trust in interns is the key to a good site supervisor. When a supervisor entrusts an intern with specific responsibilities that are necessary for the news operation, that intern becomes a productive member of the news team.

My supervisor would come to me and say, "I'm giving you this responsibility. I'm counting on you. I don't expect to have to put out a lot of fires. Are you up for it?" Of course, I'd say "Sure!"

I believe interns *want* this kind of pressure: It lets them know they are taken seriously and motivates them to get the job done. When you are given this kind of responsibility you feel "ownership" in the product. You are not likely to call in sick or not show up. You will be there, contributing to the news operation.

Of course, you have to show your supervisor you are worthy of being trusted. You need to work hard, be on time, not quit until the job is done, know the craft, and learn what is needed to function. Trust works both ways.

Tasks Give Experience

The specific tasks Corke performed during his internship were recording games and logging key plays, writing highlights for the sports anchor and assisting with video editing near the end of his internship. "KUSA is a non-union shop," Corke says, "so I was able to do some video editing that aired. Editing was really a dynamite experience for me. It was great to work the hands-on part of the business." Corke believes that writing was the most valuable of his tasks. Especially gratifying was the fact that the anchor used most of Corke's news copy verbatim. Recording and editing also were very beneficial in broadening his understanding of the entire news process.

Corke is grateful to the internship coordinator at the University of Colorado, Beth Gaeddert, for helping him with this internship. He credits her with being an aggressive coordinator, saying: "She really worked the phones for the students. That's important. Without someone at the university hustling internships, many of the students would miss out on this dynamite experience."

> *"I think any student interested in journalism should do both print and broadcast. We all have ideas of what the other is like, but we need to try each one for ourselves."*

In addition to his internship at KUSA, for which he received college credit, Corke had two other non-credit internships that he got on his own. In 1986 he worked on "The Tom Miller Show" and put together student packages that aired on KCNC TV-4, an NBC affiliate. This is where he did his first "stand-ups" for broadcast. Corke also interned at the Adolph Coors Co., where he wrote for the corporate newspaper.

"My internship at Coors was great because I got to see what writing was like in the corporate environment," Corke says. "It gave me a chance to see if I was in the right field. I learned that this was *not* what I wanted to do, and that's also an important part of interning. I think any student interested in journalism should do both print and broadcast. We all have ideas of what the other is like, but we need to try each one for ourselves."

Career Path

Corke's first "professional gig" after college was at KRDO TV-13, the ABC affiliate in Colorado Springs. There he worked in the tape feed room, recording satellite news feeds. The work was not reporting, the tape operation was rather simple and the pay was relatively low, but the job was a start in the business at a commercial station. Corke comments: "It is critical, if you get a chance, to take a job in commercial television, whatever the job is. *Get the job, any job to get into the business.* That's when you find out about other jobs, and when something up the line becomes available, you're in line to get it."

This advice came true for Corke. After working as a tape operator in Colorado Springs, he moved to Pueblo to take a position as a videographer, or field camera operator, for KRDO's southern bureau. Although he was still not an on-camera reporter, he held a production position in news, moving closer to his goal while gaining valuable experience behind the camera.

From Pueblo, Corke moved back to KRDO in Colorado Springs to work as a videotape editor, after which he was promoted to chief editor. In 1989 Corke took another editing position as a staff editor at KMGH TV-7, a CBS affiliate in Denver. These behind-the-scenes editing positions offered valuable production experience to Corke, and his move to Denver positioned him in a larger market and helped him in networking.

Freelancing Is Important

While Corke was recording, shooting and editing for KRDO, he did some freelance reporting. Because reporting was his goal, he wanted to get as much experience as he could while still working behind the scenes in the field.

"There were no full-time reporting positions available at KRDO," Corke says, "so the people at the station advised me to do some freelancing. I produced some selected packages, such as the 5K and 10K runs on Pike's Peak. I shot my own stand-ups. Even though there was no extra pay for this, it let me try my hand at on-camera, broadcast news reporting. The experience made me sure that this was what I wanted to do."

From KRDO, Corke moved to his current broadcast station, KUSA. Through his networking in Denver, he learned of a reporting position there, and the people at the station remembered him from his internship. He was hired to work an eight-hour day shift, 10 a.m. to 6 p.m. He didn't like the long stretch of hours, but eventually he became a sports anchor-reporter, and he now works a split shift, 4:30 to 8:30 a.m. and 2 to 6 p.m., hours he much prefers.

Role of Education

Corke is also continuing his education, studying for a master's degree in Journalism at the University of Colorado. A graduate degree is not necessary for his employment, but he values education and wants to continue studying in his chosen field. In addition to his research and theory courses, he hopes to take some communications marketing and other business courses to move into management. For those starting communications courses, Corke suggests:

- "Take typing! I know that sounds silly, but it is so basic to reporting. I see interns who can't type, and I wonder about their commitment to a journalism career. You must be able to type.
- "Communications law and policy courses also are important. I plan to take a graduate law course.
- "A history of broadcasting course is also key. You need to be well rounded in the journalism field. You probably won't start out doing on-camera reporting; you need to know about all aspects of the business to land that all-important first job and to do it well."

Corke believes that an internship "is the quickest and smartest way to find out about jobs in the field." When he hears people say there are no jobs in broadcast news, he gets upset and retorts,

There *are* jobs. There is always room for talented people who are willing to work hard. You need to be flexible. You need to be willing to do any job to start out. If that's you, you will get a job of some kind: writing teasers, recording news feeds or something. The important thing is to take the work, whatever it is, and begin to work with people. They will see your interest, and when a higher-level position opens up, you'll be in line for it.

I have helped place six former interns in jobs in five states: one each in Colorado, Iowa, Nebraska and Oklahoma, and two in Wyoming. Friends of mine in these states told me about these jobs, and I recommended former interns of mine who had really impressed me. I was happy to be able to help them get their first paying gigs. These are entry-level jobs in small, "feeder" markets, and from here—if these interns decide this is the career for them—they will move up. They worked hard when they were my interns, and they showed that same ambition in accepting these jobs.

S he Got to Do It All!

Current Job

S ONJA GANTT is a black general assignment reporter and weekend morning anchor at WGN TV-9, Chicago, one of the nation's major independent stations. An internship helped her change career directions from law to broadcast journalism. She is a University of North Carolina graduate.

Sonja Gantt's internship saga is one of a woman who truly valued the practical experience available through internships. She landed her first internship the summer before her freshman year. It was with a law firm because at that time she planned to enter the legal profession. This non-credit internship put her into contact with the community affairs director of Charlotte, N.C. With the director, Gantt served on a committee on teenage pregnancy. The community affairs director introduced her to key people, including some broadcasting professionals who remembered her later when she interned and worked at different TV stations in Charlotte. Because of these contacts, Gantt realized the value of her first internship.

Gantt changed her mind about law and decided to try journalism. She studied both print and broadcast journalism at the University of North Carolina, Chapel Hill. For her next internship she settled on a television station, WSOC, an ABC affiliate in Charlotte.

Gantt found her internship at WSOC to be so valuable that she interned there for all three summers before her senior year. Each intern position was paid. Although Gantt believes that just about any internship can be valuable, she found that being a paid intern seemed to carry more responsibility than being unpaid. She says:

There's greater respect. I found that I was expected to perform as if I were on the regular staff. For example, my supervisor simply assumed that I would meet deadlines with the writing assignments I received just as if I were a reporter.

The station pays its interns, so my boss rightfully made sure the station got its money's worth out of me! I was expected to perform like any employee of the company. I liked that. It gave me a chance to experience the "real world" of broadcast news as a paid worker, and it taught me the seriousness of working hard and completing all assignments on time.

For her first two summers as an intern at WSOC, Gantt worked as a promotional assistant. Her duties included writing "over-credits"—any spoken words for airing, such as "tune in tomorrow"—and other such copy. Before writing the over-credits, she screened the videotapes that were scheduled to be aired the next day and wrote the copy to those programs. In the afternoons she went to the sister radio station of WSOC where she wrote news headlines and teasers that WSOC's television news anchors would read for the radio station.

During her third summer as an intern, Gantt worked in the news department on these principal tasks:

- Wrote voice-overs for the anchors.
- Served as a file librarian to locate video clips and other materials for the newscasts.
- Collected and assembled the wire copy for the news team.
- Shadowed the reporters to observe what they did on assignments.

Each internship was a practical lesson in the operations of television and radio stations. These experiences added up to a real education and preparation for her first job in broadcast news.

That First Job

Gantt's first job was as a general assignment reporter at WBTW, a CBS affiliate in Florence, S.C. She describes her work there:

I was a "one-person band." I shot, wrote, edited and voiced my own news packages. I got to do it all, and the experience was fabulous! I admit, I did not like this at first: It was hard. For example, when I went out to shoot an interview, I had to set up the lights, put the microphone on the person, frame and focus the shot, then leave the camera while I sat down to do the interview and hope the picture and sound came out all right since I couldn't monitor them!

But the experience paid off: I came to understand what each person does on a video crew. For example, I had heard the term "videographer" but didn't understand fully what it meant until my work at WBTW.

I also learned to appreciate the amount of time needed to plan, shoot and edit a story. Today when I work with other crew members, I can work positively with them because I know what their needs are. I know the terminology they use and I know the capabilities and limitations of the equipment they operate. Also, I know how much time they need to complete a project.

I was grateful for the interviewing skills I had learned as an intern at WSOC. Learning to ask the appropriate questions of the person you're interviewing is paramount in the news business. This requires planning: sitting down before you go out, thinking about the topic and why you selected this person to be interviewed, and designing the questions to elicit the information you want.

Interviewing skills must be learned, and an internship is a great place to learn them! By shadowing reporters as an intern I was fairly well-prepared to handle my own interviews as a reporter. Of course, you only get better with practice so I'm still polishing my interviewing technique!

The Career Continues

After two years at WBTW in Florence, Gantt accepted a position as the medical reporter for WBTV, a CBS affiliate in Charlotte. She worked there for three years, then moved to her current assignment at WGN in Chicago where she continues to achieve success as a broadcast journalist.

> *"This ability to write with no wasted words has proved to be very valuable in my career."*

Gantt enthusiastically credits her internships, all three of them, with helping her launch her career.

Perhaps the best learning experience I had was during my third internship at WSOC when I wrote voice-overs. That taught me how crucial it is to write very tightly for broadcast. I had to get across the most important information in 20 seconds, without losing the viewers with too much detail. I learned to weigh every word—to decide if each word was really needed, and if so, if that were the best word. This ability to write with no wasted words has proved to be very valuable in my career.

For example, when I was a medical reporter

at WBTV, I had to weed through the professional jargon of the medical field to report my stories accurately without turning off the audience with too much technical terminology.

Writing Is Important

In addition to her internships, Gantt credits writing courses as being a key to entering the field of journalism.

You should certainly take courses in journalistic writing. These will teach you to structure information and convey it in a simple, straightforward manner that readers can understand. If you plan to work in broadcast journalism, it is also vital that you take radio and TV writing. The style for broadcast is different from the style for print. For example, broadcast writing is less formal than print. You write conversations for the reporters and anchors to deliver to the listeners.

Broadcast stories also are much shorter than print stories so your writing must be very concise. You must be able to get the points across with a minimum of words. Additionally you'll learn that broadcast news is written "to the pictures" in television and "to the sound bites" in radio. This means you write copy around the available footage or sound.

This last point really hit home when I was at WBTV and covered a story about foster parents of children with AIDS. I kept wanting to shoot more but the deadline was approaching. Finally, I just had to go with what I had and write the story to the video that was already shot.

When I reviewed the tape to write my copy, I saw there were some technical problems with the video that made it unusable. So all the time I spent gathering the information went down the drain; the story never aired. I learned that pictures are everything in television news, and the writing must complement the available video. This is one of the characteristics that makes broadcast journalism unique. It is a combination of pictures, sounds and words—each of which is necessary to deliver the news.

I have some friends in broadcast journalism who were English majors in college. They had learned good, basic writing skills, which got them their jobs, but they have told me how different broadcast writing is from the kinds of writing they did in school. Conversational style, cutting unnecessary words for time, writing to pictures and meeting tight deadlines were all skills they had to develop on the job.

Some Advice

Gantt has tips for budding broadcast journalists:

- "Start early in looking for internship sites for interviews. Focus your goals to narrow the number of sites. Then apply well in advance of deadlines.
- "Be open to any assignment. You will not hit the streets as a reporter right away. Volunteer for phones or any work that moves you closer to reporting. Work the wire. Do not consider yourself too good for any job. I had to do mundane tasks on my internships, but I did them and I did them well. This established my commitment as an intern.
- "Learn the importance of time. Everything in broadcasting is timed to the second. You must learn to write and edit stories within tight time constraints. A missed deadline can mean a hole in the newscast where your story was supposed to air. And it could cost you your job.
- "Read a lot. First, read the news: stay current with newspapers, magazines and even the office mail. It's worthwhile to look through the mail for story leads. Second, read literature. Reading is a good release from the daily stress of reporting. You can learn effective writing skills from good authors. Good literature dovetails with good writing. You can pick up some ideas.

Sonja Gantt found internships to be so valuable that she did three of them in broadcast journalism. During her internships she learned every facet of the broadcast news business because she worked in many different areas. Writing for the tight time constraints of television, which requires consideration of each and every word, was one of the most important skills she developed as an intern. Additionally, by shadowing reporters she learned about the day-to-day tasks of the

reporter's job: interviewing, setting up, shooting, editing and meeting deadlines. Her internships proved to be valuable training for her career.

Photojournalism: More Than Aiming a Camera

Current Job

RAY WONG is the systems editor of the *Nashville Tennessean*. He supervises the overall design and format of this daily newspaper. Included in his duties are the operation and upkeep of the computer systems for the paper, both Apple- and IBM-based.

As he earned his bachelor's degree in journalism at Arizona State, Ray Wong landed an internship at the *Philadelphia Inquirer*. For his internship he was a general assignment photographer, one of about 35 photojournalists at the paper. Although Wong did not tap into any minority organizations—such as the Asian American Journalists Association—to locate an internship, he urges students to use any available resources to find good internship sites, including professional organizations for minorities.

Wong later earned a master's degree in photojournalism from the University of Missouri, specializing in picture editing. This education and the experience at his internship prepared him well for his profession.

The *Inquirer* as a guild paper gave me the chance to learn both the opportunities and the limitations of guild requirements. For example, the guild works hard to guarantee work for its members, but that means non-members, such as photo interns, are not allowed to take certain assignments.

I also learned at this internship the importance of meeting deadlines. The newspaper had a very tight printing schedule, and there was no grace period for work that was even a few minutes late!

One helpful aspect of my internship was the size of the newspaper: I was able to work for a large-market publication. This introduced me to the realities of photojournalism in a way that a smaller-market paper might not have.

One story I remember in particular was very demoralizing. The home of a mob family in New Jersey had exploded, killing some of the family members. The photographs from the scene were quite graphic. I came face-to-face with the ethical decisions photographers and photo editors face regarding what is acceptable to print.

From Intern to Picture Editor

After his *Inquirer* internship, Wong accepted a job as one of five picture editors at the *Toronto Star*, Canada's largest newspaper. His portfolio of published news photographs from the *Inquirer* impressed the editors at the *Star*, helping him get the job.

In his new position Wong was responsible for deciding what photos to print. He had prepared for this work during his internship by observing and consulting with *Inquirer* editors, learning the day-to-day decisions picture editors face.

Wong learned about the job in Toronto through some friends in the newspaper industry. "I was hired because of some contacts I had made," Wong says. "Someone who knew me found out about the position at the *Toronto Star* and asked me to apply. *Getting this job showed me just how valuable professional contacts are in this business.* In addition to learning about job opportunities, it's wonderful to have friends I can call for advice. Today I'm in a position to hire people, and I often call my friends for recommendations.

Increasing Responsibilities

Wong left the *Toronto Star* to become the picture editor for the Jackson *Clarion-Ledger* in Mississippi. Wong describes this job as "unique" because of the way his responsibilities evolved there:

My first assignment in Jackson was to establish a new department of photography, which I did. After that, my responsibilities grew into other areas of design, and eventually I was assigned the task of redesigning the entire format of the newspaper. I included much more photography and graphics in the new design to make the paper more visually appealing.

After the new format went on line, I started a separate graphics department to support the more visual look of the paper. This department, which was separate from photography, handled all of the charts and diagrams that accompanied the stories. The *Jackson Daily News* then hired me to work on redesigning that paper, so for a time I was working on both of the major newspapers in Jackson!

Wong applied for, and received, another position, this time at the *Nashville Tennessean*, where he continues to work today. He was hired as the graphics editor, again assuming responsibility for all of the diagrams, charts and figures used to illustrate stories. In 1993 he was promoted to his present position of systems editor, giving him full responsibility for the overall format and look of the paper as well as for the computer systems used in publishing the paper.

Politics in Journalism

Through his years of experience, one issue of working at a newspaper that Wong stresses is the importance of learning, and learning to live with, the "politics of the business." By this, Wong means that the editorial decisions made at every newspaper where he has worked are made with the social agendas of the editors in mind. Wong elaborates:

It shouldn't come as a surprise that editors make their decisions based on their personal political views. This is not necessarily a bad thing: It is unavoidable human nature for people to bring their own biases to their work, even in the supposedly "objective" news business.

The important aspect of politics for new journalists is to evaluate their own beliefs and work ethics in light of the political agenda of the newspaper. If you are comfortable with the political views of the editors where you work, and you can tailor your assignments for that paper, you'll do fine there. If you discover you are uncomfortable at that particular paper, you need to be honest enough with yourself to look for another job at a different paper.

Politics are a part of every news environment. The political agenda of the editors may not affect you at first as you learn the day-to-day routine of the paper, but when that agenda impacts you personally, you will need to evaluate whether or not this paper fits with your own ideas.

> "The important aspect of politics for new journalists is to evaluate their own beliefs and work ethics in light of the political agenda of the newspaper."

Ethics in Journalism

Another aspect of photojournalism that Wong believes is important for all journalists to address is the issue of ethics. He illustrates this with one example:

In photojournalism, nothing is more controversial than dead bodies. Every picture editor asks, "Do we run this or not, and if we do, do we run it on the first page or put it inside?" It's a tough call each time. The editor has to weigh the perceived newsworthiness of the photo, the level of gore, the types of readers the publication has and other factors like that.

I remember one instance in particular. A local commissioner in Pennsylvania had called a press conference, and in front of all the media he stuck a pistol in his mouth and killed himself. There was an abundance of pictures of this suicide. My photo editor at the time could have chosen pictures from any moment—before, during or after the death. There was a great deal of

discussion among the editors over this story.

The picture editor decided the story was absolutely newsworthy and belonged on the front page, but he didn't want to enrage too many readers, so he opted for a front page photo of the politician with the pistol in his mouth *before* he pulled the trigger, followed by a second picture inside that showed the corpse *after* the suicide from an angle that didn't reveal too much blood and brain matter. Even though we did not print the most graphic pictures, we still received quite a number of angry calls and letters, more than we had expected.

And speaking of angry calls and letters, I want to say that I'm often amazed at the hypocrisy of American news readers when it comes to dead bodies. Nothing gets a paper more hate mail or phone calls than corpse pictures. If you show a corpse in America, especially if it's on the front page, the readers will let you know in no uncertain terms how much they despise your choice to exploit the victim for crass commercialism, or to upset their children with explicit photography, or to damage society in some other way.

Pictures of corpses from outside America, though, don't get much hate response. Perhaps the proximity of the death has something to do with it: The closer the corpse is to home the more upset the readers become.

These two important issues, politics and ethics, come together in Wong's own philosophy of which photos to print: "Personally, I'm rather liberal in what I choose to run. If it's a major news story and has a dramatic impact on the way we live our lives, I'll print even a gory photo and risk some angry responses. I believe news is news and 'damn the torpedoes.' But I won't print a shocking photo just for the sake of shocking people."

On the Job Today

Today, Wong no longer makes those daily decisions of what pictures to run. That's the job of a picture editor. As the systems editor for the *Nashville Tennessean*, his day-to-day decisions concern the format and layout of the newspaper and the use of the editorial computer system. But Wong's education and training as a photojournalist, picture editor and graphics editor led him to his current position. A big part of that education and training was his internship as a photojournalist in Philadelphia.

From Cuba to Florida to California

Current Job

JEORDAN LEGON, a Cuban-American, is a general assignment reporter for the *Orange County Register* in California, where he began working as an intern in 1990.

Jeordan Legon traces his love of journalism from elementary school. He moved with his family from Cuba to Miami when he was in the fourth grade. Neither of his parents was a journalist, but he became interested in reporting when, as a sixth-grader, he learned of other elementary school students who were producing their own radio news show:

I was watching TV one evening and saw a report about some students in one of the southern states who had started their own radio station over the loudspeaker in their school. I thought that was a great idea, so I asked my teachers if I could do the same thing at our school.

They agreed, so I started station WROQ. We did live announcements, some packaged reports and played music. I was the station's roving reporter.

Making It Happen

Legon landed his first internship when he was a 15-year-old high school sophomore. He had always admired the *Miami Herald*, and his dream was to work there. One day he went to the personnel office and asked for a job.

His timing was great. He had attended a high school journalism workshop at the University of Miami, so he had some training, and the *Herald* had decided to take on some high school interns. Legon was hired, along with a few carefully selected other students. They began to work on the neighborhood sections of the paper, covering community events. Legon worked at the paper 16 to 24 hours per week while attending high school.

In addition to neighborhood reporting, he performed other tasks, including maintaining the community calendar for the paper, opening mail and entering information in the computer. Soon, Legon wanted more responsibility: "I asked for more reporting assignments and less clerical work. After about six months I finally groveled my way into some additional stories. I was given some religious features and some profiles of people in the community."

The Big Break

Eventually, Legon's "big break" came:

One day I learned about a Cuban woman who was coming to America. Her story was very interesting. Years earlier, she had prepared to leave Cuba with her family on the Mariel Boat Lift. After getting on the boat, someone discovered that she was a doctor, a gynecologist, so she was taken off the boat and forced to stay behind. Her family made it to the U.S. and began saving every penny they could. Now, after seven years, they finally had saved $25,000—enough to buy her freedom.

I asked for the assignment to cover this woman's arrival in Miami, and I got it—at the age of 15! The story ran on the front page: quite a feather in the cap of a teenage reporter, especially since that same day Oliver North admitted to shredding documents! I'm proud to say I still hold the record at the *Miami Herald* for the youngest reporter ever to get a byline on the first page.

From Miami to California

Legon worked at the *Miami Herald* for one year. When he was a junior, his family moved to Stockton, Calif. He worked on his high school newspaper and also did some freelance reporting for Stockton's local newspaper. He was honored as Northern California's High School Journalist of the Year during his senior year in high school.

After high school, Legon attended the University of Southern California (USC) in Los Angeles, where he worked on the *Daily Trojan*, USC's newspaper. He also went to the *Los Angeles Times* to seek out an internship. There, he encountered some resistance to his enthusiasm for work.

"The *Times* was not interested in a college freshman for an internship," Legon says. "I was told to slow down, chill out, take it easy. No one understood, or appreciated, how badly I wanted to work there. The whole initial experience was rather depressing."

Legon did manage to get an internship at the *Modesto Bee*. He was assigned clerical work rather than reporting and writing, but he was happy to have the job. He discussed his desire to get some reporting assignments with his supervisor, and for the last six weeks of his internship he was able to write for the features and metro sections of the paper.

"I really enjoyed the *Modesto Bee*," Legon remembers. "It had the feeling of small town journalism. The paper was family-owned, and the atmosphere in the office was like a family. I got to know everyone quite well and I was made to feel like one of them. This internship was a nice contrast to my internship at the *Miami Herald*."

Internships Continue

In the spring of 1990 Legon finally found work at the *Los Angeles Times*. Because of his persistence, his demonstrated skills as a reporter and his ability to read, write and speak both Spanish and English, he was given the opportunity to write some articles for "Nuestro Tiempo," a bilingual section of the paper. He also applied for an internship at the *Orange County Register*, a

large newspaper south of Los Angeles, and was selected as one of only eight students to intern there that summer. Legon describes the experience:

After I had been there a few weeks, the Metro reporter for the city of Placentia left, and I was asked to fill in. I was miserable at first because I wanted to be in the newsroom, not in a small bureau office.

That summer the Nixon Library opened in the neighboring city of Yorba Linda. I covered and interviewed some of the major players from the Nixon administration, including John Dean, Alexander Haig and H. R. Haldeman. That was a great experience!

I was also given the freedom to develop my own ideas. One issue that particularly interested me was the plight of the migrant workers in Orange County. I was able to do a story on that. So the summer turned out to be one of the most wonderful internships I had!

After the summer internship ended, Legon continued to work part time, mostly on the weekends, for the *Register*.

From California to Boston

The following summer, 1991, Legon learned from some professional contacts about an opportunity to intern at the *Boston Globe*. He had been planning to spend his summer at the *Orange County Register* again, but his supervisors encouraged him to go to Boston to broaden his experiences. It was a difficult summer for Legon.

I found that East Coast journalism is radically different from West Coast journalism. There is a definite East Coast bias: an unstated assumption that news about people who are most like the editors is more important than news about other people. This bothered me.

Boston has a reputation of being a wonderful mecca of liberal thought, so I was really excited about going there at first. But once I got there, I found that many of the people are actually quite bigoted in their daily lives. The city is very divided along the lines of race and social class.

In particular, the editorial staff of the *Globe*

practically ignored the African-American and poor sections of the city: They didn't put many resources—specifically reporters and money—into those areas. They seemed most interested in covering wealthy, Anglo news. I definitely did not "click" with this bias. I enjoyed the history and architecture of the city, but I was greatly dismayed at the appalling divisions among races and classes of people, both in the city and at the paper. I gained some good newsroom experience and got some good clips, but it was a very hard summer for me emotionally.

Back to Orange County

After returning from Boston, Legon went to work full time as a general assignment reporter for the *Orange County Register*, the position he holds today. Interestingly, he has not yet finished his college degree at USC. With his determination, he was able to make doors open and find employment in his chosen career without a university diploma. He hopes to finish his degree, but neither he nor his family can afford it at the moment. He plans to apply for fellowships to complete his studies, and if that proves unsuccessful, he will have to wait until he has saved enough money to finish his schooling.

Road to Success

Finding work as a journalist without a university degree didn't just happen to Legon. Here are the keys he credits with having led him to success:

> "Dogged determination is necessary in this field. If you just sit back waiting for opportunities to come to you, they never will."

■ "I was really determined to get any work experience I could find in journalism, paid or not. Dogged determination is necessary in this field. If you just sit back waiting for opportunities to come to you, they never will. I made a lot of phone calls, knocked on a lot of doors, and visited a lot of offices in order to get the internships I did.

■ "Internships themselves are important to launch a successful career. The practical training and experience is simply invaluable when a student applies for a 'real' job.

■ "It is also important to become a member of whatever journalism organizations you can. *Networking is a key.* I learned about some of my career opportunities through networking. I'm a member of several journalistic organizations: the Hispanic Journalists Association, the Chicano News Media Association (through which I got my initial contact with the *Orange County Register*) and I'm a board member of the Press Club of Orange County and of the Southern California National Lesbian and Gay Journalists Association."

H is Internship Launched a Career

Current Job

IAN KAWATA, a Japanese-American, is a freelance art director preparing print advertisements for two corporations that distribute and sell multimedia computer products in the San Francisco Bay area. He also does some freelance video work for a small production company.

Every day Ian Kawata uses skills that he learned as an intern. In 1992 he read an article in the *L.A. Business Journal* about an innovative program called the Minority Advertising Training Program, or MAT. This program places 30 interns per session in 14-week-long internships in advertising agencies throughout Southern California. Those interns are chosen out of about 250 applicants. Kawata decided to apply.

MAT is sponsored by the Chiat/Day advertising agency in conjunction with the West Coast Advertising Association. Each MAT intern is asked if he or she prefers an internship that emphasizes the creative side or the account side of the business.

The internship supervisors are instructed to give the interns a well-rounded experience in both creative and account work, but some of the agencies emphasize one more than the other. MAT attempts to match each intern with a location that best fits his or her goals.

The interns are given specialized training, such as creative writing seminars, scripting workshops, field trips and the like. There are also social mixers with the students and the agencies to enhance networking among industry professionals and future employees.

Beyond these opportunities, the students work at the agencies and learn the business "hands-on." The internship sites are expected to treat the interns as professionals, giving them real creative or account assignments. The pay is about $250 per week.

To be selected as a MAT intern, each applicant must demonstrate strong potential based on his or her résumé and portfolio. Applicants must go through two separate interviews, each with a different panel member. Each panel member then nominates his or her top two choices from all the applicants interviewed, and the candidates with the top 30 scores are chosen.

Successful Candidate

Kawata had the second highest score in his MAT class. He was placed with the Kresser Craig agency, where he was given an overview of the account side of the business and a heavier emphasis on the creative. He worked primarily in the broadcast production department helping to produce commercials, most of them for the agency's largest client, Clothestime. He was an assistant producer.

The experience and knowledge he gained was so valuable that Kawata considered applying for a second term with MAT, which interns are allowed to do, but he decided against this because he didn't want to take away a spot from another applicant who could also benefit from a MAT internship.

When his internship ended, Kawata continued to work for Kresser Craig as an independent contractor, serving as a freelance assistant producer for its commercials. He hoped for a staff position to become available, but that didn't happen. He was growing tired of living in Los Angeles, so in July of 1993 he moved north to the Bay Area. In San Francisco, Kawata became a freelance video producer and director, work he had done before his MAT internship.

As a college student in Long Beach during the late 1980s, Kawata studied video production. On his own, he shopped around for a television internship and found one at NBCTV in Burbank. He worked in on-air promotions, the NBC department that produces all of the spots for upcoming programs.

A typical spot shows a few highlights from an episode of a program, and a voice-over teases the audience to watch that show. Kawata observed the producers as they took an idea from concept through completion, and he also worked with scheduling, billing, dubbing, trafficking and setting up satellite feeds. In short, he learned a tremendous amount about television from this internship.

This internship, coupled with his college work in video production, qualified him for a production job when he graduated. Kawata, employed by Corporate Video and Film in Newport Beach, worked as a camera operator, director and producer of corporate videos. They were primarily sales, training and trade show projects.

In 1991, Kawata's supervisor left Corporate Video to start his own multimedia company called McKnight Visual. His supervisor hired Kawata to produce and direct for him.

> *"If you want creative control [in advertising], take design courses in school."*

After moving to the San Francisco area, Kawata continued to do some producing and directing for McKnight Visual and continues to freelance for this company today. His current project is shooting video for Bio-medic, a McKnight client.

Career Plans

Kawata plans to stay in advertising but would like some new challenges. He enjoys the independence of freelancing, but he would also like the security of daily employment. Ideally, he would like to work for a small, hot, creative shop, or start his own agency one day that does both print and film/video ads. In his present position Kawata finds it difficult to get full creative control over his projects. He explains:

I've learned in this business that once a person is channeled into the broadcast production side, as I was, it's very difficult to get promoted to a position with full creative power. The people with creative control in advertising tend to come from graphic design backgrounds. Typically, they begin working in design, then move to assistant art director, then art director, and finally creative director. In production, people tend to hit the ceiling as directors or producers, which means they have control over the "look" of a spot and have some input on the concept, but they do not have the final say for the concept. That is given to the art director or creative director.

This is frustrating for me. I've learned the graphics side of the business through my internships and work with art directors, but because I came from a broadcast production background, I'm not seen as a likely candidate for art director or creative director. That's why I'd like to work in a small shop, or start my own, so I can apply all of the design experience I have gained over the years and have creative control for the concepts of the ads I generate.

Some Advice

With his wide array of experiences, Kawata has some advice for future advertising professionals:

- "If you want creative control, take design courses in school. If I had my education to do over again, that's one of the areas I would have included. This would have helped me develop a portfolio as a creative person, and that would have complemented my production portfolio. Personally, I would still major in production because I really enjoy that, but I would have rounded out my education in art and graphic design.
- "I would also have started earlier to seek out internships, and I would have done more of them. Internships are the key to getting into the industry because of the practical experience and networking they offer.
- "It is also vital that interns be open-minded. You don't always get to do exactly what you want to do, but you need to do it anyway. That establishes you as a team player with a strong work ethic. Of course, you should let your supervisor know what you would like to do. Your supervisor won't know if you don't tell him or her! Then, when an opportunity comes along that you would like, your supervisor may give it to you. Be responsible with all your assignments, but don't simply be complacent about tasks you don't want to do.

Conclusion

These profiles of eight successful communications professionals show that some of their experiences are common whereas others are unique to individual situations. This demonstrates that there is no one path to career success. Each person charts his or her own course through school, internships, other work experiences and job opportunities. Whatever course you choose, one or more internships will be a very important—and perhaps even a necessary—part of the path you make for yourself as you move toward success in your professional career.

For Thought and Discussion

1. In several instances, some of the professionals told how they stayed abreast of developments and opportunities in communications. Discuss at least three examples of what these people did to keep current.

2. Discuss three of the jobs, either full- or part-time, held by the professionals on their way up the career ladder. Tell why you're attracted to each job.

3. Give three examples of "management tasks" from the current jobs of any of the professionals to show the level of responsibility they have in their positions.

4. Assume that you are the person who hired McKean for her position at Cathay Pacific. What do you think was the one principal strength of her experiences, her résumé and her background that stood out? Why was it so important?

5. What do you think are the most important threads of activities or experiences that weave through these stories that point to successful career outcomes?

6. Writing skills seem to be important to each professional. Give at least a half-dozen examples from the chapter that directly illustrate experiences that improved their writing.

Sources for Internship Leads

Academy of Television Arts & Sciences
5220 Lankershim Blvd.
North Hollywood, CA 91601

The Academy of Television Arts & Sciences' Student Internship Program is designed to give college undergraduate and graduate students in-depth exposure to professional facilities, techniques and practices during an eight-week summer period in Los Angeles. Twenty-eight internships are offered in 24 areas of the television industry. They are: Agency, Animation, Art Direction, Broadcast Advertising & Promotion, Business Affairs, Casting, Children's Programming/Development, Cinematography, Commercials, Daytime Programming, Development, Entertainment News, Episodic Series, Editing, Movies for Television, Music, Network Programming Management, Production Management, Public Relations & Publicity, Sound, Television Directing (single-camera film), Television Directing (multi-camera film/videotape), Television Scriptwriting and Videotape Post Production.

Hosts in each category are working professionals who agree to take one intern for the eight-week summer session. Interns work a 40-hour week. The Academy pays a stipend of $1,600 plus a $300 travel allowance if the intern lives outside Los Angeles county. It's a very competitive program with more than 800 applicants from all 50 states. Information on the program is available in University Career Placement centers and radio/TV/film departments in January each year. You must have one of their yearly updated flyers to apply. The deadline is March 31.

American Advertising Federation (AAF)
Coordinator of Educational Services
1101 Vermont Ave. NW, Suite 500
Washington, DC 20005
Phone: 1-800-999-2231

The AAF publishes a directory from information submitted by club and corporate members. The annual publication is $10 for non-members and $8 for members. Paid and unpaid internships are listed, but some states have few listings. Internships are mostly in advertising or marketing, with fewer numbers in television, radio and journalism. As a student you may write or call for a free "Careers in Advertising" guide.

American Business Press Association
Phyllis Reed, Director of Intern Program
675 Third Ave.
New York, NY 10017-5704
Phone: (212) 661-6360

These are paid summer editorial internships on trade magazines and the business press nationwide. Juniors, non-graduating seniors and graduate students in journalism, communications and technical writing can get applications in October. Faculty can write for additional information.

American Society of Magazine Editors
919 Third Ave.
New York, NY 10022
Phone: (212) 752-0055

141

A 10-week internship program begins each summer with an orientation in June. Interns are assigned to consumer and trade magazines, mostly in the New York area. Each magazine pays a stipend of about $300 per week. Applications are given out by deans and directors of schools of journalism and communications and in career offices of liberal arts colleges. Only one application from each university or college is accepted. Candidates must have some newspaper experience, either on or off campus, to be eligible. Most candidates meet this requirement by working on their college newspapers.

Direct Marketing Educational Foundation
6 East 43rd St.
New York, NY 10017

This foundation does not have internships at present but publishes and circulates a directory of available paid and unpaid internships across the country. You can write to the above address for a free copy. You should have an interest in marketing. Most internships are for eight to 10 weeks in the summer. They are open to juniors, seniors and graduate students not returning to school in the fall. The Women's Direct Response Group sponsors the directory.

Editing Intern Program for College Juniors, Seniors and Graduate Students
The Dow Jones Newspaper Fund
P.O. Box 300
Princeton, NJ 08543-0300
Phone: (609) 452-2820

Up to 50 summer internships will be offered to college juniors, seniors and graduate students to work as copy editors at daily newspapers. All interns will attend a two-week pre-internship training program (paid for by the Newspaper Fund and participating newspapers) before beginning work. Interns are paid regular wages by the newspapers for which they work and receive a scholarship at the end of the summer to apply toward their following year in college. Students returning to undergraduate or graduate studies will receive a $1,000 scholarship. This program is open to minority and non-minority students at the time they apply. Applications are available only from September 1 through November 1. Application deadline is November 15.

Entertainment Employment Journal
7095 Hollywood Blvd., No. 815
Hollywood, CA 90028
Phone: (213) 969-8500

This is a twice-a-month publication that includes a number of full-time jobs in the film and television industries. Some internships are listed. Two special issues (February and September) at $10 each including postage feature internships with those seeking interns listed in Hollywood, New York, and various locations of cable stations. For orders: 1-800-335-4335. Six-month subscription is $60.

The Harris Internship in Television Production
WTTW/Channel 11
5400 North St. Louis Ave.
Chicago, IL 60625

This public television station in Chicago offers two one-year internships in television production each year. You must be a graduating senior or possess a bachelor's degree in any major. Previous television production experience is desirable. Pay comparable to entry-level salaries is arranged through a grant-in-aid. The internship runs from September 1 to August 31. Applications are available in December and are due back by a February deadline. Write for more information.

The Institute on Political Journalism
Larry Guillemette, Director
The Fund for American Studies
1526 18th St. NW
Washington, DC 20077-6098
Phone: (202) 986-0384

This program is a combination of study

and internship from early June to late August each summer. Six units of college credit are awarded. It is open to sophomores or juniors only. You need not be a journalism major, but clips from your campus newspaper are required. You must have a 3.0 GPA, and you can apply for numerous scholarships. Deadline each year is in March. The two courses—Economics and Public Policy, and Ethics and the Media—accompany the 30-hour internship, which is on a major Washington newspaper, magazine, broadcasting station, network, etc. Tuition is $2100 plus $775 for housing. Only 60 students are accepted.

International Association of Business Communicators (IABC)
One Hallidie Plaza, Suite 600
San Francisco, CA 94102-2818

Some career information is available. There is a job referral service for professionals. Students interested in internships or jobs should contact their local IABC chapter. There is a $25 fee for membership, with national plus local chapter dues.

Journalist's Road to Success
The Dow Jones Newspaper Fund
P.O. Box 300
Princeton, NJ 08543-0300

Published annually, this guide includes information on job opportunities, how to get scholarships and where to prepare for journalism study. $3 a copy.

National Council on U.S.–Arab Relations
1140 Connecticut Ave. NW, Suite 1210
Washington, DC 20036
Phone: (202) 293-0801

The council sponsors the Joe Alex Morris Jr. Journalism Internship Program, which provides for approximately six summer and fall internships for journalism graduates. Interns work with English-language newspapers and magazines in various host countries including Egypt, Jordan, Saudia Arabia and Kuwait. The three-month internships pay a housing and living stipend and round-trip airfare from Washington or New York. Call for a brochure. Applications are available in the fall semester.

National Press Photographers Association
3200 Croasdaile Dr., Suite 306
Durham, NC 27705

The association publishes an annual internship guide for photojournalism students. Daily and weekly newspapers are listed. Most of the internships are paid. Write for an application for student membership ($30 a year) or professional membership ($55 a year).

Public Broadcasting Service
System EEO Support
901 E St., NW
Washington, DC 20004

Although there are no specific internships at this office, you can write in March each year for a free internship guide listing PBS stations with internships available throughout the country for the following summer. For information on the Employment Outreach Project's Talent Bank, a service of the Corporation for Public Broadcasting, call (202) 879-9600. This is for people seeking careers only in public broadcasting.

Public Relations Society of America
33 Irving Place
New York, NY 10003
Phone: (212) 995-2230

Internship assistance is provided to members through local chapters. Several scholarship programs are open to members only. Information is available through student chapters. Membership is $38 a year for college students, who can join only when there is a student chapter at their schools. Two $1,500 Multicultural Scholarships are open each year (deadline in spring) for any junior, or higher, student with a 3.0 GPA. Write for information.

Pulliam Journalism Fellowships
Russ Pulliam, Director
The Indianapolis News
307 North Pennsylvania St.
Indianapolis, IN 46204
Phone: (317) 633-1240

Twenty internships on newspapers in Indianapolis and Phoenix for 10-week summer period. Stipends in 1994 were $4,000. Must be a top graduating senior interested in an editorial career on a newspaper. Previous internships, college newspaper experience and good writing samples are more important than actual major. Write or call for application in January. Deadline is March 1.

The Society of Newspaper Design Foundation (SND)
Box 4075
Reston, VA 22091

SND compiles and publishes as an internship project a listing of available internships each year. The newspapers are arranged by states and include a few international newspapers seeking interns. You must have good graphics/layout/design skills although any major is acceptable. Both paid and unpaid internships during all semesters are included. Write for more information.

Society of Professional Journalists (SPJ)
P.O. Box 77
Greencastle, IN 46135
Phone: (317) 653-3333

An internship directory listing newspaper and broadcasting internships in journalism is published annually. Cost is $10 plus $2 postage. Internships are listed by states, with information and salary and qualifications. The organization's Foundation sponsors a Project Sunshine internship for an incoming senior or graduate student and two Pulliam/Kilgore internships for spring semester or summer. The 10-week First Amendment internship is for graduate students in journalism or law with some FOI activities. Write for application details and also for information on a high school essay program.

United States Olympic Committee
Coordinator of Educational Programs
1 Olympic Plaza
Colorado Springs, CO 80909
Phone: (719) 632-5551

Five to 10 journalism students are accepted each semester for internships in the information/media division of the U.S. Olympic Committee. This is a full-time program with all meals and lodging provided plus a stipend equivalent to minimum pay. You must have strong writing skills and basic computer skills. You must be an undergraduate (at least two years of college are required) or graduate student. The summer terms run from June through August. Write for more information and an application.

Women in Communications, Inc. (WICI)
3717 Columbia Pike, Suite 310
Arlington, VA 22204
Phone: (703) 920-5555

Unpaid internships are offered from time to time at WICI headquarters. It is best for students to contact local WICI chapters for internships in specific regions.

Minority Opportunities

American Association of Advertising Agencies (AAAA)
Minority Advertising Intern Program
666 Third Ave.
New York, NY 10017
Phone: (212) 682-2500

Designed to give minority students (applicants must be returning to school in fall) a realistic view of advertising, the program is open to any major who has completed the junior year in college. It is from June through August, with application deadline the preceding January. Contact the association for application.

The summer internships pay about $350 a week, depending on the agency. Major agencies participating are in New York, Chicago or Los Angeles. Allowances are granted for both 60 percent of housing costs and 60 percent of one round trip from the student's home and internship site. About 25 percent of students have accepted positions with advertising agencies, and many others have taken related jobs with advertisers or media.

Asian American Journalists Association
1765 Sutter St., Room 1000
San Francisco, CA 94115
Phone: (415) 346-2051

$1,000 scholarships are available to high school seniors. Call the above number for an application. Deadline is usually in early April. The association also publishes a quarterly newsletter and a job hotline and publication that lists a number of internships throughout the country. A student membership is $12.

The Associated Press
Summer Minority Internship Program
Jack Stokes, Director of Recruiting
50 Rockefeller Plaza
New York, NY 10020

Each summer about 15 to 17 minority students are placed for a 13-week period in internships in AP bureaus throughout the country. These are reporting internships for juniors, seniors and graduate students with some experience and good academic records. Write for an application. Deadline for applying is in February.

Chicago Sun-Times
Tom Sheridan, Assistant to the Editor
401 N. Wabash Ave.
Chicago, IL 60611
Phone: (312) 321-3100

One $1,500 scholarship is awarded annually to any qualified minority student entering his or her junior year. You must have an interest in print journalism. A paid summer internship will follow, if a "B" average is maintained. The deadline is in May. Write to the above address for more details.

Hallmark Minority Scholarship/Internship Program
Hallmark Cards, Inc.
P.O. Box 419580
Kansas City, MO 64141-6580
Phone: (816) 274-8511

Designed to assist talented minority students in the visual arts and advertising/editing writing communication arts, the program has two awards: (1) a $4,000 scholarship for the senior year of school and (2) a paid summer internship at Hallmark in Kansas City. Pay is $395 a week, subsidized housing is available, and the company pays round-trip airfare. You must be a junior (second semester before the internship) with a 3.0 major GPA and a 2.5 overall GPA. Your major does not have to be journalism, but you need some writing/editing background. Clips may accompany your application due each March 1. Write to the above address for more details and an application available each November.

Hispanic Link News Service, Inc.
1420 N St. NW, Suite 101
Washington, DC 20005
Phone: (202) 234-0280

Hispanic Link publishes a weekly report of news items of interest to the Hispanic community. From time to time, unpaid internships and some work-study programs are available. Spring is the best time to apply.

Knight-Ridder Minority Training Program
Arlene Morgan, Senior Editor
The *Philadelphia Inquirer*
P.O. Box 8263
Philadelphia, PA 19101

Four minority entry-level journalists who are interested in specialized fields of reporting or editing will be selected for two years of training at entry-level salaries of the host newspaper. You must be interested in one of the following areas: medical/science, legal affairs/courts, business, features/criticism reporting, graphics or news editing. You must have a minimum of one professional newspaper internship, have a college degree and make a two-year commitment to Knight-Ridder. The deadline each year is usually in December. Write the above address for more information.

In addition, some individual Knight-Ridder newspapers offer summer minority training programs. These are for 10 weeks or longer. Deadlines for the following summer are usually in December. For example, the *Philadelphia Inquirer* has had a couple of openings in photo and reporting in recent summers plus a minority copyediting internship. Pay is Guild minimum. Applicants must be returning to school in the fall. No graduating seniors are accepted. Contact individual newspapers for more information.

Minority Editorial Training Program (METPRO)
METPRO Reporting Director
Los Angeles Times
Times Mirror Square
Los Angeles, CA 90053
Phone: 1-800-283-NEWS, Ext. 74487

An intensive two-year career-entry program for minority journalists. Reporting and photography trainees receive 11 months of full-time instruction and employment along with a regular stipend, paid housing and utilities; medical insurance is available after three months. Applications are available in September with a January 1 deadline. The program begins each June. For information about METPRO/Editing write: METPRO/Editing Director, Newsday, 235 Pinelawn Rd., Melville, NY 11747. A college degree is preferred for both programs. In addition, the *Los Angeles Times* operates reporting, editing, photojournalism and infographics internships for college students during spring, summer and fall semesters. Call the above number for application material.

National Association of Black Journalists
P.O. Box 4222
Reston, VA 22091
Phone: (703) 648-1270

Paid journalism internships are available in print and broadcasting starting in July. Student membership, $20 per year; professional, $60. Applicants must be full-time students in communications or journalism. Write for internship (by November 1) or membership application. A job hotline is available for members only.

National Association of Hispanic Journalists
National Press Building, Suite 1193
Washington, DC 20045
Phone: (202) 662-7145

There is a paid, one-year, full-time journalism internship available for a student or graduate to work on the *Hispanic Link Weekly Report*. Inquire about starting date, which varies. Pay has been $17,500 including benefits and travel allowance. In addition, the association has a nationwide job placement and internship referral service for members only. Student membership is $15 a year; professional, $35. Internships are mostly print and mostly unpaid.

Native American Journalists Association
1433 East Franklin Ave., Suite 11
Minneapolis, MN 55404

Two or four (depending on funding) paid summer internships are offered to Native Americans each year. These print and photojournalism internships are arranged in conjunction with Newhouse Newspapers. Preference is given to placing students in a region near home. Apply through the association by March 1.

Newspaper Association of America Foundation
Summer Residency Program
11600 Sunrise Valley Dr.
Reston, VA 22091
Phone: (703) 648-1053

Information is available on newspaper internships and summer seminars. Write in January of each year for the following summer's list of participating newspapers.

Newspapers, Diversity & You
The Dow Jones Newspaper Fund
P.O. Box 300
Princeton, NJ 08543-0300
Phone: 1-800-DOW-FUND

This is a special guide for minority journalism students co-sponsored by a number of professional organizations. Included is career information, jobs and salary report, and listings of internships by news organizations. Write for a free copy.

Radio-Television News Directors Foundation
1000 Connecticut Ave. NW, Suite 615
Washington, DC 20036

The foundation offers scholarships and internships. Three six-month internships (approximately $1200 per month) are for any minority graduates in an electronic journalism sequence from an accredited university program. Also, three summer internships for three months with a television or radio station near your home are underwritten. These are for students interested in broadcast management. Several minority student scholarships (open to sophomores, juniors or seniors fully enrolled in college) are available. Write the above address for information and applications. Deadlines are usually around March 1. (Note: Another association, The National Association of Broadcasters, does not publish any internship guides but assists professionals with job placement.)

Books and Directories

A number of books that will help you in the process of searching for an internship are available in career sections of bookstores. Some have pointers on writing résumés, creating cover letters and responding to interview questions. Here are a few directories and books of interest to students, professors and employers or site supervisors.

America's Top 100 Internships
Mark Oldman and Samer Hamadeh
New York: Villard Books, 1993

Internships in a variety of fields are evaluated through interviews with former interns and other sources. Many take students with any major. Communications organizations included are the *Washington Post, Rolling Stone, Spy,* the *Wall Street Journal,* MTV:Music Television, Backer Spielvogel Bates, National Public Radio, Hill, Holliday, Connors, Cosmopulos Advertising and Ruder-Finn.

Bob Adams Resume Almanac
Holbrook, Mass.: Bob Adams, Inc., 1994.

Approximately 600 résumés are listed. There is a chapter on communications résumés and résumés for special situations. Tips are included for recent high school graduates preparing résumés, as well as for college graduates. Samples are included of cover, follow-up and thank-you letters.

Broadcasting & Cable Yearbook
New Providence, NJ: R.R. Bowker, published yearly

A complete listing of all television, radio and cable stations throughout the country. In addition to complete addresses, the directory has many contact sources for internship inquiries. This directory is available in many libraries. Addresses of networks such as ABC and CNN are included.

Career Directory Series
Gale Research Co.
P.O. Box 71701
Chicago, IL 60694-1701
Phone: 1-800-877-4253

A series of six directories for newspapers, advertising, marketing, public relations, magazines and book publishing are updated every two or three years. Includes sections on jobs and internships. For example, the 1993-94 newspaper directory has a section on available internships plus comprehensive information on the industry written by publishers and editors. Each soft-cover volume is $17.95. Call for more information.

Careers in Communications (1994)
Shonan F. R. Noronha
VGM Career Horizons
NTC Publishing Group
4255 West Touhy Avenue
Lincolnwood, IL 60646-1975

A discussion of careers in journalism, photography, radio, television, film, multimedia, public relations and advertising. Valuable job search resources, including appendices on trade associations, publications and directories are listed.

The College Student's Resume Guide
Kim Marino
Berkeley: Ten Speed Press, 1992

This book is all about résumés and cover letters relevant to those being prepared in communications.

Directory of Internship/Placement Coordinators
Beth Gaeddert and Don Heider
School of Journalism and Mass Communication
University of Colorado
Campus Box 287
Boulder, CO 80309-0287

Arranged by states, this new directory includes faculty coordinators, their addresses and phone numbers in journalism and communications programs in colleges and universities throughout the country. Write for a copy.

The Experienced Hand: A Student Manual for Making the Most of an Internship
National Society for Experiential Education
3509 Haworth Dr., Suite 207
Raleigh, NC 27609

The book has sample learning contracts, résumés, letters, etc. It has information on various steps to search for an internship and is helpful for those who must arrange their own internships. Write for current price or check your library.

Great Careers: The Fourth of July Guide to Careers, Internships and Volunteer Opportunities in the Nonprofit Sector (1990)
Devon Cottrell Smith, editor
Garrett Park Press
P.O. Box 190B
Garrett Park, MD 20896

More than 37 of the 48 contributors to this 600-page book are career planning and placement professionals working at universities and colleges across the country. The book includes a number of leads on internship directories, career books, job information, nonprofit organizations, international internships, etc.

Inland Press Association
777 Busse Highway
Park Ridge, IL
Phone: (708) 696-1140

An internship directory is published annually in the fall. There are usually 75 to 100 daily and weekly newspaper and photojournalism internships listed, both paid and unpaid. The directory is free.

The Internship Experience
Lynne Schafer Gross
Prospect Heights, Ill.: Waveland Press, Inc., 1987

This book was prepared as a practical guide to aid students seeking internships in radio, television, film and broadcast journalism. It serves three audiences: students just starting out to interview for an internship, faculty interested in setting up programs and companies wishing to consider establishing internships. A valuable appendix section for faculty coordinators contains forms, contracts, applications and other materials. Also, information from several schools shows course requirements.

Internships in the Communication Arts and Sciences
Susan A. Hellweg and Raymond L. Falcione
Scottsdale, Ariz.: Gorsuch Scarisbrick Publishers, 1985

Detailing the steps of finding and completing an internship, the book is of interest to students and faculty. Sample application, agreement and evaluation forms should be noted by faculty coordinators.

The National Directory of Internships
National Society for Experiential Education
3509 Haworth Dr., Suite 207
Raleigh, NC 27609
Phone: (919) 787-3263

The 600-page directory published biannually lists thousands of internship opportunities by field of interest, location and name of sponsor. Under communications are a number of newspapers, television stations, publishing companies and public relations and advertising agencies. Many PR internships are also listed under arts, consumer affairs and other titles. Mail a check for $26.50 (includes postage) to the above address for the 1993 edition.

Internships 1995
Peterson's Guides
P.O. Box 2123
Princeton, NJ 08543-2123
Phone: 1-800-338-3282
Updated annually in November, this is a big directory of 1,700 organizations with internships available in various fields. Both paid and unpaid internships are included. Has communication section with sites in advertising, broadcasting, journalism, public relations, film and book publishing. Cost for the 1994 edition is $29.95.

Resumes That Get Jobs
Jean Reed
New York: Prentice-Hall (an Arco Book), 1994 (7th ed.)
Some good advice on improving your résumé. Included are very detailed cover letter strategies.

Southern Newspaper Publishers Association (SNPA)
Information Department
P.O. Box 28875
Atlanta, GA 30358

Publishes annual directory each October. For a copy mail $2 to the above address. Internships in almost all southern states are included with both large and small newspapers. Circulation of each paper and time (mostly summer) when internships are available are listed. Mostly editorial and photo internships are listed, but a few papers offer advertising internships.

The Student Guide to Mass Media Internships **(1993)**
Ronald Claxton, Editor
Journalism Department, Eastern Illinois University
Charleston, IL 61920
Formerly published annually, this guide is appearing again after an absence of several years. Volume 1 (print) includes internship opportunities on daily and weekly newspapers by states. A second book covers radio and television and some cable internships. It is the best directory for newspapers. Most print internships are paid. Cost of each volume (prepaid) is $35.

Internships Rank High

These excerpts are from Louis Gwin, "Prospective Reporters Face Writing/Editing Tests At Many Dailies," *Newspaper Research Journal* 9 (Winter 1988): 101-11. (Reprinted with permission of *Newspaper Research Journal*.)

This national study confirms a trend that daily newspapers are using writing and editing tests to evaluate prospective reporters. It finds that nearly 45 percent of responding newspapers administer such tests and that the likelihood of testing decreases as circulation size increases. Those managing editors who do test consider test results a key factor in reaching a hiring decision on both experienced and inexperienced candidates for reporting jobs.

The overall rankings of hiring factors do not offer any major surprises except in the relatively high ranking for "internship" for both experienced and inexperienced candidates, indicating that managing editors regard internships as a key factor in evaluating whether to hire a reporter, regardless of his or her experience.

Tips for Photo Interns

Following are excerpts from a column with tips to photo interns from two veteran photographers supervising interns on two large daily newspapers. Their comments were published in a newsletter. Reprinted with permission from the National Press Photographers Association.

First, check carefully on spelling and grammar. Misspelled words in caption information, a resume, or a letter usually eliminate a candidate. If you cannot take the time to check spelling in something as important as a job application, you probably will not be careful enough in handling caption information.

Next, I'm becoming more concerned with slide portfolios. It's very difficult to tell if a student knows how to process film and make prints from a slide. I would like to see a few prints included in the portfolio. Nothing fancy, just a few 8'10s.

How a person dresses is important. An intern should dress appropriately for the job. We are, after all, professionals and it's important that we project that image in the field and in our newsrooms.

If applicants want to know if a portfolio has reached its destination, then I suggest that they include a self-addressed postcard for an editor to return. Don't drive me nuts with phone calls.

Students should plan to subscribe to the newspaper for about a month before they actually show up for work. The responsibility of getting a subscription is theirs. We send the newspaper to our intern, but many newspapers don't. Students should call the circulation department themselves if a subscription isn't offered.

Come prepared to work. Leave your boyfriends and girlfriends at home. Don't abuse company phones. Be responsible with meeting deadlines and taking care of equipment. Take advantage of the opportunity, not advantage of the company.

Finally, don't apply to a newspaper that's going to be over your level of experience and talent. An internship is supposed to be a learning experience. Even if you're lucky and get the internship, you could spend the summer mixing chemicals when they find you can't carry your own weight.

* * * *

When you put together a portfolio, think of it as a sample of your personal vision. Sure, it's important to show that you're proficient at setting up lights or shooting high school football at night, but the portfolio that draws my interest reveals something about the person who made the photographs. I'd rather not see another car wreck recorded in an attempt to fulfill some sort of breaking news hole in a portfolio.

From my own experience of being an intern as well as supervising interns, I think pacing is important. You're here for three months and you can't burn out in the first six weeks. That means taking time for dinner occasionally. Maintaining your energy level helps your ability to photograph at a high level of concentration when you're on deadline.

Professionalism can't be emphasized enough. That includes spelling names correctly in cutlines, not wrecking staff cars unless it's absolutely unavoidable and being open to critiques from well-intentioned picture editors who've been in the business a while longer than you.

If you don't know, don't be afraid to ask.

Sample Test Questions

The following examples of test questions were taken from exercises prepared by newspapers, public relations firms and various organizations. The examples change each year, but the format remains about the same. These are the kinds of questions for which to prepare if you are required to take a writing test as part of the interview process for a newspaper, magazine or PR internship.

Part 1 — SPELLING If a word is spelled correctly, do nothing. If it is spelled incorrectly, write the correct spelling on the line to the right.

---

1. teamstor _____

2. appleate _____

3. liason _____

4. limousine _____

5. politicking _____

6. privilige _____

7. academys _____

8. vacume _____

9. gague _____

10. naval orange _____

Part 2 — GRAMMAR AND WORD USAGE There are four underlined words or phrases in the sentences below. If you find any error, find the number beneath that error and write the number in the blank at the left side of the page. Then write the correct usage below that number. If you find no error in the sentence, write a "5" in the answer blank.

Error Number ____

Correction _____

1. On <u>any</u> given day, a newspaper <u>throws away</u> almost as
        1   2
    many <u>stories</u> as <u>they use</u>. <u>No error</u>.
              3   4   5

Error Number ____

Correction _____

2. He <u>went</u> to the opera <u>since</u> he <u>was offered</u> <u>a lot</u> of
         1   2   3   4
    money to write a review. <u>No error</u>.
                                 5

Error Number ____

Correction _____

3. The police officer <u>took</u> a <u>hands-off</u> position when the
                        1   2
    reporter asked why no one <u>would issue</u> a statement after
                                    3
    media <u>were</u> barred from the accident scene. <u>No error</u>.
          4   5

Error Number ____   4. <u>Everybody</u> <u>but</u> George and Sue <u>decided</u> <u>to enter</u> the
                              1   2   3   4

Correction _____   writing contest. <u>No error</u>.
                                                   5

Error Number ____   5. <u>Each</u> one of the students in the <u>class</u> <u>hope</u> for a passing
                          1   2   3

Correction _____   grade on the test the professor <u>gave</u>. <u>No error</u>.
                                                    4   5

Part 3 — VOCABULARY   Circle the best definition:

1. ravenous: ferocious / famished / exhausted / delighted

2. motley: dirty / multicolored / dull / unusual

3. vociferous: talkative / demanding / noisy / strident

4. vague: unknown / incorrect / imprecise / inadequate

5. to transfix: to surprise / to make motionless / to change / to make useless

6. to disperse: to scatter / to pay / to ignore / to reward

7. to entreat: to delay / to oblige / to suggest / to implore

8. transcend: bypass / surround / surpass / overlook

9. capricious: good-humored / erratic / stubborn / extravagant

10. ingenious: resourceful / dishonest / curious / naive

Part 4 — USAGE   Correct each sentence:

1. Two homes in the fire's path were rendered totally destroyed, and three others were

   partially demolished.

   _____

2. The suspect alluded police pursuit over the weekend, a police spokesman said, but the

   search will continue this week.

   _____

3. The union has demanded that wages be increased by 10 percent, and a reduction in mandatory overtime.

_____

4. Attendance was scarce at the first annual city-sponsored Food Fest Sunday.

_____

5. Despite claims that it's design made it the most unique theatre in Hollywood, the 70-year-old building was razed to the ground to make room for a parking garage.

_____

Part 5 — PUBLIC RELATIONS WRITING   If the sentence is correct, do nothing. If there is any kind of spelling, punctuation, grammar or word usage error, circle the incorrect material and write the correction in the blank.

---

1. Jones, who is building the shopping center adjacent to the new theater, owns some housing tracks in the area.

_____

2. Winner of a new design award, the complex accomodates about 300 patrons in each of its ten theaters.

_____

3. The sight of the new staidium is just east of the shopping center.

_____

4. Under terms of the agreement, Sanbar receives exclusive marketing rights of the product in select markets in all of North America and South America accepting Brazil and Peru.

_____

5. The USTR Telex Board which enables the microcomputer to be used as both a transmission and reception Telex station, thereby replacing the need for a separate Telex machine.

Part 6 — LEAD WRITING   Type a three-sentence news story for tomorrow morning's Newark, Del., newspaper. The time now is 11:45 p.m., and your deadline is midnight. You have already made all of the necessary phone calls to gather the information below, and you must go ahead and write the story, even though the prime suspect has not been caught.

Source: Delaware state police.

What: Woman shot by .357-caliber revolver and pronounced dead on arrival at Dover General Hospital.

Dead: Jane Williams, twenty-eight years of age, from Philadelphia, PA. She was wife of Arthur Williams. The couple lived in Dover, Delaware.

Place of shooting: The couple's home.

Time of shooting: Twenty minutes past eight in the evening.

Other times: Police arrived at house at eight thirty. Ambulance arrived two minutes later. Ambulance arrived at hospital at 8 fifty-five.

Prime suspect: Fred Johnson, who lives in Wilmington, Delaware. He was Jane's first husband. Police are searching for him at deadline.

Witness: Arthur Williams of 23 Front St., Dover, Delaware. He was married to Jane only one week before shooting. He told this reporter over the phone that Fred was drunk when he smashed in the bedroom window and crawled through, shouting nasty words at Jane. Arthur said Fred's actions prove he is, to quote Arthur, "a nasty man."

APPENDIX B

Introduction to Faculty

Materials and guidelines in the chapters and appendices of this book can assist faculty in coordinating an internship program. Interested faculty can become involved in several ways: A faculty member can start out with a few interns; faculty can give half time or more to coordinate a number of interns from several sequences; or faculty can teach a seminar or class for interns.

A starting point is to review the basic facts of what an accrediting council (the Accrediting Council on Education in Journalism and Mass Communications) says about internships (see page 160). Note the implications of these words: "carefully monitored," "supervised experience," "formally structured and supervised program," and "faculty visits to the site of the work."

Also review information presented on two programs in this appendix. The first, of a Midwestern program, shows prerequisites, application procedures, credit requirements and evaluations useful for a small to medium-sized program. The second at Fullerton is a model for a large program. Many topics discussed, such as pay, timing of internships and alumni connections, are explored in chapters and other appendices.

John De Mott wrote guidelines for initiating or revising university journalism internship programs in a manual published in 1981 (*A Manual for Journalism School Administrators*, published by the American Newspaper Publishers Association Foundation). His recommendations (see excerpts on page 169) are still relevant and useful to any professor starting a program in journalism or communications. As Prof. De Mott points out, there is no typical or "best" program among colleges for a model. Many factors are at play at each university.

If you are interested in getting a program underway, you need to accomplish three basic tasks:

1. *Determine objectives and the basic design for an internship program at the outset.* In building a program one must consider a number of issues and questions: Will interns be working full time, part time or both? Who will be eligible? Can sites be developed nearby? Which sequences and faculty will be involved? What will be the policy on pay and credit?

There are many other questions to consider. Some answers may appear in the WICI and the advertising surveys showing current practices and recommendations. For more answers check your campus internship or cooperative education office or those working with business or education majors in similar programs. Or write to the National Society of Experiential Education for information on starting a program (see address in Appendix A).

2. *Design some kind of contract form or "learning agreement" to show the responsibilities of the employer, university and intern* (see examples page 174).

3. *Draw from job descriptions models of achievable objectives for interns to reach.* Faculty coordinators must take the lead and

158

assist employers and site supervisors new to a program to formulate work assignments based on objectives. Many site supervisors have very good intentions. They sincerely want to train interns. But for many reasons, they may require assistance in designing specific work assignments for interns.

A few models are easy to outline. You can ask a photo intern to produce a half dozen feature photos and give him or her tips on where to go. Asking an advertising intern to handle various media tasks for an agency requires more-detailed statements.

It's true that many internships are similar to entry-level positions and are unfairly loaded with routine clerical chores. A bal-ance can be developed by adding significant assignments, projects and portfolio products to be produced. Some basic objectives as part of the job description can help. Examples can assist supervisors in creating these (some pointers are listed on page 173 and in Chapter 2).

A class or seminar concurrently with or after internships are completed can add an attractive component to the program. Credit can be given for the combination of internship and class attendance. Through this course students can build a bridge from their internships to career planning by discussing their experiences and reporting their work.

Accrediting Council Rules

For faculty starting internship programs in journalism and communications, these statements from the Accrediting Council on Education in Journalism and Mass Communications (ACEJMC) explain the current guidelines. Credit and supervision requirements should be noted.

Internships/Work Experience

Quality experience in journalism and mass communications should be encouraged. Academic credit may be awarded only for carefully monitored and supervised experience in fields related to journalism and mass communications. Academic credit may be awarded for internships in fields related to journalism and mass communications, but should not exceed one semester course (or its equivalent) if the internship is away from the institution and, for the most part, supervised by media professionals rather than academics.

Schools may have up to two semester courses (or their equivalent) at an appropriate professional organization where the institution can show ongoing and extensive dual supervision by the institution's faculty and professionals. Schools may have up to three semester courses (or their equivalent) at a professional media outlet owned and operated by the school where full-time faculty are in charge and where the primary function of the media is to instruct students.

Explanation

Journalism and mass communications internships, practicums and student publications can add a significant and realistic component to a student's education. Innovative programs in this area of the curriculum are encouraged. Many schools allow academic credit for work on campus student or quasi-professional publications. To ensure fairness, faculty also can craft equally outstanding academic experiences at cooperating professional media.

For that reason, the focus is on internships not in isolation, but in the larger framework of how they contribute to the quality of the education that students possess when they reach graduation. When academic credit is awarded for such experiences, the unit should develop a formally structured and supervised program monitored by a regular member of the academic staff.

Supervision should include consultation with the organization or business offering the internship or practicum, specification of the duties to be undertaken, regular reports from a designated supervisor at the employing firm and from the student, and faculty visits to the site of the work. When students receive academic credit for student publication work, that work should be under the direct supervision of a regular member of the academic staff.

Evidence

a. The structure and supervision of work experience programs as described in the self-study report and interviews with students, faculty and cooperating employers.

b. Student interviews about the quality of their work experience.

c. Credit for work experience on official student transcripts, whether the credit is given by the unit or by any other department of the university.

Two Programs

The two examples of internship programs below will provide some guidelines for assisting faculty coordinators and administrators as well as employers and site supervisors in setting up internship programs. The first description of a Midwestern university program is part of the accreditation self-study material prepared before an accreditation visit to this campus by an ACEJMC team. By request, the school is not identified. The second at California State University, Fullerton, is outlined in these excerpts from a 30-page manual that includes the history and development of the program. Limited space here permits only some highlights. The manual was originally prepared for faculty coordinators in various Fullerton departments under a grant from the University Internship Center. In their last two visits to Fullerton, members of the accreditation teams said that the program should be a model for large programs, particularly because of the large alumni participation. A copy of the manual can be ordered from the author.

A Midwestern University Program

Journalism 400, Media Internship, is described in the catalog as "application of classroom knowledge and skills in supervised mass media activities at internship sites approved in advance by the Department of Journalism." Journalism 400 has five prerequisites. The student

1. must be a journalism major or minor
2. must have achieved junior standing
3. must have a grade of C or better in qualifying classes designated within department sequences
4. must have completed pre-intern orientation
5. must be approved by the department.

Site locations are developed by mail survey, phone calls and personal contacts. Sometimes a student, through personal initiative, will develop an internship. However, the site still must receive departmental approval. Work site supervisors are identified, and a description of the duties of interns must be submitted.

A three-person departmental committee representing each of the sequences (news editorial/print, broadcast news and advertising) reviews qualifications and screens applicants. Particular attention is paid to journalism courses taken by the student applicant. One faculty member serves as Intern Coordinator. The qualifying courses are:

Intern Area	Required	Recommended
Advertising	Advertising Copywriting	Advertising Layout
News/Print	News Reporting	News Editing
Radio News	Broadcast News Reporting	
TV News	Radio-TV News Editing	

Of course, all applicants would have completed Mass Media Writing and Visual Communication just to enter the sequence courses listed above, and many will have taken Introduction to Photography, the department's most popular elective course. A rare exception to the requirements for qualifying course work may be made for a student with related professional experience.

The department does not have a public relations sequence but gets requests from employers and students to administer PR internships. This usually requires one or more of the above courses plus one of the department's three PR courses.

In addition to listing qualifications, applying students also must prepare a brief essay discussing why they believe an internship would be valuable. The essay also gives reviewers an example of the student's writing ability.

A student whose application is successful becomes eligible for an approved internship. This may put the student into competition with other qualified classmates. Some internship providers hope for a good field of candidates, believing that the interview process is valuable in itself. At other times, our candidates are in competition with students from other colleges and universities.

Once selected by the employer, a student must complete at least 80 hours at the work site for one credit, 160 hours for two credits and 240 hours for three credits. (A student may have more than one internship but may accumulate no more than three credits.)

The student must keep a diary of daily work-related activities, write an essay on strengths and weaknesses of the internship and submit work samples to the faculty person serving as Intern Coordinator.

A public presentation during which the intern discusses experiences at the work site completes the requirements. This presentation is made at an informal buffet dinner sponsored by the campus chapter of the Society of Professional Journalists. All students are invited and attendance is mandatory for those participating in the department's intern program because hearing the presentations is a part of both pre-intern orientation and post-intern debriefing. Interns enjoy hearing about one another's experiences, and younger students are inspired to try for their own internships.

A faculty member receives a part-time summer teaching appointment and a modest travel budget to visit interns and internship sites that may be at some distance from campus including other states. During the fall and spring semesters, interns are usually much closer to campus, which permits visits by the faculty coordinator during school days. A report is prepared by the faculty visitor following each visit.

Internship supervisors and interns are questioned jointly and separately. Any problems are resolved on the spot. For example, at an advertising agency a student was found to be doing too much clerical work and too little creative. This was pointed out to the work site supervisor, and a change was made in the student's assignment. At a newspaper, a student was doing only feature stories but no hard news. The faculty coordinator discussed this with the work site supervisor, and a change in assignment was made.

Two evaluations are prepared by the intern's on-site supervisor. The first report, at the midpoint of the internship, is given to the student to help correct performance flaws and provide direction. The second evaluation summarizes the intern's performance and is mailed to the faculty coordinator. The contents of this evaluation are discussed privately with the intern.

This second evaluation is influential in determining the student's grade. Also considered in determining the grade are the quality of the work samples and the intern's essay on the strengths and weaknesses of the internship. The essay is evaluated on both content and writing quality.

Most of the interns enrolled during regular semesters serve their internships in this city or nearby communities. These sites may be continuing opportunities; for example, a hospital or radio station will take one or more interns every semester and in the summer sessions. These repeat sites are well-known to the faculty, and the student interns are on campus daily. If any problems develop, a call or visit may be made to the work supervisor, or a call may be received from the work supervisor.

The Program at California State, Fullerton

THREE FACTORS FOR SUCCESS

An internship program in communications at Cal State Fullerton is a natural because of the huge media and communications market in Southern California and the numerous available sites for interns 45 miles away in Los Angeles and Hollywood. Also, the department's phenomenal growth in the '70s and '80s guaranteed increasingly large numbers of interns. The internship program, established when the bachelor's degree was approved more than 30 years ago, requires a mandatory internship from all majors.

These three factors also can be said to have played a major role in the program's success:

1. A large enrollment of interns in the summer session. All students pay tuition, which has permitted a budget to hire faculty coordinators. Summer enrollment has reached 175 to 200, frequently exceeding fall or spring numbers.

2. The advantages of increasing alumni participation in the program has greatly aided new site development and even financial support for interns.

3. Close attention to changing employment trends in communications has resulted in more development of advertising, public relations and marketing internships. This comes at a time when both advertising and public relations enrollments have increased. The number of journalism majors has decreased, so more newspaper sites were not needed.

The summer has numerous advantages. Many companies budget for summer interns. Opportunities for pay are better in the summer. Many companies are willing to underwrite a scholarship to pay the $300 to $450 summer tuition fees for an intern. Students can arrange internship schedules without the conflict of classes, often a disadvantage in spring or summer semesters. More hours may be available to spend at the site.

Probably a chief advantage for students interning in the summer has been the greater employment possibilities. With all graduation requirements out of the way, students are free to concentrate on an internship of 25, 30 or 40 hours a week. If their work performance is good, a full-time job might follow the internship. A University Summer Sessions study in 1985, looking at communications graduates completing summer internships, found that in the advertising sequence 53 percent or 24 interns obtained full- or part-time jobs at their sites. (A small number returning to school in the fall accepted part-time employment.) It was a 36 percent placement for public relations interns and 35 percent for those in journalism. Because of a number of factors, including recession periods, the percentages have dropped considerably in the early '90s.

A full-time faculty member and a part-time assistant, a former newspaper editor, direct the program. Clerical support includes an excellent four-fifths–time secretary and student and graduate assistants. This office also handles functions related to job placement of graduates. Summer tuition supports the hiring of two, three or four (depending on enrollment) regular faculty members to work part time several months in the summer visiting with internship site supervisors.

The program benefits from this summer faculty support. Sites are scattered over a wide area of the Los Angeles market, so it is difficult for regular faculty coordinators, who need to be in the office several hours a day for conferences with students, to make these trips. The part-time coordinators arrange a schedule to visit a number of sites in a day. In addition to contacting the intern's supervisor for an on-site visit, the part-time coordinator also meets other company personnel and human resource people to see if additional internship sites can be arranged.

All of the part-time faculty seemed to enjoy the experience. In addition to representing the department well, the coordinators became more supportive of the intern program after meeting and talking with interns and their supervisors. They are assigned by sequence so that, for example, a journalism professor would visit a newspaper. Most visit 40 to 50 sites in one summer.

It should be pointed out that none of

the extra staffing and clerical support would be possible without the internship class offering academic credit. Many state universities and colleges support cooperative education and internships through staffing formulas based to a large extent on enrollment numbers. Even if numbers are small, particularly when an internship program is first underway, some teaching units should be awarded to show department or school support for the program.

A second factor in Fullerton's success is the participation and strong support from students and alumni. The internship class has ranked as the number one course in popularity in all alumni surveys. Many alumni feel an obligation to help the department and the school, especially those faculty members who have earlier helped them find internships and job leads. Many alumni are site supervisors.

In addition, some alumni regularly send leads for sites to the faculty coordinators. These may be difficult-to-reach companies not normally participating in intern programs. Or alumni sometimes help students locate places to intern in other markets.

The employment outlook, a third success factor, requires checking trends for numbers of majors and graduates, requests from sites for special skills and discovering new companies and new organizations willing to participate in the program.

Placing journalism majors into non-newspaper sites such as magazines, publications and technical writing and editing positions has become more important. Many area newspapers, hit hard by the recession in 1990, dropped paid internships.

Advertising seems to gain the most from the accrediting process. Many major Los Angeles advertising agencies—the first of which was Foote, Cone & Belding—have accepted only Fullerton interns because they favor an accredited program that provides credit to interns. And Fullerton is the only ACEJMC-accredited advertising program in Southern California.

SUPERVISION IS IMPORTANT

Site supervisors are the people responsible for assigning an intern tasks, checking to be sure that he or she does them and then working closely with the school in evaluating the intern's progress. It is useful to focus briefly on supervision since this can make or break an internship for a student. There are at least three ways that an employee of a company or organization ends up in the role of working with an intern.

■ In the first place, a company may decide to offer internships in specific areas of the company's workforce, and usually someone in a department is appointed as a supervisor. This person could be a volunteer, but more often a person is asked to take charge of an intern or two. This may work well. But frequently the new supervisor may have an already heavy workload and only a limited amount of time to devote to the intern. In some cases, the overburdened supervisor may get other employees to assign the intern work from time to time. Since the latter situation can lead to a need for more work for the intern and/or a complete lack of supervision, a better policy is to have one person responsible for the intern's supervision and assignments.

■ A second and more successful route toward good supervision occurs when a company employee volunteers and approaches his or her manager with the idea of using the skills of an intern. This person may be someone interested in teaching or working with students. The idea of contracting for an intern may have come from a fellow worker or someone at a similar company. Or perhaps a contact from a nearby college has suggested the possibility.

The person who volunteers should have a workload that would allow him or her to carve out sufficient time to monitor an intern. Especially in the beginning the intern may require more time to ask questions, to clarify assignments and to learn some of the company's procedures and work rules.

Some highly qualified interns may take charge of assignments and produce quality work at once. Others may require more supervision and direction and take longer to adapt to the demands of the workplace. Good supervisors can map out a plan of work adjusted to the differing entry-level skills and work habits of interns.

- A third way to get site supervisors is through your own school's alumni. This has been most effective at Fullerton in attracting supervisors for communications interns. Participating in the program is a way of paying back the university for past favors. Some alumni have been active in the program for many years, taking responsibility for an intern almost every semester. In fact, in some semesters close to two-thirds of the supervisors either have been Fullerton alumni or have been referred to the intern program by an alum. This keeps them in touch with the department and the university.

Graduates of the department can become excellent role models. They are familiar with the internship requirements and know that they should assign meaningful work. They understand what the coordinators expect in terms of work samples and projects. Their background prepares them to do a good selling job to their managers and supervisors on the overall value of internships and how the company benefits from working with students at a local university.

Fullerton has been able to put a touch of frosting on the internship cake through receptions for many of these alumni as well as others who supervise interns. This idea was developed years ago, but serious budget problems, which have also affected site visits, have eliminated such events for now. Once a year an afternoon wine and cheese reception can be held with invitations to most of those who presently or have recently worked with interns. Some interns can assist in planning. For some supervisors this may be their first contact with the university and the department. It is valuable for them to see the facilities of the department as well as meet some of the faculty, also invited. Funding for such receptions has been through department and university funds.

Screening Applicants

For a large program such as Fullerton's, a formal application form is necessary. In fact, a number of forms are required to handle the numbers of students enrolled.

Students apply at different times of the year. Many change from one semester to another before completing the requirement. In a program in which most of the majors eventually will need an internship, it is necessary to carefully screen applicants after they submit applications to see if they are qualified to proceed.

Some students complete two or three non-credit internships, hopefully moving into more responsible and valuable experiences each time. The internship office assists in these placements. By the time students are ready for a credit internship they have work experience that may be very relevant and useful.

A majority of faculty participate in the screenings. Often high recommendations by faculty may help interns get into more competitive sites. Some students may be disqualified on the basis of poor faculty recommendations. Screening is necessary in a large program to identify and advise those who represent poor performance risks.

At Fullerton, students must submit a résumé with their application. The screening process takes place three times a year prior to the semesters of the student's actual internship. Applications are requested at orientation although provision is made for those who apply late for approved reasons.

When the faculty are screening at the bottom of the academic ladder, marginal students may get the green or red light based on how they are doing in skills classes. Faculty comments are important. Some recommendations or approvals may be conditioned on interns being restricted to less-demanding sites.

If a student has a 2.0 GPA on a four-point scale or is below 2.0 and is on probation, an alternative course to the internship is required. As long as the student is on probation, he or she is automatically rejected. The alternative course is arranged by the student's adviser.

A number of students with low GPAs have outside work experience and can become excellent interns. Perhaps they are working too much outside of school to concentrate on their academic work. Thus, grades are low. Some faculty want to raise admission requirements so that only those with a major GPA of 3.0 are eligible. This change would eliminate some successful interns. The point is that relevant work experience seems to be an important criterion for internship success.

Studies of those 10 to 15 percent who get "poor" or "very poor" evaluations from site supervisors show that they are from scattered grade point ranges. Some of the high-GPA students have little or no work experience and are simply very shy and nonproductive under work conditions. The outstanding success rate of some of those with lower GPAs and work experience would seem to indicate that many factors enter into screening applicants. An application form may help in this process.

After the prospective interns attend orientation, screening is completed. Letters of acceptance and rejection are mailed to interns applying for the following semester. It is important that they get notification well in advance of the internship semester so that they can apply for interviews or make other plans to take an alternate class.

As the Los Angeles/Hollywood/Southern California market is one of the largest media markets, communications internship opportunities are numerous. There is competition among several schools with communications programs. Some good sites may have dozens of applicants. A key to Fullerton's success

has been to get faculty coordinators to speak individually with prospective interns immediately after the approval process. It may take too much time for many outstanding intern applicants to uncover opportunities. Thus, the process often works along these lines. Companies will call, seeking interns. A faculty coordinator will select a number of the top candidates from each sequence. Selection is made on the basis of faculty recommendations, work experience, skills, computer knowledge, résumé, GPA, etc. Calls are made and information given to the students about opportunities. Students are told how to apply. Some sites want students to call immediately for an appointment; others request cover letters and résumés so they can collect a number for review by the people interviewing prospective interns.

A Directory Helps

Because of the large numbers of students involved, the campus bookstore publishes a directory of internship sites every September. Formerly, each of the five sequences had their own small directories. For the past seven years, the one directory has been enlarged to include the more than 600 sites in the program plus detailed information and forms necessary to acquaint students with the program.

Students purchase a copy of the latest directory for the orientation meeting. The program is completely explained in the directory. All rules and procedures to obtain an internship are detailed, and samples of necessary forms and requirements are included. The directory lists the sites alphabetically by the name of the company. Sites include a sequence designation although many sites take interns from several sequences. A brief job description follows each listing.

The key to the use of the directory is a large file of sites available in the university library's reserve book room. Students are able to check out for library use only a limited number of files at a time.

The directory saves much faculty time in answering questions. Late applicants or students who miss orientation can get up to speed by reading sections of the directory dealing with requirements for credit. Freshmen and sophomores may use the directory to find out how to get a non-credit internship. The information in the directory matches up with a site's file in the library. By the way, files are updated periodically.

Orientation Answers Questions

Orientation meetings scheduled three times a year are held by the internship coordinators primarily to answer student questions. The meetings run about 50 minutes each. Of that time, about 25 minutes is spent answering specific questions from those in attendance and in describing some sample sites.

Although time is limited, some special sites may be discussed at orientation. An example would be to help a journalism major looking for a public relations site. Or a broadcast journalism major, with a couple of internships already completed, may be searching for cable sites where reporting/anchoring experiences may be possible. Some similar sounding sites may have very different requirements as well as expectations.

These are the four requirements for the program:

- Register for credit (Communications 439) and attend orientation.
- Complete 150 hours at a site, evidenced by report forms every other week signed by the site supervisor.
- Prepare two copies of a final report following a form in the directory. One copy will go to the reserve book room of the university library for future interns to review, and one copy goes into the intern's file in the internship office.
- Schedule a final conference with a faculty coordinator. This 15- to 20-minute meeting allows the student to discuss thoroughly the experiences and the site. Any problems encountered by the intern affecting future interns should be explored. The evaluation form, also in the directory, is completed by the site supervisor and may be on hand for the coordinator to discuss with the intern.

Sites, Interviewing and Visitation

In a program with a large number of interns each semester, it is necessary for prospective interns to set up several interviews. Similarly, many sites want to interview numerous candidates before making a selection.

The pressure is more likely to be on the student than on the site. At Fullerton interns have a deadline to obtain a site (usually June 1 in summer). If they cannot get acceptance at a site by the deadline, they are automatically moved to the next semester.

Follow-up studies show that Fullerton graduates rate as one of the most important characteristics of the program the opportunity to get interviewing experience for an internship at several potential sites. Some say they gain much confidence after two or three interviews and believe this experience prepares them well for later job interviews. Some report as many as 10 or 12 interviews.

A site report form is filled out when the intern accepts a site's offer. This form shows where the intern interviewed and the results of the contacts. When they accept a site, students are encouraged to promptly notify other sites where they may be waiting to hear about an offer. This may enable another Fullerton student to move up in the selection process, and it shows that the student is caring and responsible. Later, a verification form showing the site and supervisor's name and phone number and other details is mailed to the internship office for the student's file. All forms are the responsibility of the student intern, not the site.

Sometimes as high as 30 percent of the interns in a semester will be in sites not in the program directory the previous semester. These new sites come chiefly from three sources: one-time-only sites from students for the semester, leads from the University Internship Office, and sites that are either new to the program or that have been unable to employ an intern for several semesters or years. In the first two categories, some sites may join the directory, especially if a visit is made.

Fullerton is unique among Southern California universities in scheduling its site visitation to meet with supervisors of interns. As mentioned earlier, many of these visits are accomplished in the summer when additional department faculty join the internship program for this specific purpose.

Since Southern California is a very large and scattered media market, sites to be visited need to be organized by areas for more economical site visit time and travel.

Although sometimes difficult to schedule, meetings between a faculty coordinator and the site supervisor are usually successful. The company's representative appreciates the university connection to the program. The meeting includes a discussion of the intern-

ship program and any concerns expressed about the job description and/or the intern's progress. Often a tour of the facilities and especially the work station of the intern are arranged.

Visits generally are not planned until about a third of the way into the semester so that the intern and site supervisor have had time to get acquainted and adjust to a regular schedule. Coordinators in a number of departments applaud the site visit, especially when the intern can be included in the meeting with the supervisor. Often the intern will show marked improvement after the visit and will ask the supervisor for more assignments.

The best part of site visitations are those contacts with alumni of the university who serve as site supervisors. Many alumni continue as site supervisors for years. They are very successful in locating new sites, not only in their own company or organization but also where they may have friends working. Since most are aware of the goals and requirements of the program, they are very conscientious supervisors. Some increase their interest in the university by joining the alumni association or taking part in school advisory committees.

A Manual for Administrators

The excerpts are from the manual edited by John De Mott mentioned on page 158. This manual is useful for faculty starting a new intern program or revising an existing one. Although prepared for journalism departments and schools, recommendations can apply to any communications internship with an agency, company or organization. (Reprinted with permission of the Newspaper of America Foundation, Reston, Va. Originally published in 1981 by the American Newspaper Publishers Association Foundation.)

Developing and Conducting Internships

Regardless of a journalism school's approach to internships, those developing a new program or conducting an established program need to:

1. Focus the faculty's interest on a proposed internship program, articulating its objectives; obtain approval for the program and determine its relationship to the curriculum.

2. Draft a proposal for newspapers whose cooperation is to be sought.

3. Mobilize support from alumni in the field.

4. Educate everyone involved on how the program works.

5. Inform prospective participants among the area's newspapers, prospective interns and others about the program.

6. Organize to recruit prospective interns.

7. Establish guidelines for selecting interns.

8. Develop criteria for evaluating performance of interns.

9. Devise ways to obtain effective feedback from interns.

10. Publicize program's success as means of building support for continuing growth.

11. Execute a written agreement between the student and university (with courtesy copy to the newspaper) to spell out rules and guidelines for length of internship, type of work, etc. The contract will not be binding on the newspaper, but will make clear the general agreements.

12. Review the program periodically.

Program Objectives

The overriding objective of any internship program is to improve the professional skills of the intern. To achieve that goal, however, many other objectives must be considered and, whenever possible, satisfied. Take a look at them from the perspective of the three parties involved:

For the newspaper:

■ Support and contribute to the education of future journalists.
■ Give newspaper managers a look at prospective employees.

The intern looks at an internship as a way to:

■ Improve skills learned in the classroom.
■ Learn what it's like in the "real world."
■ Speed apprenticeship.
■ Open the door to a job.

The educator views the internship as a:

■ Lab to supplement teaching.
■ Device for getting feedback about students and the quality of teaching.
■ Way to maintain relations with the newspaper business.
■ Way to find jobs for graduates.
■ Way to expand/improve curriculum.

Measuring Objectives

An effective internship program, new or established, provides criteria for measuring how well the program fulfills its objectives. There are questions that should be asked routinely during the procedures adopted for selecting interns, monitoring their work and determining their grades. While grades are not given to the employer and the educator, the procedures established for conducting the internship should ensure that questions concerning their performance are answered satisfactorily.

The newspaper's (employer's) role can be assessed by asking:

- Are you providing instruction or otherwise contributing to the growth of the intern?
- Are interns being given real work to do?
- Are interns given the same work and responsibilities as regular staffers?
- Are some interns good enough to earn a place on the staff? Should you be making plans for his or her future employment?

To assess the intern's performance ask:

- Are you applying yourself?
- Are you using the experience to learn?
- Are you developing and sharpening skills, knowledge and professionalism?

Educators should be asked:

- Are you in control of the program?
- Are you evaluating internships on a regular basis and making use of the feedback?
- Are you communicating with the employers and interns?
- Are you acting to maintain standards?

These questions must be asked regularly. They must be asked by the intern, the employer and, most importantly, by the person who controls the program, the educator.

Full-Time and Half-Time Programs

There are two recommended program designs. The first is a full-time eight-week internship during the summer. The other allows half-time work for a full semester during the academic year. Both offer advantages over other fragmented programs.

- They allow time for the student to get involved in a full range of newspaper activities.
- They result in the student being given some kind of substantial work assignment.
- They provide an opportunity for the socialization process of the newspaper to affect the student.
- They give the student a real opportunity to improve skills on a continuing basis.
- They give the student enough time to confirm, question or dismiss the idea of a career as a newspaper journalist.

These program designs allow enough time to arrange some kind of job rotation to allow students to explore their aptitudes and interests to help them find their niche. One arrangement that has worked well is to have the intern have one job each week for the first half of the program, then a permanent assignment for the second half. This will give enough variety to permit the student to experience several kinds of work and enough consistency to allow the employer to realize some benefits as well.

Accrediting

As mentioned in the above, the Accrediting Council on Education in Journalism and Mass Communications has adopted the following guidelines concerning credit for internships: "No more than 10 percent of a student's journalism and mass communications credit should be earned through such internships. Work on student media may be defined as an internship."

The latter are sometimes ignored or overlooked as sources for journalism internships. The campus newspaper and radio station, the yearbook staff and the school's public affairs office are built-in resources offering excellent opportunities and valuable experience.

They should be used to augment your off-campus internship program and to provide a testing and evaluation ground, especially for marginal students who are not yet ready for the "real world" or need closer supervision and monitoring.

To Pay or Not to Pay?

This choice is not all that difficult—try for a paid position at the entry-level scale. The difficulty may come when you try to get the newspaper to go along with your choice. Be prepared for the newspaper publisher who says that journalism students should work free for the experience and college credits they receive.

Keep in mind that it's not only the student who benefits from a paid internship program. It's a mutually beneficial approach. The advantages of a paid, versus a non-paid, internship are great.

- The relationship automatically becomes a professional one.
- The intern feels the self-respect and the obligations that a paying job brings.
- The employer has a vested interest in furthering the training of the intern; since the newspaper is paying for the work, it has the right to expect quality performance.
- The full-time staff will respond more directly to a fellow staffer.
- The intern is less likely to be treated as a "go-fer."
- An editor will feel free to let a paid

employee go if standards aren't met, whereas the volunteer intern will probably be put up with—a disservice to all parties involved.

- A student who is expected to work free for the experience may learn an unintentional lesson—newspaper journalism doesn't pay.

There is another important reason you should try for a paid internship. It's not just that the student wants money for time spent on the job, it's that students these days must earn while they learn. Tuition and living expenses go up every year. (Any editor who has a son or daughter in college can certainly appreciate that.) Students have worked for pay all summer and reported a net loss after paying metropolitan rent, food and transportation.

If you've given it your best shot but the newspaper remains adamant, insisting on a non-paid internship, a scholarship is a possible alternative. The newspaper can make a scholarship contribution in the student's name. This would probably be a tax deduction for the newspaper.

If all else fails, you may want to settle for a non-paid internship program.

Whatever the case, be certain the student (and the student's parents, if applicable) knows the situation well in advance. Some students may not be able to participate in a non-paid program for financial reasons. Others may have to seek student loans or scholarships elsewhere. Part of your job is to make every effort to inform students of alternative sources of financial assistance.

On the Job

A set of academic assignments for each student in addition to the on-the-job activities will add to the richness of the internship experience. A good first assignment is to put the student to work studying the publication and its market. The assignment can accomplish the desired end of familiarizing student with style, with types of news considered important, and with characteristics of the community. This assignment can be completed while the student is still in school and still on campus.

A good second assignment might be one that helps the student become familiar with the publication itself—interviewing the supervisor, perhaps, to see how that person got to that position with the newspaper.

The publisher could be interviewed for views on the role the newspaper serves in the community. Naturally, newspapers of varying size will call for different treatment.

The idea throughout these assignments should be to use reading and writing by the student in ways that enhance the student's understanding of the newspaper itself and of newspapers generally. Merely keeping a log or diary doesn't quite do it, although such a requirement is useful.

Aftermath

As the internship ends—before the next semester comes in with a lot of distractions—obtain a self-assessment from the student and a confidential evaluation from the employer. If you've done the other work well, both student and employer will trust you enough to give perfectly frank assessments. It's important, too, that you be perceived as a listener, so respond to these

evaluations. You will find, we think, that as your intern program grows more extensive your ear will pick up hints as to what you should be doing differently.

As a last phase of this year's program and a first phase of next year's, try to arrange some kind of reporting device for the interns. Some schools have an intern course, which sometimes doubles as the credit section of the intern program. Students take turns reporting on their work. That can be a good technique, especially if you lure other students and faculty to attend. Another method is to have a public program or two devoted to the interns talking about what they did and learned. The Society of Professional Journalists/Sigma Delta Chi chapter is an excellent vehicle for this type of program. Early in the semester after the internship has been completed seems like the ideal time for programs of this sort. And of course, the purpose of such a meeting is only partly to report on past success. A larger purpose is to whet enthusiasm for internships.

A final important suggestion, we think, is to assemble most if not all student assignments and work samples into a scrapbook for showing faculty and other students. Such a collection of work helps the entire faculty appreciate the value of the intern program and is also useful in doing publicity on the program.

Competency-Based Internships

Competency-based internships break the job down to a number of basic objectives and tasks. A series of instructional objectives are posed along with specific activities that the intern must do to reach each objective. Assessment or evaluative activities represent the evidence that the intern has reached the goals set.

Stating clear objectives helps the students to visualize educational goals that must be attained for a job. Also, they can understand what assignments must be accomplished during the internship. Better job descriptions are the result. This can benefit employers, site supervisors and company personnel managers in knowing exactly what the intern will be doing. Faculty coordinators can improve evaluation procedures, too.

As shown in Chapter 2, it works something like this: (1) State an objective saying what the intern will do, (2) then list a number of specific work tasks involved in meeting this objective, and (3) indicate some ways that all involved in the process will know when the intern reaches the goal.

Obviously, communications interns show off a number of skills in writing, editing, interviewing, producing photos, completing art and graphic projects, etc. But there are less-direct objectives that may be useful in communications internships. These might include persuasive skills for use in handling media relations and skills in research, planning, formulating strategies and organizing plans.

Let's see how this works. A faculty coordinator is responding to a company representative and a proposed site supervisor to see how the firm can start a public rela-

tions/marketing internship program and acquire a student to work. Here are some instructional objectives that the group decides will nail down a job description:

- The intern can research and develop leads to assist the company's sales representatives to make calls.
- The intern can plan and participate in a special event (company picnic).
- The intern can plan and set up a booth for the company for an upcoming trade show.

Let's take the third objective, setting up a trade show booth, to illustrate the next two final steps:

- The second step requires a listing of tasks or activities which will show that the intern can reach the initial objective. Some of these could be checking with trade show personnel to determine the booth's location, painting or ordering signs indicating the company's name and other information, checking with company personnel on what equipment and materials will be needed or arranging for personnel to staff the booth.
- The third step is an effort to evaluate the intern's progress. For this particular objective, evaluation could take several approaches. The intern could be asked to use the calendar and prepare a series of reports to the supervisor showing progress toward setting up the booth. Or a report at the end of the trade show could detail the steps taken, which problems were particularly difficult and what recommended changes seem appropriate for the fair next year.

Sample Forms

(The following forms are courtesy of Women in Communications, Inc.)

TERMS OF THE LEARNING AGREEMENT

This agreement must be completed and signed by all participants.

Name of student _____

Social security number _____

Address _____

_____

Phone _____

Sponsoring employer _____

Address (placement location) _____

_____

Name of employer supervisor _____ Title _____ Phone _____

Name of faculty adviser _____ Title _____ Phone _____

Amount of credit to be received _____

Number of hours per week on the job _____

Number of weeks on the job (length of internship) _____

Intern's wage _____

Other reimbursement (housing, travel, meals) _____

Intern's learning expectations and goals:

Specific activities and assignments to be completed by the intern to meet goals and objectives:

Supplementary activities to be completed by intern (reading, research tasks):

Procedures for evaluation:

Daily log: Yes _____   No _____
(Intern)

Written progress reports:
(Intern)

How many? _____

Due dates? _____

Other assignments: _____
(Intern)

Conferences with faculty adviser:
(Intern and employer supervisor)

Number of conferences: _____

Dates of conferences: _____

Location: _____

Final evaluations
(Intern and employer supervisor)

Due dates: _____

Other provisions for evaluation: _____

Requirements for early termination of internship:

As participants to this agreement, we have each accepted the responsibilities and terms as stated on this form

_____

(Student's signature)   (Date)

_____

(Faculty adviser's signature)   (Date)

_____

(Employer supervisor's signature)   (Date)

SAMPLE EVALUATION FORM
(Employer Evaluates Intern)

_____ Interim
_____ Final

_____ is an intern under your supervision.
INTERN'S LAST NAME   FIRST   MIDDLE

Please provide an interim evaluation of the intern's performance midway through the internship period and a final evaluation at the conclusion of the period. Please return your evaluation to the Coordinator of Student Professional Development at the address above.

INSTRUCTIONS: Below are listed several dimensions that we believe are important to the successful completion of an internship experience. Please evaluate the intern on each of these dimensions by making a check in the appropriate boxes: (E-Excellent, AA-Above Average, A-Average, BL-Below Average, P-Poor, NO-Not Observed).

	E	AA	A	BL	P	NO
Is dependable						
Is creative/innovative						
Can work independently						
Can work under supervision						
Can work as a member of a team						
Meets deadlines						
Meets job responsibilities						
Shows leadership ability						
Shows initiative						
Seeks additional work opportunities						
Is highly motivated toward profession(s)						
Readily accepts challenges						
Readily applies instruction						
Positive attitude toward learning						
Readily accepts constructive criticism						
Appreciates importance of internship experience						
Dresses appropriately for job						

Please describe in some detail the nature of the assignments given the intern:

Date	Official Position
Institution/Organization	Typed Name
City and State	Signature

1. In your judgment, how well overall did the intern perform assigned tasks?

    ____ Superior ____ Good ____ Average ____ Satisfactory ____ Unsatisfactory

2. Please evaluate the QUANTITY and QUALITY of work accomplished by the intern.

3. Relative to the tasks assigned, what were the intern's strengths?

4. Relative to the tasks assigned, what were the intern's weaknesses?

5. Based on your experience with the intern, do you believe the intern has the basic skills, intelligence and motivation to pursue a successful career in this field?

    ____ Yes ____ No (Please elaborate)

6. If you had a full-time position open in the area of the intern's experience, would you consider seriously this intern as a likely candidate for that position? (This is not a commitment of a position to the intern.) ____ Yes ____ No

7. If you had to grade the intern, what grade would you recommend? _____

SAMPLE EVALUATION FORM
(Employer Evaluates Internship Program)

_____ has been an intern under your supervision from

INTERN'S NAME

_____. We would like your comments on the structure

COLLEGE OR UNIVERSITY

and quality of our Internship Program and need your suggestions for improvement. Please take

time to answer the following questions and return to _____

NAME

faculty adviser, _____, _____

SCHOOL   ADDRESS

_____.

1. Are you satisfied with your role in the selection of this intern?
   ___ Yes ___ No Please comment:

2. Had the intern completed sufficient course work in preparation for the internship?
   ___ Yes ___ No If not, what courses would you recommend as prerequisites?

3. Did the faculty adviser provide frequent direction and support to the student?
   ___ Yes ___ No If not, what would you recommend?

4. Did the learning agreement between you, the adviser and the intern adequately explain responsibilities and expectations for all parties?
   ___ Yes ___ No Please comment:

5. Do you feel the internship was mutually beneficial to you and the intern?
   ___ Yes ___ No Please comment:

6. Would you offer another internship?
   ___ Yes ___ No   Please comment:

7. Do you have any other suggestions for improvements in the program?

8. Do you feel your role in the student's evaluation was sufficient?
   ___ Yes ___ No   Please comment:

9. Did the college/university provide adequate direction to you as "adjunct professor"?
   ___ Yes ___ No

SAMPLE EVALUATION FORM
(Student Evaluates Internship Experience)

Name ————————————————————————————————————

Internship site ————————————————————————————————

Name of faculty adviser ———————————————————————————

Name of employer supervisor ————————————————————————

Were you well "matched" with your sponsoring employer?
___ Yes ___ No Please comment:

What objectives were you to reach during your internship?

Did you achieve these objectives?
___ Yes ___ No Please comment:

Did your faculty adviser help you to achieve these objectives?
___ Yes ___ No Please comment:

Were your assignments and responsibilities clearly explained to you?
___ Yes ___ No Please comment:

Did assignments provide sufficient challenge for you?
___ Yes ___ No Please comment:

WICI Survey

In 1980 Women in Communications, Inc. (WICI) conducted a national survey to determine the status of internship programs for college students. A different questionnaire was mailed to groups of universities, employers and former interns. A total of 2,207 questionnaires was mailed. Responses from chairs of journalism and communications schools reached 34 percent, from employers 10 percent and from former interns 44 percent. An analysis of the responses provides the profile of intern programs around the country.

This study is somewhat dated because a number of internship programs developed and grew during the 1980s. Credit, wages and other factors have changed somewhat. An example is the trend toward providing interns with credit/no credit as opposed to letter grades. However, excerpts from the report do point to useful factors in evaluating programs. Also included here are the recommended WICI guidelines helpful in establishing programs (guidelines and study reprinted with permission of Women in Communications, Inc.).

Universities and Colleges

Most colleges and universities emphasize a need for better communication between schools and employers. While a faculty member often must approve the sponsoring employer, colleges report the final decision in selection of the intern usually lies solely with the employer.

One of the most important ingredients in a successful internship is the "learning agreement." This document should be in writing, should clearly outline responsibilities of all parties involved and should be signed by the intern, the employer and the school prior to the internship.

Among respondents, educators and students had the clearest concepts of the elements of good learning agreements, while employers were less familiar with the formal agreements. Of the 73 colleges and universities responding to the survey, 60 indicated contracts are required.

Many respondents who attached learning agreements to their surveys indicated the following as common elements in a good learning agreement:

- Objectives of the internship
- Proposed learning activities to achieve objectives
- Methods of feedback and evaluation
- Employer's role in supervision
- College or university's role in supervision
- Intern's responsibilities/assignments
- Length of the internship
- Credit, if any
- Wages, if any

The learning agreement was compared by educators to a "course outline." These respondents expressed a desire for employers to consider the internship as an extension of the curriculum.

The solution for better matches and better communication, according to most colleges and universities, is increased availability of internships. One respondent says, "I wish more firms in print, broadcasting and PR would make internships available—not only for students but for faculty. We teach a lot better if our skills are fresh."

According to the survey, there is a need for better supervision and on-the-job evaluation, which is left almost exclusively to the employer.

Only 10 percent of the colleges evaluate their students throughout the internship, yet in nearly all cases, final grade is determined by the faculty adviser. Ninety-seven percent of the colleges say there is room for failure, but exactly how failure can be determined is vague.

Budget restraints and teaching loads were blamed for inadequate faculty supervision and evaluation during the internship.

Employers

Many employers feel students come to the internship unprepared—lacking basic communications skills and holding an unrealistic view of the working world. One public relations respondent says, "We generally find student interns to be woefully lacking in writing skills and journalistic training."

A newspaper respondent says, "I'd like to have prospective interns required to work on a student newspaper or magazine before the internship. This eases the burden of training on us."

Broadcasters share a similar concern for students to be "better prepared in broadcast journalism, [to have] better previous training on equipment and more emphasis on writing."

In most cases, employers feel the responsibility of placing qualified students lies with the college or university. Most employers want better screening of applicants by the school and more candidates from whom to choose their interns.

Benefits most employers derive from offering internships are that they help to ensure a pool of trained people "for the good of the industry"; internships serve as a training ground for prospective employees and offer the employer an opportunity to "inspect" potential employees with no obligation to hire the interns after graduation; and, for the most part, interns bring enthusiasm and fresh ideas to the organization.

The importance of the intern's evaluation of the program was underscored by one employer, whose program was completely restructured after invaluable constructive comments from a former intern.

Generally, contracts are verbal and

there are few standards to follow as different colleges and universities have different requirements, according to employers.

Some employers place the responsibility of establishing a learning agreement with the university or college, saying the school does not clearly set objectives. Many employers say, "[We] need more specified guidelines" and "more guidance from [the] university."

Fifteen percent of the employers say there is a possibility of failure, with several defining failure as early termination of the internship. One employer considers the intern a failure if the student would not be considered for full-time employment.

Former Interns

Generally, the senior year is the best time to take an internship, while the junior year ranks second and graduate school, third. Most educators indicate students are not eligible for an internship until they have fulfilled basic requirements in the subject area, i.e., broadcasting, public relations, advertising or newswriting sequences.

Students are equally divided on the issue of advanced preparedness. About half feel they are prepared for the working world. One respondent claims, "My university prepared me very well; nothing was strange to me. I had heard it all before."

Others agree college training left them unprepared for the internship experience. One student says, "More specific written information on how to prepare copy and technical data [would have been helpful]."

Many students suggest employers should be screened just as closely as the employer screens the student. One student says, "I was very fortunate to intern with a professional who saw the internship program as a valuable means of gaining experience. Others in my college, however, were asked to complete nothing but menial tasks. Their experiences were often worthless.

"I think the college and the internship program adviser must take a more active role in selecting organizations and individuals to participate in the program and must more carefully evaluate the student's interests in determining the site of his/her internship."

Timing can be an important factor in the matching process as one student's negative experience points out: "[Since] the newsroom was in the middle of reorganization, most of my time was wasted just sitting because the paper was disorganized."

Two-thirds of the students responding indicate they filed an agreement of some sort before the internship experience. Their responses reveal, however, that while learning agreements take many forms, so do student responsibilities that are outlined.

Some agreements require term papers and some establish general requirements if credit is to be awarded. Others require daily logs, schedule mid-term evaluations or ask both employer and student to file a report at the end of the internship.

One former intern considers wages imperative, saying, "I couldn't have done it without a salary."

To some students, wages are not that critical. One intern who earned minimum wage says, "The experience was so valuable to me that I considered the salary adequate." Another says, "I was more than willing to accept the internship without monetary compensation. I only wanted experience. I was pleased and surprised when I received the check at the end."

One-third of those who didn't receive wages did receive financial remuneration in another form such as mileage (most common), a farewell gift, and in a few instances, housing.

Most interns accept their colleges' policies on credit with little comment. Several, however, emphasize the importance of receiving academic credit.

One student, who earned two credits for a full-time 10-week internship, said, "I battled with the amount of credit an internship should give. I do feel an internship gives better experience than many four-hour courses. I feel strongly that an internship should not hinder a student from graduation."

Another student was involved in a part-time (20 to 30 hours per week) internship that lasted one and one-half years. Because the intern earned a salary ($3.15 per hour), no credit was given. "In my case, it [the internship] was a low-paid learning experience," the intern says. "I needed both the money and the experience so I took it. Never got credit—my university doesn't give credit to paid interns—it's like being penalized for working."

Students express an overwhelming need for more direction and feedback from employers. Although they enjoy being treated no differently from permanent staff members, extra direction is needed to compensate for lack of experience.

"A closer relationship between myself and my supervisor would have helped me a lot. I was capable, but someone needed to let me know what was expected of me. I would have performed much closer to the peak of my capabilities," one student says.

"In effect, I had no supervisor after the first day. They were very shorthanded. [The only feedback I received] was when I made a mistake," says one intern.

Most students feel even greater neglect from faculty advisers who in some cases are virtual non-participants in the internship. Only 26 percent of the advisers are involved in ongoing evaluations, although in nearly all cases faculty advisers determine the final grade. Employers decide the grade in 9 percent of the internships, and employers and advisers collaborated on the final grade in 37 percent of the cases.

Recommended Guidelines

Recommendations are based on interpretation of survey results, including an analysis of statistical data as well as an analysis of the subjective comments from former interns, employers and colleges and universities.

Former interns typically view a well-structured internship as the single most valuable segment of their college careers. This endorsement, coupled with employers' concerns for more relevance in the academic curriculum, makes it apparent that internships should become an integral part of every communication major's education.

Because internships are first and foremost learning experiences, the majority of recommendations are directed to colleges and universities. However, employers who have a vital interest in the caliber of in-coming professionals should also take an active role in the development of quality internships.

UNIVERSITIES AND COLLEGES

■ An internship should be mandatory for all communications majors. The anticipated problem of a shortage of employers is not evident at surveyed universities with required internships.

■ There should be a mandatory counseling session at the end of the sophomore year at which time faculty advisers tell students whether they appear to be adequately developing skills necessary to complete a satisfactory internship. Students who are not qualified for internships are not qualified to hold a communications degree or professional job and should be advised to reconsider career goals in line with demonstrated academic strengths.

■ The university should take responsibility for developing quality internship programs with a wide range of communications employers—not to be limited to the school's immediate geographical area—in order to offer a selection of employers to prospective interns.

■ Approval of an employer to be involved in an internship should be contingent upon the employer's willingness to enter into a learning agreement and on the appropriateness of the work site to the student's skills and career goals.

■ Universities should develop written learning agreements that clearly outline expectations and responsibilities of all parties—employer, university and intern. Parts of this agreement could be standardized: objectives of the internship, a statement that assigned duties will be of a professional caliber, duration of employment, amount of academic credit, employer's role in supervision and evaluation, university's role in supervision and evaluation, methods of direction and feedback. Portions of the agreement could be individualized to accommodate needs of each employer and student: student's on-the-job responsibilities, amount of wages.

■ Internships should be equivalent to a three-month professional experience with no less than a full academic term spent at the work site.

■ The faculty adviser should visit the work site at least three times during the internship. The first visit should come before the internship begins to discuss the requirements of the learning agreement and to answer any questions the employer may have. The second visit should come about three to four weeks after the internship begins to monitor the quality of daily supervision, direction and feedback and to evaluate the intern's demonstrated strengths and weaknesses.

After separate conversations with the intern and employer, the faculty adviser may be able to offer suggestions to one or both parties that will enhance the learning experience while making the intern a more valuable employee.

The third visit should come at the end of the internship to allow for a joint final evaluation session among intern, faculty adviser and employer. If distance or other factors make on-site visits difficult, the faculty adviser should make telephone contact with intern and employer at the above stated intervals. In addition, the university should send one faculty member on biennial trips to all employers not visited in person during the course of internships.

EMPLOYERS

- Employers should be willing to meet requirements set forth in a learning agreement, with emphasis placed on those conditions relating to direction, feedback and evaluation beyond that offered to permanent employees.

- Employers who accept interns from universities that do not supply learning agreements should take the lead in developing such agreements.

- Employers should have the right of final selection of interns from a field of several applicants, based on personal interviews with applicants.

- Employers should provide interns with daily directions and feedback. This task could be delegated to a senior staff member. The employer—preferably the senior supervisor—should meet regularly with the intern to answer questions regarding past assignments, discuss problems, evaluate performance and offer suggestions for improvement.

- Employers should take an active role in the final evaluation of the intern and determination of the final grade. If a written evaluation form is not provided by the university, the employer should submit one.

- Employers' payment of wages to interns guards against exploitation, ensures professional assignments and guarantees employer interest in quality programs. A suggested salary level is three-fourths of that paid to full-time first-year employees; however, lower levels could be accepted if the university is convinced of the value of the employer's internship program. Under no circumstances should an intern be paid less than minimum wage.

INTERNS

- Interns should be willing to meet all requirements set forth in the learning agreement and should realize that successful completion of the internship will rest, in part, on meeting those requirements.

- Students should have an active role in choosing an internship. They should interview with employers on an approved university list or find new employers willing to participate in the internship program, subject to approval by the university.

- Interns must take responsibility for informing both the employer and the faculty adviser if direction or feedback is not adequate or if the caliber of assignments is below professional standards.

- The intern should feel free to inform the department head if the faculty adviser is not meeting requirements under the learning agreement or if the intern feels the quality of the internship is jeopardized by a lack of communication with the faculty adviser.

- The intern should be involved in the final joint evaluation among intern, faculty adviser and employer. The intern should understand why a particular final grade is given or why the internship is deemed satisfactory/unsatisfactory if the course is graded on a pass/fail system.

- When the internship is completed, the intern should have the opportunity to evaluate the employer and the university, offering suggestions for improvement. Despite willingness to participate, some employers may not provide students a true learning experience. These employers should be encouraged to change their programs or be dropped from the university's list of approved intern employers.

Similarly, some universities may not offer students an adequate pre-internship curriculum or may have weak spots in the structure of their internship programs. These universities should be encouraged to review their curricula and internship programs.

Advertising Survey

Prof. Kevin Keenan of the University of Maryland completed an informative study of advertising internship programs ("Advertising Field Experience and Experiential Learning," *Journalism Educator* [Spring 1992]: 48-55), excerpted below. The article describes the two-page questionnaire mailed to 109 schools with advertising education programs. The response rate was a good 77 percent. These excerpts from the results and discussion sections of the article give interested faculty and advertising employers insights into current internship practices. (Excerpts are reprinted with permission from *Journalism Educator*.)

Results

Internships are a part of the curriculum at all but two of the 84 schools included in this study. Using the full sample as a base, 19 percent *require* that students serve an internship and 79 percent offer internships as an optional or elective part of the advertising major.

Of those schools that do offer internships (N=82), the traditional letter grading system is used slightly more often than pass/fail or credit/no credit systems.

Faculty are usually responsible for grading interns. In some cases internship workplace personnel also assist in assigning grades, and in fewer cases some other arrangement is used.

Nearly every school requires that certain prerequisite courses be completed before students can serve an internship. The most common prerequisite is the Introduction to Advertising course. Some schools require specific additional classes or an option of one or more from among selected groups of courses (e.g., Media Planning *or* a Copywriting course) prior to the internship.

Internships exist in many different settings and types of organizations. Advertising agencies are the most common intern sponsors and account for the largest percentage of all internships.

There is some flexibility in the scheduling of student internships.

Over one-quarter of all internships result in the student receiving a job offer from the sponsoring organization.

Most advertising internships are located or arranged through the school rather than by the students themselves. The majority of these internships are not paid.

Discussion

Academic credit is awarded for internship work at 93 percent of the responding schools. While it is possible that these numbers are slightly inflated due to non-response by advertising programs that do not include internships, it is clear that internships are considered an important and accepted component of the advertising major at most colleges and universities.

There is a range of positions regarding the number of internship credit hours that can be applied toward a degree. Limits range from a low of two credit hours through a high of 21 hours, perhaps reflecting different views on the value and contribution of internship experiences.

Most schools use some formula for translating the number of hours spent on the internship into academic credit hours. The range here is from a minimum of five work hours for each credit hour at one school through 100 or more work hours per credit hour at 13 percent of the schools studied. The most common arrangement is to require 40 work hours for each hour of academic credit. Estimating that students in traditional classroom courses spend an equal amount of time on in-class and out-of-class work (e.g., a total of six hours per week for a three-hour class, or 30 hours of real time for each academic credit hour in a 15-week semester), internships tend to require greater expenditures of time per credit hour.

Where there is concern about grade inflation or grading criteria for internships, it may be useful to consider some pass/fail system or other alternatives to traditional letter grades.

Faculty are solely or partially responsible for assigning grades at 90 percent of the schools that offer internships.

Data on employment resulting from internships indicate that around one-third of all interns receive job offers from the sponsoring organization and that two-thirds of these offers are accepted. These findings reflect positively on advertising education in general and on internship programs as valuable for job placement purposes.

One potentially troubling discovery of this study involves the kind of assignments required of interns. Related to the distinction between "how" and "why" philosophies of advertising education, assignments are predominantly of the "how" variety, emphasizing the practice of advertising with little attention to the theoretical. There is a missed opportunity for bridging the gap between the two approaches here. Internships offer the perfect setting for examining and applying points of theory that may seem amorphous to students when presented in the classroom. By incorporating assignments of a more academic or theoretical nature into internship programs, both the practical value and educational objectives of the internship experience would be better served.

Some final areas investigated here show a desirable flexibility in terms of the source, scheduling and compensation of internships. It was found that most students locate their internship through the school but that in some cases they may seek out an internship on their own. Internships through the school have the advantage of more direct "quality control" and should contribute to closer industry-educator relations. But in cases where the school lacks resources or time to oversee internship screening and placement, or for especially bright and ambitious students, the option of student-arranged internships seems a wise one.

Finally, unpaid internships outnumber those that are paid by almost two to one. From a pedagogical perspective this variable may make little difference, but students are likely to consider it important. Monetary compensation of interns is something that deserves the attention of sponsoring organizations and academic programs.

Interns in Recession Times

The following article was published in The *Wall Street Journal*, Thursday, April 25, 1991 (reprinted by permission of *The Wall Street Journal*, ©1991 Dow Jones & Co., Inc. All rights reserved worldwide).

Christine Sparta works full time as an assistant editor at Meredith Corp.'s *Ladies' Home Journal*. She sits in on story meetings, covers press conferences and researchers articles. Her first byline will appear in the July issue.

But Ms. Sparta, who graduated from New York University in December with a bachelor's degree in journalism, is no ordinary junior executive: She is a $6-an-hour intern.

Without her, the magazine's health department would have to hire a salaried assistant editor, says her boss, health editor Nelly Edmondson Gupta. But that's "not in the budget," Ms. Gupta explains, adding: "The interns have been lifesavers. We're getting the best and brightest for a very low rate."

Tough economic times are changing corporate attitudes about college interns. Only a few years ago, companies could afford to design internships around the interns, investing time and money to squire them through the business, hoping to woo the most promising to full-time employment after graduation. Now, as more companies cut their salaried staffs, they are increasingly tapping interns as a source of inexpensive labor.

In some cases, interns are offered temporary jobs not just for the summer but for the next three seasons, too. But then, instead of being offered permanent spots, they are replaced by new interns.

For some students, it can be a boon. Instead of scrambling for a limited number of spaces, they have an easier shot at even the best firms. And there is the chance to take on real responsibilities while rubbing shoulders with seasoned professionals.

Because many of the interns are supported by financial aid or their parents, they acquiesce to working for little or no pay, no benefits and no promise of a future at the company. Instead, they earn something they say is worth its weight in gold: the name of a Fortune 500 company at the top of their resume.

"I like to tell my interns this is the best of times and the worst of times," says Jason Berger, a communications professor who oversees an internship program at Duquesne University in Pittsburgh. "It's the worst of times for business, but the best of times for interns. Two or three years ago, a lot of [intern] jobs would have been entry-level positions."

Consider the Moody's Investor Service Inc. unit of Dun & Bradstreet Corp. Shorthanded, one of its bond departments quadrupled the number of so-called ongoing interns—those who work indefinitely—to eight this year. Among other things, the interns help analysts rate bonds.

The extra manpower helps because "we don't necessarily have approval to hire more people on a permanent basis," says one employee, who calls the arrangement "a cost-effective way to use staff without increasing head count."

To be sure, some strapped companies are eliminating or cutting internship programs. Merrill Lynch & Co. still pays business-school finance interns $1,000 a week but has shelved plans made last fall to start a similar program for college students. "We're kind of coming off a tough year," says John Rae, director of recruiting. An intern program "is pretty expensive and time-consuming," he says.

For those companies now turning to interns for critical manpower, there can be a downside. While the interns are energetic and motivated, they are, after all, lacking the experience deemed necessary by some to make major decisions. As long as students simply assist decision makers, "I think it's a good thing," says Richard L. Rowan, co-director of the Center for Human Resources at the Wharton School. But, he adds, "if they are indeed being put into real decision-making jobs, that could cause some problems."

While more companies are taking chances with inexperienced interns, others plug the students into clerical spots or use them for grunt work. Companies now call "all the time" requesting interns to fetch coffee and make copies, says Trudy Steinfeld, director of the office of career services at New York University. "They call the position an administrative intern, but we won't list it," she says.

"This is the seedy side of it," adds Mr. Berger of Duquesne, who once yanked a student from a marketing internship that involved tabulating customer-response cards. "Interns shouldn't be used to fill short-term labor needs."

Some companies say they have no choice in the matter. At Ford Motor Co.'s accounts-payable department, for instance, manager Ronald Fiscus realized he would need extra hands to do work that will be phased out in July by computers. The work requires little skill because it's highly automated, he explains.

Lacking permission to hire new workers, or even temporary ones, Mr. Fiscus enlisted the help of six paid student interns this semester, double the number of past periods. "We're using them almost as full-time employees," Mr. Fiscus reports. But he can't hire them, he says; there's a hiring freeze on.

Eastern Airlines made ample use of interns before it declared bankruptcy. Last fall, for instance, it used five interns to help answer calls in a three-person Pittsburgh sales office. Maureen Healey, an intern from Duquesne, says she enjoyed the work but was relieved when Eastern finally supplemented the staff with a secretary. "They needed another employee in the office instead of so many interns," she recalls.

While Ms. Healey, who has since graduated from Duquesne, says she learned a lot working for a company teetering on the brink of bankruptcy, most of her duties involved answering phones. And in the end, she never received her full pay. That's because Eastern paid its interns with one free round-trip ticket for every 50 hours worked. By the time the carrier filed for bankruptcy, Ms. Healey had earned five tickets and used only two. One of her fellow-interns was stuck with 10 tickets; others had to cancel trips to Cancun.

Overall, the experience was worth it, she says. But she adds: "It was almost free labor."

No Pay, No Credit Is Unlawful

The following excerpts from a *Daily Variety* story (April 4, 1991) by David Robb touch on a number of issues including pay, credit and conditions under which trainees or interns are lawful under a 1981 Supreme Court ruling. (Published with permission from *Daily Variety*.)

The use of unpaid workers—so-called interns—is widespread in the film, television and broadcast industries. In many cases, particularly those where the interns are not receiving college credit for their work, the practice is unlawful—a violation of state and federal minimum wage laws.

California's minimum wage law states that "every employer shall pay to each employee wages not less than $4.25 per hour for all hours worked." Effective April 1, the federal minimum wage was also raised to $4.25 an hour.

One exception to California's minimum wage law covers the employment of "learners," who may be paid 85% of minimum wage—or $3.60 an hour—during their first 160 hours of employment in occupations in which they have had no previous similar or related experience.

Many industry employers, however, believe that they can hire "interns" and pay them nothing at all.

Jose Millan, senior deputy labor commissioner for the state of California, said that such practices are "unlawful" unless the individual is receiving college credit for the internship.

"The internship category is one that requires the individual intern to be pursuing some professional course of study," Millan said, "and as part of that course of study, there is this on-the-job work experience called an internship. We have traditionally viewed interns primarily as students who are pursuing a course of study at an accredited college."

Many unpaid Hollywood interns, however, are not receiving college credit and are being recruited off the street through want ads placed in trade publications, including *Daily Variety* and *The Hollywood Reporter*.

In the last few months, more than a dozen different companies—including Chanticleer Films,

the Stephen J. Cannell Co. and producers of "The Love Connection"—have placed ads looking for unpaid interns.

The Melinda Jason Co., a small independent production/management firm with offices at Touchstone Pictures, placed such an ad recently stating that it was looking for "part-time, non-paid interns."

The ad, which used Touchstone Pictures as its mailing address, caught the attention of Disney's labor relations office, which then notified the entire company that it was running the risk of violating minimum wage laws.

"I told them," a Disney official said, "that if their interns were not students receiving credit or in a training program, they'd have to hire the people and pay them minimum wage, at the very least.

"You can have a training program and not be paying people, but this was clearly not one of those situations, and we at Disney did not want to be identified with a company that was violating state and federal labor relations laws."

A spokeswoman for the Melinda Jason Co. said that the firm has heeded Disney's advice and has not hired, and will not hire, any unpaid interns.

"We have not hired any interns," the spokeswoman said. "We have been informed that that may be against the law."

As the Disney official pointed out, "interns" must be paid minimum wage unless they are receiving college credit for their work or unless they are part of a bona fide training program.

Basically, then, there are two types of bona fide internship programs that allow interns to work without pay or for pay below minimum wage.

One such program requires interns to receive college credit for their work. Such programs are supervised by local colleges and universities and are exempt from state and federal minimum wage laws.

Another program allows employers to engage in non-college trainees or college students who are not receiving college credit for their work, so long as the training program meets with six criteria set down by the U.S. Supreme Court. (Employers who engage college-credited interns need not meet these six criteria).

Just what constitutes a bona fide, non–college-accredited training program was the subject of a Supreme Court ruling handed down in 1981 in a case involving a flight attendants training program run by American Airlines.

In that case, the Court ruled that a training program must meet six criteria in order for trainees not to be considered "employees" as defined by the Fair Labor Standards Act of 1938. If any of those six criteria are not met, the Court said, the "trainees" would have to be considered "employees," and be paid at least minimum wage.

The Court, in determining the six criteria for a bona fide training program, ruled that:

- The training, even though it includes actual operation of the facilities of the employer, must be similar to that which would be given in a vocational school;
- The training must be for the benefit of the trainees or students;
- The trainees must not displace regular employees but work under their close observation;
- The employer that provides the training must derive no immediate advantage from the activities of the trainees, and on occasion his operations may actually be impeded;
- The trainees are not necessarily entitled to a job at the conclusion of the training period;
- The employer and the trainees understand that the trainees are not entitled to wages for the time spent in training.

Most, if not all, of the industry's employers who hire unpaid, non–college-accredited interns have training programs that meet most of the Court's six criteria. Very few such employers, however, have established training programs that meet all six criteria.

Howard Ostermann, chief of the Department of Labor's branch of special employment, said that there is "not much elbow room" in the Court's six criteria—all of which, he said "have to be met" in order to qualify as a bona fide internship program.

Of the six criteria, Ostermann said, the "most difficult" for employers to satisfy is the one that states that employers will derive "no immediate advantage from the activities of trainees."

"There's not much elbow room there," he said. "It's not much of a matter of degree. If these [interns] are doing the kinds of things that are clearly necessary for the organization to operate—such as filing, copying, office chores and things like that—it would certainly raise a lot of questions."

Ostermann said that "the problem comes in when [trainees] spend extended periods on the work site." This, he said, may result in employers reaping some "economic benefits" from the work performed by the interns. It can also have "the potential for displacement of [paid] employees," he said.

Ostermann said that the DOL has no problem with employers whose interns are receiving college credit—that's protected by the law.

"But when you don't have college credit," he said, "it's going to be much more difficult [for employers] to prove that an employment situation doesn't exist [between the employer and the intern]."

Ostermann said that "the best way" for employers to find out if their non–college-accredited internship programs are in compliance with the law is to contact the local office of the DOL's wage and hour division.

Ostermann said that it would also be a "good idea" for employers to have written internship programs to ensure that the programs are being "implemented as designed." Many employers interviewed by *Daily Variety* said that they have no such written internship policies.

Asked about companies that place ads for unpaid interns, Ostermann said: "There could be some public spirited companies, but [such ads] would raise questions about whether [the hiring of interns] was something the company needed to operate."

An ad that ran recently in *Daily Variety* stated: "Part-time interns wanted. Major film production company seeking bright, motivated interns for errands and clerical work. Great opportunity to experience the business."

This would apparently be in violation of state and federal labor laws, which do not permit unpaid trainees or interns to run "errands" for their employers.

The company that placed the ad did not list its name, address or telephone number. Applicants were asked to send their resumes to a mail pick-up box in care of *Daily Variety*.

APPENDIX C

Introduction to Employers

At first glance, starting an internship program looks easy. First, print some hand-outs describing the internship and then call a school asking students to apply. Choose the best applicant. Finally, assign the intern to someone in the company with extra time.

Establishing a good internship program is not difficult, but the above scenario creates problems. Noting a few rules will ease your working relationship with faculty at the university, the young people who will intern for your company and your employees who will be involved. Here are a few pointers:

1. You probably will want to involve a nearby college in your search for interns. Once the internship is listed and a job description disclosed, you can publicize your opening to many schools. It is important at first to select a university with a department or school teaching the skills required in your proposed internship work. Although many students may be bright and interested in your position, they may not have the background or skills required to perform satisfactorily.

2. When contacting an internship office or the chair of the department potentially interested in your internship, clearly state your needs. This can reduce the time required to find candidates. If you are a personnel manager for a newspaper or station and are looking for an intern capable of public relations, advertising or marketing work, you may want to look beyond the journalism department. Some time spent detailing what skills are required can pay off

with more and better-qualified applicants.

3. Selection of a site supervisor is next. You may have to choose more than one if you have several different internships to fill. The supervisor should be willing to work with an intern, have an interest in education or training young people and have a good understanding of the assignments to be given to the intern. Do not assign one intern to two supervisors, if possible, as in most cases the intern will be neglected. The supervisor should be working the same hours or shift as the intern. The choice of a supervisor may depend on the intern's assignment to full- or part-time status. Supervisors are sometimes graduates of nearby colleges.

4. Before you can publicize your internship and begin interviews, you need to consider topics such as pay, schedule of work (hours, days), credit, preparing forms for the university, etc. Some of these are discussed in the first two chapters of this book. In this appendix, an article on local government internships tells what needs to take place in any internship, regardless of the field. Information is presented also on benefits of internships to the company and to students.

5. Both the supervisor and the intern need to understand that the chief purpose of the internship is to learn. If the intern spends most of his or her time on clerical duties, then he or she should not receive credit. Nor should the company use the intern as a cheap source of labor (see Appendix B).

194

To advance the educational benefits that a challenging internship can offer, it is necessary for both the employer and the supervisor to meet with the faculty representative of the university to develop an adequate job description. The Women in Communications, Inc. (WICI) survey guidelines and steps toward basic objectives in Appendix B can facilitate an effective learning agreement.

The best way to attract more interns is to run a good program in which students get maximal opportunities to work. Word passes around quickly. Students will seek your site next semester if it stands out as a good place to learn. To inform next year's class of opportunities, see the examples on page 199. A simple announcement can be mailed to interested schools in your area. Competition sometimes aids in recruiting.

Of course, the company supervisor at the site has responsibility for evaluating the intern's progress. However, the bottom line is that the faculty coordinator and the university are required to monitor progress, record reports and award grades and credit. A successful internship is a positive result for the student, the company and the university.

Guidelines for Internships in Local Government

For Employers and Site Supervisors

The following excerpts are from "Effective Local Government Internships." by Joy Pierson (*Public Management 74* [February 1992]: 16-19). It should be of interest to any business or company wanting to start an internship program. In fact, some communications majors, particularly with public relations backgrounds and courses, have become excellent interns in local, county and state government agencies. (Excerpted with permission of *Public Management (PM)* magazine, published by the International City/County Management Association (ICMA), Washington, D.C.)

Internships have traditionally been the practical learning experience for people entering the local government management profession. An internship program should focus anywhere in the organization where staff are committed to providing a nurturing environment in which to learn. All local governments are different and should structure an internship program that best suits the organization's needs. There are several types of internships, including

- rotational full-time internship to two or more departments;
- one-year full-time internship in one department;
- part-time internship in the manager's office;
- part-time internship in a specific department—budget office, fire department, personnel, or parks and recreation; and
- cooperative education, or internships established with one or more local schools.

While every internship varies, a strong internship program is well organized and has the commitment of the manager or department head. Regardless of the type of internship or who fills the positions, all internships should include the following components:

- strong recruitment efforts and publicity;
- standard application process including a cover letter, resume, writing sample, transcripts, references, and application if desired;
- screening process with specific selection criteria;
- telephone and/or in-person interviews;
- workplans or learning contracts including the intern's and the organization's expectations of what to contribute, learn, and take away from the experience;
- regular feedback and adjustments in workplans if necessary;
- exposure to professional development opportunities, meetings, key decisions makers, training, etc.;
- career counseling and assistance with job placement; and
- constructive criticism and evaluation in exit interviews.

Anyone interested in learning more about local government (or a specific department) could be a great intern. This includes undergraduate students, graduate students, post-graduate students, employees who want a rotational assignment/cross-training, mid-career professionals, and high school students (with some limitations).

Interns can do many things that full-time staff do since their skills and interests are varied. When deciding what responsibilities to give interns, think about what they will get out of the task or project and explain that to them. Granted, some work will not be as satisfying as others, but that is reality. Try to give interns tasks that have a clear beginning and end, and explain how their work fits into the bigger picture. Start the interns with relatively easy tasks and progress to more challenging assignments. Writing a press release, for example, is an easier first task than performing an analysis of solid waste methods. Consider these responsibilities:

- handling citizen requests;
- researching how other local governments provide services;
- representing the organization at neighborhood meetings;
- writing short memorandums, newsletter columns, and news releases;
- analyzing service delivery alternatives; and
- preparing annual reports, budgets, and progress reports.

All internships emphasize different skills needed to best fill the position. For example, interns in the manager's office might need an interest in local government management, but engineering interns need technical competence in drafting. After determining desired knowledge, skills, and abilities, specific interview questions can be determined. Some ideas are listed below for criteria to use in selecting interns:

- strong writing skills;
- effective interpersonal skills;
- familiarity or experience with computers;
- customer service experience;
- past work or volunteer experience that might be applicable;
- applicable academic coursework and grade point average;
- leadership experience;
- references from past supervisors and professors;
- interest and familiarity with local government, budgeting, recreation and parks, or whatever area is applicable; and
- self-motivation; ability to work well with minimal supervision.

While most interns stay with an organization or department a short time, it is vital to give them an honest evaluation of their strengths and weaknesses. This input will help interns improve their skills and marketability.

- Consider using your current personnel evaluations.
- Use the established workplan.
- Ask interns to evaluate their own performance first, then add yours. Often they know exactly where they need to improve, but might not know what they have done well.
- Talk about any misperceptions or disappointments interns might have. Frequently, interns are new to the work environment and have high expectations.
- Explain what interns have contributed to the organization.
- Explain specifically the skills interns can use in future experiences.
- In some part, each internship will be evaluated differently as each intern will want to learn different skills, experiences, etc.

All internships are learning experiences—for both the student and the local government. Remember it is supposed to be a 50/50 deal. Interns should be learning 50 percent of the time and working 50 percent of the time. This means they should be given adequate opportunities to attend meetings and other professional development experiences, such as computer training.

When deciding to establish (or renew) internships, do a critical analysis of the costs and benefits for both the intern and the local government. Here are some of the costs incurred by local governments:

- initial start-up costs to create an internship program;
- time and money spent for recruitment, screening, and interviewing;
- resources devoted to orientations and training; and
- continued commitment to provide strong supervision, direction, assistance (estimate roughly 10 percent per intern for supervision).

The benefits, however, can outweigh those costs. Local governments, for example, receive:

- new energy and enthusiasm;
- completed projects and reports;
- new ideas and fresh perspectives on challenges;
- an opportunity to test employees for full-time positions;
- the flexibility to hire without constraints of civil service;
- contributing to the local government management profession; and
- the personal satisfaction of teaching and helping someone.

It is important to realize interns are making sacrifices to receive the benefits of internships, accepting:

- low or no wages;
- little or no benefits or leave;
- restricted work hours;
- additional clothing costs;
- the stress of juggling school and work;
- adjusting to a new organization and environment; and
- sometimes must pay moving costs.

Interns do benefit from:

- practical, significant experience in local government;
- the opportunity to test skills and discover who they are;
- experience in interpersonal communication, group dynamics, and organizational politics;
- networking with practitioners and other interns; and
- the opportunity to learn from others through coaching, strong supervision, and mentoring.

Sample Internship Announcements

At a Local Hospital

INTERNSHIP OPPORTUNITY

Mountain Valley Regional Hospital and Medical Center has an immediate opening for a paid internship/part-time job in its Marketing and Community Relations Department.

Position Title:	Marketing/Public Relations Intern
Duties:	Intern will assist in marketing, public relations and communications projects including planning special events, writing newsletters and news releases and assisting with the development of flyers, brochures and other promotional materials.
Hours:	20–30 hours weekly between the times of 8:00 A.M. and 6:00 P.M.
Compensation:	$7 per hour
Skills and Requirements:	—Communications, Public Relations or Journalism major —Class level should be Junior or Senior —Excellent written and verbal communications skills —Proofreading skills —Familiarity with Associated Press style and proofreader's marks —Organization and planning skills —Basic computer skills —Desktop publishing experience a plus
To Apply:	Send résumé, cover letter and two writing samples to: John Long, Community Relations Coordinator Mountain Valley Regional Hospital Anywhere, USA
The Hospital:	Mountain Valley Regional Hospital and Medical Center is a 413-bed, full-service acute care facility located in Mountain Valley. The hospital is for-profit and physician owned. There are nearly 1,500 employees and approximately 750 physicians affiliated with the hospital.

At a Newspaper

NAME OF NEWSPAPER

- Up to four internships will be awarded for 8 to 12 weeks beginning in May or June, depending on availability

- Candidates will be considered for internships in these areas:

      Reporting: news, features, sports
      Copy Editing
      Photography
      Graphics

- Pay of at least $400 per week

- An internship is no guarantee of a full-time job, but if we have an opening at the end of the summer, we will consider outstanding interns.

APPLICATION PROCESS

Juniors, seniors and graduates with previous experience are more likely to be chosen, but we will consider younger students or non-students with special qualifications. Minorities are encouraged to apply. Application:

1) A letter telling us about yourself, the work you've done, what you want to accomplish in journalism, why you want an internship with this newspaper, and your area of preference from the categories above.
2) A résumé detailing your experience and academic background. Include three references.
3) Up to 12 samples of your best work (articles, layouts, edited copy, photographs, artwork).
4) One letter of recommendation.

To make sure we received your material, you may enclose a stamped, self-addressed postcard or envelope. We'll send it back to you as soon as we receive your packet.

Finalists will be contacted for interviews.

We will inform all candidates, whether they are chosen or not, by mail or phone. Please refrain from calling after you have submitted your application unless you have new information to convey.

Deadline: All materials to Joy Smith, Director of Human Resources at the address above for receipt by January 7.

Model Training Program

This network-affiliated television station is launching this trial program in 1994. Officials did not want identification of or publicity for the program until it has operated one year. If successful, it will be continued. It is open to both minority and non-minority college students in their junior or senior year. These details may be of interest to stations seeking to attract better students for internships.

[Station name] is instituting a very exciting training opportunity for university/college students in their junior/senior year who are majoring in journalism, communications, or radio-TV-film.

The Training Program is designed to recruit qualified and talented students and provide them with an intense, comprehensive 12-week formal training program. Every effort should be made to encourage minority students to apply for this program.

Students selected will be expected to spend 15-25 hours per week, for which they will receive an hourly wage of $8.00. No one will be considered who is unable to meet the minimum 15-hour requirement. **We hope you will consider giving academic credit to the student to accommodate these hours. Aforesaid, however, it is not a necessity.** Upon the successful completion of the Training Program, the station will offer a $500 scholarship to the student, paid to the school, to help cover academic costs for his/her senior year.

We invite your department to pre-screen and recommend *2 finalists* to participate in the program. Following are the criteria for selection: (1) minimum GPA of 3.0, (2) some evidence of financial need and (3) a major or minor in journalism, communications or radio-TV-film. Attached are materials that you may use to alert and facilitate the selection.

The student candidates will enter a competition with 12 other finalists from campuses in this region. The 14 finalists will be asked to submit a 500-word or less essay on "How the Training Program Can Be of Value to Me." A blue ribbon community committee will then judge the essays and select five students to participate for the first 12 weeks. The process will be repeated approximately every 12 weeks to ensure a steady flow of participants.

Training positions will be available in the following departments: sales, news, technical operations, programming, community affairs and promotions. Students will be asked to state their areas of interest, indicating first, second and third choice. Where possible, students will be assigned to those departments first. Each participating department will have a manager assigned to supervise and monitor the work of the students to maximize the benefits of their 12-week training program.

The station will commence the first 12 weeks of the training program on June 27, 1994. Our *deadline* for student selection from your department is *April 29, 1994*. Finalists will be notified no later than June 15, 1994.

Ad Agency Tips

Robert Utley, principal in a 20-person advertising agency, says that hosting an intern is an investment in time that can't be billed to clients. But it is an invaluable experience to the next generation of talent, and he urges agencies to do the necessary planning. He comments:

Agencies should not contract to take an intern unless there is a good deal of planning. We no longer take interns in the summer since this is often a low spot for business. We think it is easier to assure the intern of significant experience in the fall or spring semester or quarter.

Our experience has led to some simple guidelines which we recommend to other agencies:

- Prepare a 10-week schedule for both the intern and the agency to follow.
- Assign one agency person to coordinate the intern's activities and for the intern to consider as a "mentor."
- Give the intern real hands-on work to do. Get the intern involved. Avoid putting someone in the corner for busy work.
- Try to treat the intern as a regular employee.
- Ask your intern to critique you. You should be able to learn, too, you know.

Our first experience with an intern was several years ago when a talented young advertising woman from the University of Oregon worked with us. It worked so well that we made it an annual event.

One of our account executives, a former ad intern himself, took charge of screening applicants and planned the intern's schedule. Her first two weeks were in account management, working with the agency's executives.

When it was appropriate, she visited clients, participated in budget and planning sessions, and got an overview of agency/client relations. Our clients were eager to meet the intern and were impressed that we were contributing to the future of advertising.

After a week or two in the copy department, the intern's notes read, "I knew that I would be getting experience here, but I never expected to write copy that would be used. This week I wrote a magazine ad and a corporate profile for a brochure."

She spent a week in the art department and a week with the production manager and toured printers, color separators, and film houses. After her time in the media department, the intern wrote, "I learned that cheapest isn't best and that subjectivity counts. Like my media professor pointed out, it's not an exact science when it comes to business and trade publications."

The intern said that she was pleased to have worked in a small agency because she was not treated as "just an intern."

INDEX